REAGAN'S LEGACY IN A WORLD TRANSFORMED

Reagan's Legacy
in a World Transformed

Edited by **JEFFREY L. CHIDESTER**

and **PAUL KENGOR**

 Harvard University Press

Cambridge, Massachusetts

London, England

2015

Library of Congress Cataloging-in-Publication Data

Reagan's legacy in a world transformed / edited by Jeffrey L. Chidester and Paul Kengor.
pages cm
Includes bibliographical references and index.
ISBN 978-0-674-96769-4 (alk. paper)
1. United States—Foreign relations—1981–1989. 2. United States—
Foreign relations—1989– 3. Reagan, Ronald—Influence.
I. Chidester, Jeffrey L., editor, author. II. Kengor, Paul, 1966– editor, author.
E876.R423 2015
973.927092—dc23 2014035126

Contents

III. A New National Strategy: Reagan's Defense Policy Revisited

IV. The Great Debate: Reagan and Negotiating the End of the Cold War

V. Reagan and Multilateralism: Two Voices

Foreword

BRIAN MULRONEY

Reagan's Legacy in a World Transformed is all about remembering Ronald Reagan, his presidency, and the manner in which he changed the world.

During his centennial year in 2011, individuals of great distinction the world over shared their personal reflections of the fortieth American president and bore witness to his life's work. Many knew Ronald Reagan longer and better than I did. Some worked with him daily for years. I knew him as a fellow G-7 leader with whom I shared moments of high drama on the world stage during one of the most explosive decades in modern history. We became friends, and I saw him often when questions of world peace or war were being determined. In that most scalding of political cauldrons, I observed Ronald Reagan closely. That is the perspective I bring with me to open this volume.

Some years ago the legendary *New York Times* columnist Scotty Reston came to lunch with me at 24 Sussex, the prime minister's official residence in Ottawa. After an impressive "tour d'horizon," Mr. Reston said: "You know, Prime Minister, for the last 25 years I have opposed every single policy that your friend Ronald Reagan has ever stood for." Then he added: "And during that same period, Ronald Reagan was twice elected governor of California and twice elected president of the United States."

This self-deprecatory observation—I thought memorable because of its infrequency at the *New York Times*—was delivered somewhat ruefully, as if Mr. Reston were perplexed by his own admission. But to so wise an observer as Reston, the answer surely should have been very clear. It's called leadership— that ineffable and sometimes magical quality that sets some men and women apart so that millions will follow them as they conjure up new visions and invite their countrymen to dream big and exciting dreams.

In his seminal work on leadership, James MacGregor Burns segregates "transactional" from "transforming" leadership. He writes that it is the transforming leader who "raised the level of human conduct of both leader and led . . . who responds to fundamental hopes and expectations and who may transcend and even seek to reconstruct the political system rather than simply operate within it." Many suggest that great, inexorable currents of history themselves—and not individual leaders—seal our fate. In my judgment, however, Carlyle was on target when he observed that the right man in the right place at the right time can completely change the course of history. I believe that to be true because I was there to see it happen.

In a brilliant address delivered some years ago in Canada, Theodore Sorenson—himself a skilled observer of powerful leaders—said:

> Once in office those who wish to stand up and stand out and leave something enduring behind must build new institutions, not new images. They must look to the next generation, not merely the next election. They must talk in terms of fundamental values, not merely costs. They must appeal to our hopes as well as our needs, to what we long to be and what we know is right. That's leadership.

Does this remind you of anybody?

Now, if today you asked the American people if they think Ronald Reagan was a "transforming" president or simply a "transactional" one, what do you think they would reply? Look around you, they would say, the Reagan Revolution and its powerful effects on freedom, economic prosperity, the private sector, and the public good are clearly visible both to contemporary America and to history.

President Reagan's personal qualities defined his presidency in interesting ways. One day at lunch in Tokyo during a discussion of leading personalities in public life, I asked him who he really disliked in American politics. He thought for a moment, looked at me quizzically, and said: "You know, Brian, I just can't think of one at the moment. I'm fixated on what looks like an eel in my soup." This was a very disconcerting answer for any Canadian prime minister who, on his best days, has more adversaries than friends—and who can clearly remember every insult or slight from any opponent since his fourteenth birthday. In fact, in some countries such generous detachment of attitude in politics would probably be unconstitutional. Nevertheless, under my insistent interrogation, President Reagan finally identified a former associate as someone he actually disliked. This display of vindictiveness on his part made me feel better and partially restored my faith in the American political process.

To be fully serious, however, I noted that because of this absence of malice, President Reagan's judgments were unaffected by the pettiness and mean-spiritedness that tend to make good intentions bad and tough situations worse. He never sought to get even with anybody except by the triumph of his ideas. He struck me as a leader more interested in healing old wounds than in settling old scores. In consequence, his true nature and sunny personality came through to the American people, who reveled in the choice of a president who clearly made policy not for easy headlines in 10 days but a better America in 10 years.

I also thought that President Reagan's understanding of the nobility of the presidency coincided with the American dream. One day in Brussels following a NATO meeting, President François Mitterrand of France, in referring to Ronald Reagan, said to me: "Tu sais, Brian, notre ami Ronald Reagan a vraiment la notion de l'État." Rough translation: "You know, Brian, our friend Ronald Reagan really has a sense of the State about him." The translation does not fully capture the profundity of the observation: what Mitterrand meant was that there is a vast difference between the job of president and the role of president.

In fact, many people can do the job. Few, however, fully grasp that unusual alchemy of history, tradition, achievement, personal conduct, and national pride that define the special role the U.S. president must assume at home and around the world. "La notion de l'État"—no one understood it better than Ronald Reagan, and no one could more eloquently summon his nation to high purpose or bring forth the majesty of the presidency and make it glow better than the man who saw his country as a "shining city on a hill."

Ronald Reagan's mature attitude to life while in office framed his presidency forever. President Kennedy captivated America and the world 54 years ago, in January 1961, in large measure because of the excitement and promise of his youth. From that day on, the celebration of youth in public life was overpowering and pervasive. It was also somewhat misleading. But around the world, presidents and prime ministers in their thirties and forties proliferated. If you were young, you were smart, you had brilliant ideas, knew sophisticated, talented people, and could conquer the world. Suddenly, if you were older, you were quaint and pretty well out of business. Or so it seemed. I myself came to office at age 45 after a pretty solid career in law, business, and life generally. But when the hostile battering and the unremitting personal attacks began soon thereafter by the opposition, media, and interest groups, I can recall from time to time being left uncertain or undecided about a particular course of action.

Ronald Reagan came to the presidency at age 70. His principles were tested and firm. His ideas were clearly developed and straightforward. His attitude was good-natured and self-assured. He had thought his way carefully through America's challenges and solutions and was both relaxed and resolute in addressing both. He was, as the French say, "bien dans sa peau"—comfortable in his skin.

That was one principal reason that, having made all the major policy decisions himself, he felt no hesitation or insecurity at delegating the implementation to a group of strong aides and cabinet secretaries who surrounded him throughout his time in office. He could also weather a debilitating recession, cause a huge firestorm by firing all of PATCO, label the Soviet Union an "evil empire," launch military strikes against terrorism halfway around the world, propose SDI, and withstand all the criticism without changing course. He could not care less what the *Washington Post* or *New York Times* or anyone else said. He was 70 years old and had seen it all before. His imperturbability while at the vortex of great protest and convulsive change demonstrated that he had become a leader who was unshakable in his pursuit of fundamental policies because they reflected his own beliefs and values, which had resulted from a full life's work. In my judgment, this reality was not an insignificant factor in the success of the Reagan presidency.

Ronald Reagan personified the optimism and confidence of America to Americans and to the world. He bolstered the spirit of America, restored national strength and the ability to succeed. The word "malaise" was never part of his vocabulary. Even those who did not agree with him—and they were legion—respected Ronald Reagan because he was unwavering in what he believed was right for America. No ambiguity, no deception, no cynicism. What you saw or heard was precisely what Ronald Reagan meant.

From time to time, I recorded thoughts and impressions in a private journal or memoirs, following major events or particularly interesting occurrences. Here are a few brief entries as I described the Ronald Reagan I saw and knew, beginning 31 years ago. I first met with him at the White House before my election as prime minister of Canada. I was then leader of Her Majesty's Loyal Opposition.

June 22, 1984

During the meeting yesterday I was struck by the president's remarkably youthful manner, his sense of humor, and strange to say, feeling of serenity. He seemed calm and composed, solicitous of others but very much in command. We discussed arms control negotiations, acid rain, steel imports, and methods of better managing our relationship. I had been told to expect that after a few comments others would take over the discussions on his behalf. The meeting lasted 40–45 minutes and he was the vigorous and lone American participant throughout. He was humorous and courteous throughout. He listened carefully and politely as I made pretty vigorous pleas on behalf of the Canadian position on issues. My impression was that if this were not an election year, responses to our views might be more prompt and accommodating. I dwelled at some length on the peace issue and said that Canadians would regard it as an indication of strength, not weakness, if he took further initiatives to induce and persuade the Soviets back to the bargaining table. He said that he had no response at all from the Soviets, however, and referred to a handwritten letter he had sent General Secretary Andropov from the hospital to which there had been no response. "I don't even know if they got it," he said. At the end of the meeting he said, "Brian, let me know if there is anything we can do. Don't go to Ireland again without me."

At the Shamrock Summit in Quebec City on March 17, 1985

Our first round of private talks ended with Reagan telling one of his famous jokes. Chuckling throughout, he regaled his listeners with the story of the time men from separate American and British units found themselves in the same pub one day in England during the Second World War. As the British soldiers hoisted ales in honour of the king, the brash Americans returned a toast of their own. "Screw the king," the Americans said. Surprised, the Brits again held up their beers. "Screw the president," they answered. At that point the American soldiers chimed in, saying in unison, "We'll drink to that!"

That wasn't the only occasion Reagan had me laughing during his visit. In his memoirs, *Ronald Reagan in Private,* the president's executive assistant, Jim Kuhn, later described another Shamrock Summit Reaganism that helps to explain why Reagan was such a beloved leader. "Both leaders were scheduled to speak at an event . . . which required Mulroney and Reagan to walk into the event together," Kuhn wrote. "But, I earnestly explained to them, protocol dictated that they wait until the others in the U.S. and Canadian delegations had taken their places in the room first, which seemed to be taking a long time. Reagan looked at Mulroney and grinned. 'Brian, it's protocol—spelled bullshit.'"

When we discussed Reagan's approach to taxation and deficits, I was able to glimpse the brilliant politician that lay behind Reagan's sunny smile. The president said he planned to take his deficit-fighting plans directly to the American people. "What about Congress?" I asked. "It is not necessary," Reagan replied, "to make Congress see the light—just to feel the heat."

Personal Journal: April 6, 1985 (Shamrock Summit)

After some ten hours in his presence, Reagan gives me this impression: he is a kindly man, possessed of a warm good humour, generous instincts, and what appears to be a total absence of malice. He speaks ill of no one.

At meetings Reagan starts off and speaks to the main issues. He is clearly in command but defers easily to subordinates for details. They do not intrude on the discussions unless he asks them to. He is ready with a friendly quip or allusion. When I read him my notes of my meeting with Gorbachev in Moscow 10 days earlier where I said that Reagan had the strength at home to make peace, his eyes welled up. He seems deeply appreciative of small acts of friendship and truly grateful for kind words in defence of the U.S. He recognizes this may cause me difficulty in some quarters in Canada and is clearly moved by my straightforward declaration that I intend to give our friends, the U.S. included, the benefit of the doubt.

For my part, the president strikes me, as he has for some years, as one who has been persistently underestimated by the trendy commentators and analysts. He is a shrewd judge of people and character. A deeply religious man, he appears free from theories. His views are simple but sound, rooted in proven results and not uncompromising virtue. RR may, 100 years from now, be revered as a truly great president because he made America feel good about itself again—made it throw off its self-doubt, accrued from Vietnam to Watergate, and become a more proud and unsullied nation, capable of providing strong leadership. He really grasps the big picture.

Prior to President Reagan's Departure from Office
Following a Private Luncheon on June 5, 1988

Ronald Reagan has been for me a good ally and a trusted associate in international affairs. He is a deeply honourable man, unfailingly courteous and sensitive, with strongly held straightforward views. And he has been a remarkable success as President [and around the world] and a powerful friend of Canada.

The impact of significant public policy decisions is often unclear in the early years. It sometimes takes a considerable period—frequently decades—before the full consequences of an important initiative become apparent. As Reinhold Niebuhr reminded us: "Nothing worth doing is completed in our life time; therefore we must be saved by hope. Nothing fine or beautiful or good makes complete sense in any immediate context of history; therefore we must be saved by faith."

Nonetheless, if one allows a moment of reflection on the arc of history since he left the Oval Office 26 years ago, some early judgments are appropriate.

The world was a very different place when President Reagan took office in 1981 from when he left it in 1989, and worlds apart from what it has become since. Leonid Brezhnev then ruled the 15 republics of the Soviet empire, a vast federation in some decline, but still powerful, aggressive, and hostile. Cold War tensions prevailed, and regional conflicts abounded. The Soviets refused to discuss arms control at Geneva, even as they became embroiled in regional wars from Afghanistan to Africa. Communist leaders firmly agreed with Mr. Khrushchev's threat to the West that "we shall bury you"—and conducted themselves with a swagger that meant clearly it was a matter of time.

Some in the West during the early 1980s, believing both systems—communism and democracy—were equally valid and viable, advocated a policy of "live and let live." Others, while deploring the tragic human injustices and economic flaws inherent in the Soviet system, saw it as a country much more powerful and successful than it really was and viewed it as worthy at least of Western tolerance, if not muted praise. In contrast, Ronald Reagan saw communism as an insidious menace to be contained, challenged, and confronted in the genuine belief that its underpinnings of brute force, destruction of individual liberties, and widespread moral decay would fall swiftly to the gathering winds of freedom and the shining achievements of democracy. Provided, as he said, that NATO and the Western industrialized democracies stood firm and united. They did, and we know now who was right.

Ronald Reagan's role as a peacemaker has long been underreported. From the evolution of his relationship with President Gorbachev and the beneficial results that ensued, to his willingness to share SDI with all interested partners, from his support of a renewed UN to his opposition to the MAD (mutual assured destruction) tenet of national security. As he wrote in his memoir: "It was like having two Westerners standing in a saloon aiming their guns at each others' head permanently. There had to be a better way."

President Reagan believed in a better way. He believed in "peace through strength," and he delivered well beyond the dreams of many who were both skeptical and weary after years of tension and apprehension in a stultifying Cold War.

Ronald Reagan knew the patronizing sneer of the political and media elites. He didn't care. He knew the difference between simplistic and a powerful idea simply expressed. He read widely and absorbed the numbing policy briefings every leader endures. When it came to leading America, and sometimes the world, he was masterful at refining a complex policy challenge into a single ringing sentence—none more memorable or historic in its impact than "Mr. Gorbachev: Tear down this Wall!" The wall came down because of Ronald Reagan. And with it came the implosion of an empire and the strong winds of freedom that swept dictators and totalitarianism alike from the face of Europe, to the Urals and beyond.

For Canada and the United States, the post–Cold War world offered unique opportunities and daunting challenges. We began from a common heritage of democratic traditions and a common defense of liberty. There are reminders of that from the trenches of one war to the beaches of the next, places inscribed in the history of valor, where Canadians and Americans have stood together, where Canadians and Americans have died together, in the defense of freedom.

And because we have remained true to those values and had the courage and the strength to defend them over the decades in NATO, Korea, the Gulf, Afghanistan, and elsewhere, within the last two decades, the Berlin Wall fell and Germany was reunited; a trade unionist from Gdansk became president of Poland; a dissident poet sat in the castle in Prague, as communist regimes tumbled like dominoes across Central and Eastern Europe; and, in the second Russian revolution, the people of Moscow made a human wall around their parliament, and Soviet tanks that had crushed each stirring of liberty for 70 years now dared not cross.

One could forgive President Reagan a small smile of satisfaction as, one by one, his ideas triumphed and his policies found vindication.

Some commentators smirked when years ago Ronald Reagan articulated a vision of a free trade zone that would stretch from Anchorage to Tierra del Fuega, at the southern tip of Latin America. As a new prime minister in 1985, I signaled President Reagan that Canada was interested in negotiating a comprehensive free trade agreement with the United States of America. In 1987, following more than two years of challenging negotiations, we reached agreement. President Reagan and I subsequently signed the massive and quite radical agreement, which came into effect on January 1, 1989, leading to the largest trading relationship between any two nations in world history.

The Canada-U.S. Free Trade Agreement led to the creation of the North American Free Trade Agreement by including Mexico, and one day in the foreseeable future this vast trading relationship shall embrace the entire hemisphere—34 nations, 900 million people, and a GDP of $20 trillion—and another of Ronald Reagan's visionary dreams will have become reality.

There remain, of course, daunting challenges for President Reagan's successors and mine, including the most challenging question of international terrorism, but I am satisfied that, "on our watch," as he would say, we completed many of the essential tasks we took up—working for a safer world and preparing our people for the challenges of the new global economy.

I believe, as President Reagan said in his address to the British Parliament, that "we have come safely through the worst." And that we did is due in very significant measure to the calm, confident, and poised leadership that he offered to his country and the world.

In a special way, I am grateful for the enduring friendship between our two nations, described 70 years ago by Winston Churchill: "That long frontier from the Atlantic to Pacific oceans guarded only by neighbourly respect and honourable obligations is an example to every country, and a pattern for the future of the world." The relationship between Canada and the United States, so privileged and enhanced by President Reagan, remains a model to the world because, for 200 years, our people have overcome differences and disagreements with goodwill, mutual respect, and a sharp focus on those areas of common interest and shared objectives, providing a magnificent example of international comity and achievement for other nations around the world to follow.

May our common future and that of our great nations be guided by wise men and women who will remember always the golden achievements of the Reagan era and the success that can be theirs if the values of freedom and democracy are preserved, unsullied and undiminished, until the unfolding decades remember little else.

I salute all those who have been involved in the preparation and publication of this important volume. In doing so, they have contributed to an increased understanding of a crucial and historic period in American and world history. They have also, through their hard work, contributed to an increased understanding and appreciation before history of a president— Ronald Reagan—with whom it was my high honor and privilege to serve.

REAGAN'S LEGACY IN A WORLD TRANSFORMED

Introduction

PAUL KENGOR AND JEFFREY L. CHIDESTER

There have been a remarkable number of books on President Ronald Reagan, from conventional biographies of his life and his presidency to accounts of everything from his movie career to his governorship to his economic policies to his faith, and still many more. The supply seems to reflect demand. Reagan remains a very well liked president and figure. He won the California governorship twice in landslides and then did the same at the national level, taking 44 of 50 states from an incumbent president in 1980 and then winning 49 of 50 states in his reelection bid four years later—and at a time when the majority of registered voters were Democrats; that is, the party of his opposition. He twice won states that a conservative Republican presidential candidate today could only dream of winning: California, Massachusetts, New Jersey, New York, Pennsylvania, and more. Reagan's combined Electoral College margin was 1,014 to 62.

A two-term Republican, Reagan left the presidency with the highest Gallup approval numbers of any president since Eisenhower and had followed a string of presidencies (both Democrat and Republican) that had ended in defeat or despair. Of Reagan's immediate predecessors, Jimmy Carter failed to win reelection, Gerald Ford never won a presidential election, Richard Nixon resigned in disgrace, and Lyndon Johnson—who replaced a president killed in office—refused to even seek his party's renomination for another term. Reagan's successor, George H. W. Bush, who was elected in large part because of his closeness to Reagan, failed to secure reelection. Today, Reagan routinely ranks as not only the favorite president of the American public[1] and, in one striking poll, was even judged "the greatest American of all time,"[2] but also places among the most successful presidents in surveys of presidential scholars.[3]

The goal here is not to focus on the positive at the exclusion of any negatives. The point is that Ronald Reagan's success and appeal help explain the considerable ongoing interest in the man and his presidency. It also says something about his legacy. It is a legacy that extends beyond American borders, as Reagan might be even more popular in countries like Poland and the Czech Republic—former Soviet Bloc nations that Reagan once committed to liberating as president in the 1980s. It is no coincidence that Poles are building monuments to Ronald Reagan. Many of the books on Reagan have focused on his sustained effort to end the Soviet grip behind the Iron Curtain.

Yet, of all the books on Reagan, never have a group of diverse scholars come together in one volume to consider not so much the Reagan presidency in the years 1981–1989, but to analyze the global impact of Reagan and his presidency in the years during and since he left the Oval Office, 1981–2014. Indeed, it has been more than 30 years since Ronald Reagan first took the oath of office as president of the United States. In that time, the world has undergone momentous changes: the Soviet Union literally disintegrated, freedom swept through and beyond the Iron Curtain, the nuclear-weapons competition between the United States and the former Soviet Union declined and then diminished, political and economic integration has advanced in Europe, globalization has transformed countries and the international system, new global powers have emerged, the calamity of September 11, 2001, stunned America and the world, and a rising international threat (radical Islam) has emerged and continues to be confronted. Epic changes have taken place not only in the former Soviet Union, Eastern Europe, and Asia but also in the volatile Middle East, from significant shake-ups in Iraq and Afghanistan to regime changes and chaos in Egypt, Libya, and Syria, with portents of change of some sort (not always clear) blowing throughout the region. America's last president, George W. Bush, spoke repeatedly of extending Ronald Reagan's "March of Freedom" into the Middle East.

To what extent did the Reagan presidency influence these many changes? Aided by the benefit of historical perspective, it is a fitting time to reflect upon the Reagan legacy a generation later. Fortunately, a committed group of highly accomplished Reagan scholars from a broad array of disciplines have been doing just that over the course of the last two decades, researching and publishing extensively since the end of the Cold War. Unfortunately, they have failed to gather together in one house, or in one volume—until now. Here, we present such a volume, *Reagan's Legacy in a World Transformed*.

At some level, big or small, major or minor, here or there, the world today is one that President Reagan helped to transform. There is unanimity on that point among scholars, but there is disagreement over the precise details and exact level of impact. How, for instance, did Reagan aid that transformation? To what degree? And with the assistance of whom, what, where, and when? He most certainly did not act alone. When it comes to the end of the Cold War and collapse of communism, for instance, we certainly cannot neglect names like Mikhail Gorbachev, Margaret Thatcher, Pope John Paul II, Boris Yeltsin, Václav Havel, and Lech Wałesa or movements like Solidarity and Charter 77—just for starters.

Those are vital historical questions that must be answered and which the scholars in this book endeavor to address. The volume includes a varied group of thinkers: liberals and conservatives, Democrats and Republicans, moderates and independents. Certainly, not all of our contributors were Reagan supporters, nor does everyone agree on Reagan's level of impact. For that matter, we, the editors, do not agree with every statement by every scholar in this volume or with every final conclusion. Likewise, not every scholar in this volume agrees with every chapter. We, the editors, do agree, however, that all contributors are thoughtful, respected scholars who offer intriguing, worthwhile retrospectives on the Reagan presidency and Ronald Reagan's legacy today.

The contributors also addressed these questions from a disparate set of lenses. Some have served in government, while others have conducted their work within the academy; several have toiled in both spheres. The range of disciplinary specializations represented by our contributors, which includes the American presidency, diplomatic and military history, economics, international relations, and political science, among others still, provides a uniquely broad look at this topic. As such, this volume also lays the foundation for a more integrative analysis of Reagan's presidency and his ongoing global legacy.

We begin the volume with essays on Reagan's economic policies and philosophy, their impact at home and abroad, and their relevance to the world today. Alfred E. Eckes Jr. looks at the emergence of globalization, and how and when and where it was rooted in certain policies and thinking of President Reagan. Eckes says that during the 1980s, Ronald Reagan, together with British prime minister Margaret Thatcher, "succeeded in knocking down many of the barriers segmenting the global economy." Steps taken or initiated under Reagan to deregulate or loosen government regulations had the effect over time of accelerating flows of goods and services, financial transactions, and movements of people—all pivotal to the expanding global economy. Eckes believes that the present economic climate has raised questions about whether Reagan-era reforms "went too far, too fast." Nonetheless, states Eckes, Reagan's initiatives in trade and finance set the agenda for his successors.

Eckes is followed by Henry R. Nau, who takes a detailed look at Reagan's free-market policies and their emulation abroad, particularly in Europe. Nau argues that the economic policies of the Reagan administration were a "key factor in the record growth and expansion of the global economy between 1980 and 2010"—a period marked by liberalization in international trade and financial markets and the widening of the global market to include former communist and developing countries. Nau's chapter is followed by Peter Trubowitz, who examines the relationship between domestic and international conditions in Reagan's formulation of "grand strategy" during his presidency. Trubowitz delves into the military, economic, and diplomatic means that Reagan pursued to achieve certain foreign-policy ends. Trubowitz maintains that when it comes to foreign policymaking, presidents are far more partisan than conventional wisdom holds—with Ronald Reagan no exception. Yet, states Trubowitz, what distinguished Reagan's presidency from others was "how the intensely partisan imperative *reinforced* geopolitical incentives." The rise of powerful GOP constituencies favoring military spending and power projection made it possible for Reagan to abandon the low-cost versions of containment favored by other Republican presidents and invest heavily in "*internal* balancing" against the Soviets. These two chapters not only trace Reagan's global legacy, but the impact of his administration's policies on domestic policy formulation in the years after his presidency as well.

Part II of the volume, with essays by Jeffrey L. Chidester and Paul Kengor, takes us within those foreign-policy ends as the authors examine Reagan's impact on Europe, specifically Eastern Europe. Chidester examines U.S. policy toward Eastern Europe during the Cold War, demonstrating how Reagan made a decisive break from the détente-era presidents and effectively restored the strategy of "rollback," leaving an enduring imprint on the region. Reagan is remembered in Eastern Europe today not only for his support of anti-communist reformers and his broader crusade against the Soviet Union but also as a "referential figure" for supporters of greater political and economic freedom today. Kengor notes how Reagan's "*March of Freedom*" in Eastern

Europe—dramatically announced by the president in his June 1982 Westminster Address in London—was, notably, invoked by President George W. Bush some twenty years later. Bush sought to extend that march beyond the former Iron Curtain and into the Middle East after the events of September 11, 2001, and not without intense controversy. Bush believed that such an extension (as he interpreted it) could lessen the chances for violence and terrorism in the Middle East region. Whether President Bush was so justified is another question, as is the matter of whether he properly appropriated Reagan's vision. Either way, there is no denying that Bush's invocation of Reagan, correct or incorrect, wise or unwise, is a striking example of Ronald Reagan's 1980s ideas being applied to the modern world.

Kiron K. Skinner and Eliot A. Cohen follow in Part III with a broader look at American defense and foreign policy during the Reagan presidency and its legacy today. Skinner delivers a long-overdue look at Ronald Reagan's policies on Middle East terrorism and the notable relevancy of those policies in the modern era. We tend to glean Reagan's policies on Middle East terrorism through the prism of Iran-Contra (which Skinner addresses). As Skinner shows, however, there was much more to the story. Her chapter provides a detailed review of the considerable terror threats that exploded during the 1980s, followed by an examination of the Reagan administration's institutional and doctrinal responses to these threats. She sees terrorism policy during the Reagan years as nothing short of the beginning of a new U.S. grand strategy that redounds to today. Skinner writes that "the terrorism policy that evolved in the Reagan administration did provide the building blocks for the terrorism policies of future administrations, as evidenced by public statements that reflected national-security directives and laws that the president and his foreign-policy advisers championed." Skinner lists many examples of these directives and laws and concludes that "the Reagan administration did in fact commence policies to combat terror that have been path-dependent for future administrations."

Cohen maintains that Reagan's legacy in defense resembles, in certain ways, his legacy in domestic politics: unwavering faith in America's ideals and strength, a belief in simple (if difficult) solutions to complex problems, and "not too much interest in the details of how to bring the former to bear in accomplishing the latter." The good news for Reagan's successors, according to Cohen, was that Reagan bequeathed to them the world's most powerful military; the bad news is that he (or at least some of his key subordinates) left behind inadequate ideas of how to employ that military. "Partly because of

Ronald Reagan's achievements," concludes Cohen, those successors "had to cope with a world less easily adapted to the grand strategic simplicities that had made Reagan uniquely effective." Cohen also examines the Weinberger Doctrine, named for Reagan defense secretary Caspar Weinberger. Weinberger advocated and presided over the largest peacetime buildup of military force in U.S. history. In addition to the material legacies of the buildup, Weinberger also outlined an approach to the use of military force—the so-called Weinberger Doctrine. According to Cohen, this doctrine, which represented a reaction to America's Vietnam experience, "did not always square with President Reagan's actions." Nonetheless, says Cohen, the doctrine represented an important school of thought about the use of force that was influential until the beginning of a new century.

The Cohen and Skinner essays offer a transition to Part IV of the volume, chapters by Paul Kengor, Beth A. Fischer, and Julian E. Zelizer. These three essays zero in on one of Ronald Reagan's most unmistakable legacies: the crucial cut in nuclear weapons and reduced prospects of nuclear war that the fortieth president negotiated with Soviet general secretary Mikhail Gorbachev, literally creating a safer world well beyond the 1980s. Kengor, picking up from Cohen and Skinner, anchors his analysis in Reagan's "peace through strength" philosophy and tactic. Kengor details how Reagan, despite his rightly earned hawkish, anti-communist reputation, had planned all along to one day sit down and negotiate with the Soviets. Fischer focuses on the Reagan military buildup and Strategic Defense Initiative and where and when it goaded the Soviet leadership—and (at times) also complicated the plans of Soviet reformers. "Evidence shows that the buildup often made it more difficult for the Soviet leader to cooperate with Washington," states Fischer. Nonetheless, cooperation did come. Fischer calls the subsequent diminished threat of nuclear annihilation "Reagan's most enduring legacy," one that he achieved alongside Gorbachev: "Ronald Reagan and Mikhail Gorbachev envisioned a nuclear-free world, and they sought to make this vision a reality despite strong resistance from advisers and entrenched bureaucracies. It was, therefore, this visionary leadership, and not the buildup, that was Reagan's most important legacy in the Cold War."

Julian E. Zelizer likewise visits the "historic" arms agreements that Reagan negotiated with Gorbachev. Zelizer, however, considers the role of domestic liberal forces in prodding Reagan to the table. Zelizer writes: "A closer look at Reagan's presidency reveals that liberalism and its continued impact on American politics in the 1980s played an important role in constraining Reagan and pushing him toward a more circumscribed national security agenda." Zelizer concludes by considering how those constraints have affected policymakers in the post–Cold War world. He maintains that "the constraints on military intervention abroad by U.S. presidents and Congress in the post-1989 era are not drastically different from the 1980s. The American public continues to share a distaste and skepticism toward large-scale military action overseas."

All three authors in Part IV agree on one thing in particular: together, Ronald Reagan and Mikhail Gorbachev negotiated unprecedented agreements on nuclear arms. In areas like the Strategic Arms Reduction Treaty (START), they did not merely seek to limit the growth in stockpiles of long-range nuclear missiles—as their predecessors had done—but sought to actually reduce the number of missiles. With the Intermediate-Range Nuclear Forces (INF) Treaty, signed at the Washington Summit in December 1987, the two leaders took the extraordinary step of eliminating an entire class of nuclear weapons. The INF Treaty is thus arguably the greatest of agreements dealing with nuclear warheads. More so, the two superpower leaders initiated additional arms negotiations that were picked up and ultimately signed by their successors in the post-1989 era. The result, in all, was an undeniably safer post–Cold War world. The three essays by Kengor, Fischer, and Zelizer are about how Ronald Reagan got there and with the indispensable help of whom.

In the fifth and final section of the volume, Kim R. Holmes and Barry E. Carter consider lessons from Ronald Reagan on multilateralism and a "pragmatic internationalism." Holmes notes that Reagan believed that America had a special role to play in the world—as a moral leader and "beacon" and "force for freedom" for other nations and peoples. Reagan believed that the advance of freedom was necessary for a lasting peace and that America's moral and security roles as a world leader could advance both peace and freedom. This, the president believed, required a strong America capable of protecting itself, its allies, and its interests around the world. Holmes maintains that this strategy included an often-forgotten willingness by Reagan to work through international organizations like the United Nations—contrary to the common view of Reagan as a unilateralist. Holmes also looks at Reagan lessons learned or disregarded by his White House successors. Carter argues that although Reagan's foreign policy was often characterized by deep ideological conviction and soaring rhetoric, particularly in the fight against global communism, the president also "frequently engaged in pragmatic internationalism when such an

approach promised the most beneficial result for America's national interests."
Carter notes that Reagan demonstrated this in such diverse areas as arms
control—specifically, negotiations over the INF Treaty and the Law of the Sea
Treaty—and international finance and trade. These subjects are very much alive
today; indeed, in recent years, the likes of the Law of the Sea Treaty have been
vigorously debated.

As noted, not every reader will agree with every assertion in these chapters. That is not our intention. Nonetheless, we all agree that Ronald Reagan's
presidency was a historic one that made a distinct impact on the world. Now,
more than two decades later, it is time to take a careful look at that multifaceted legacy upon a world transformed, that very dynamic world of 1981–2014.
Let the reading—and the discussion—begin.

AT HOME AND ABROAD

The Global Impact of Reagan's Domestic Policy

1

Ronald Reagan and the New Age of Globalization

ALFRED E. ECKES JR.

When Ronald Reagan took the presidential oath of office in January 1981, the prolonged Cold War with the Soviet Union was the dominant theme of international relations. When President Reagan left office eight years later, the *New York Times* editorialized that the Soviet Union was "writhing in economic distress and pulling in its military horns." The Cold War would soon be history. An important reason for this outcome lies in the complex globalization process and in the economic revolution that President Reagan propelled with his words and actions. By 1988, government leaders around the world, many of whom once applauded state regulation and national economies, joined Reagan and British prime minister Margaret Thatcher in celebrating globalization and the magic of markets.[1]

This chapter focuses on Reagan's involvement with the globalization process. Globalization is a complex, synergistic process that integrates peoples and nations into larger communities and networks. The factors driving globalization include improvements in technology (especially in communications, transportation, and information processing), as well as the actions of governments to deregulate markets and open borders. Among the tangible results are vastly expanded flows of people, money, goods, services, and information.[2]

The Roots of "Globalization"

Interestingly, Reagan and Thatcher were slow to appropriate the term "globalization," although they were both aware of the underlying dynamics of change.

Futurist John Naisbitt and Harvard marketing professor Theodore Levitt were the first to popularize the term. In his best-selling book *Megatrends* (1982), Naisbitt examined the transition from national to world markets and offered some preliminary thoughts on the subject. But a 1983 article in the prestigious *Harvard Business Review* most influenced elite opinion. The author, Theodore Levitt, explained succinctly how powerful forces of technological change had created a "new commercial reality—the emergence of global markets." He asserted that the "globalization of markets is at hand."[3] Over time, others adopted this terminology, and by the late 1980s, it was widely used in public and academic discourse.

A review of Reagan's speeches indicates that he first made specific reference to globalization in an appearance before the Atlantic Council in June 1988 during the final year of his presidency, though he spoke often about matters relating to the world or global economy and free trade. Thatcher apparently did not use the term in speeches until 1996, six years after she left office, but like Reagan she was acutely aware of trends. Somewhat paradoxically, Reagan and Thatcher can be viewed as the leading architects and facilitators of globalization during the 1980s. Through their free-market rhetoric and the actions they took to deregulate and open markets, they brought political drive to the globalization process.[4]

While globalization has many dimensions, Reagan and Thatcher embraced *economic globalization*, focusing on the opening and integration of financial and commercial markets. They were united in pursuit of free trade, but both recognized that for free trade to be sustainable, it must be fair. America's motto, Reagan said in 1986, is "free and fair trade with free and fair traders." He noted that governments sometimes do not play by the rules, including using subsidies to gain "an unfair advantage." As a result, his administration used existing trade laws "aggressively" to pry open foreign markets and force others to play by the rules.[5]

Reagan and Thatcher also understood the role of technological forces—especially improvements in transportation and communications—as well as the role of governments in removing barriers to market forces. For example, in a speech to the Business Roundtable in June 1988, Reagan observed that "the greatest history makers in our time are not politicians and statesmen, but inventors, entrepreneurs, and others who are transforming the technological base of civilization and whose search for new markets is leading us into a more global economy." Reagan may have been thinking of individuals like Harvard dropout

Bill Gates, who was developing Microsoft computer software, or Silicon Valley entrepreneurs on the cutting edge in various technologies, or even Fred Smith of Federal Express, who initiated overnight air delivery and international service during the 1980s.[6]

A former radio announcer and movie actor, Reagan understood the importance of communications and the power of pictures. To promote change in Soviet-controlled Eastern Europe, he boosted funding for Radio Free Europe and Radio Liberty and initiated a satellite television network. The latter carried programs showing scenes of the American good life—including modern supermarkets without lines of impatient customers. Reagan, who lauded American exceptionalism, believed that American-style democracy, freedom, and human rights would appeal to people everywhere, particularly in areas with dictatorial governments. However, Thatcher, a conservative nationalist fearful of Europeanization, later would express misgivings about the universal, cultural dimensions of globalization, saying that they threatened the national values and traditions that unite people.[7]

When Reagan and Thatcher first sought national elective offices in the 1970s, the experiences of the Great Depression, World War II, and the continuing Cold War competition shaped policy debates and enhanced the authority of national governments over markets. During this period, the largest industrial economies pursued somewhat uncoordinated, nationalistic policies. Governments managed perhaps 70 percent of world trade through tariffs, quotas, exchange controls, export restrictions, and other border barriers. For much of the period, private capital flows took a back seat to international institutions (such as the World Bank) and national governments, which were the largest providers of development aid.

The Great Depression had resulted in an economic consensus in support of Keynesian-style government economic management, which remained influential. In the post–World War II period, governments in advanced countries assigned a high priority to combating unemployment and relied on Keynesian economics, with its heavy emphasis on government fiscal policy, to manage national economies. Most governments in the Atlantic region embraced deficit spending and government-funded programs to cushion unemployment and provide health care and social security benefits. During this period of what some scholars call "embedded liberalism," most advanced countries nationalized, or heavily regulated, the commanding heights of national economies, including basic industries like steel, railroads, airlines, and the financial sector—particularly banking. Interventionist government policies such as these necessitated high taxes on individuals and corporations. In 1980, the top individual tax rate was 73 percent in the United States, 83 percent in Britain, 65 percent in Germany, and 87 percent in Sweden.[8]

One result of Cold War economics and embedded liberalism was that the government sector consumed a growing portion of resources and crowded out private investment and consumer demand. In the 1970s, when the Organization of Petroleum Exporting Countries (OPEC) succeeded in quadrupling oil prices, the Keynesian consensus achieved not growth and prosperity but double-digit inflation, high unemployment, and low productivity growth. During this period of stagflation, countries on both sides of the Atlantic proved unable to meet public expectations for good-paying jobs and better lives. Years of inflation, high unemployment, and stagnant growth underscored the limitations of Keynesian consensus and opened the door to a resurgence of free-market capitalism. It seemed that communism, socialism, and statism had been proved intellectually bankrupt.[9]

The Rising Tide of the Free Market

Among academic economists and business and political leaders, there was a rising intellectual tide in support of a new capitalism to revive the free market through deregulation and lower taxes. The intellectual leaders were Friedrich Hayek, an Austrian, and Milton Friedman, a laissez-faire economist at the University of Chicago, both of whom won Nobel Prizes for economics in the mid-1970s for research supportive of free-market capitalism. Friedman's 1962 book, *Capitalism and Freedom*, articulated the case for deregulating industry, privatizing welfare programs, and substituting a flat tax for the progressive income tax that burdened enterprise and achievement disproportionately.[10]

Reagan and Thatcher shared this enthusiasm for free markets and entered politics determined to deregulate, privatize industries, and open markets. Growing up as a grocer's daughter, Thatcher early in life became a true believer in the power of free markets and an unbending critic of state socialism, which she thought ravaged the national economy.[11] Reagan's experiences were different. He embraced Franklin Delano Roosevelt's New Deal and backed Democrat Harry Truman in the 1948 presidential election. But Reagan became aware of the burdens of high taxation on individual enterprise during the 1940s as an actor in the highest tax bracket and during the 1950s as a spokesman for General Electric.[12] He was a Democrat for Eisenhower, then a Democrat for Nixon. By 1964, when he backed conservative Arizona senator Barry Goldwater, Reagan called himself a Republican. Together, Thatcher and Reagan pursued neoliberal economic agendas in public life, and their successes spread around the world, inspiring imitation during the 1980s.

Some of Reagan's and Thatcher's most significant and enduring accomplishments involved knocking down walls. Almost everyone is familiar with President Reagan's speech at the Brandenburg Gate in June 1987 when he challenged Soviet leader Mikhail Gorbachev to "tear down this wall." In that speech, he also reminded listeners that openness and freedom could transform the world. He lauded countries in the Pacific region, where "free markets are working miracle after miracle of economic growth. In the industrialized nations, a technological revolution is taking place—a revolution marked by rapid, dramatic advances in computers and telecommunications."[13]

In terms of the emerging global marketplace, some of the most significant contributions involved reducing barriers to international trade and finance. Steps taken or initiated under the Reagan administration to deregulate or loosen government regulations had the effect over time of accelerating flows of goods and services, financial transactions, and movements of people—all essential to the expanding global economy.

Efforts to reduce trade barriers had their origins in the reciprocal trade agreements program of Secretary of State Cordell Hull, who served in that position for 11 years under Roosevelt, and in post–World War II efforts to establish the General Agreement on Tariffs and Trade (GATT). When Reagan took office, that multilateral process was producing diminishing returns, and deadlocks over agriculture and nontariff barriers raised questions about the future of trade liberalization. A large number of developing countries had little interest or stake in the multilateral process. Over time, the Reagan administration succeeded in reviving the multilateral process, engaging more nations, and broadening the negotiating agenda to include trade in services, investments and intellectual property, and dispute settlement, among other issues.

After difficult and protracted negotiations, the Uruguay Round, which President Reagan launched in 1986, succeeded eight years later. The results included a permanent trade organization, the World Trade Organization (WTO), to replace the provisional GATT, a broad framework of rules for international business in the twenty-first century, and a more effective dispute-settlement mechanism to resolve conflicts. Eleven developing countries joined the GATT during the Reagan administration, including several important emerging-market nations: Colombia, Mexico, Hong Kong, Thailand, and several others from sub-Saharan Africa.[14]

To energize the multilateral process, Reagan's chief trade negotiators, Bill Brock and Clayton Yeutter, signaled a willingness to pursue bilateral and regional agreements in competition with multilateral talks. Fear of exclusion from bilateral pacts, they thought, would prompt governments to make more concessions in the GATT negotiations. The U.S.-Israel Free Trade Agreement of 1984 and the U.S.-Canada Free Trade Agreement of 1988 were first steps toward a more active bilateral and regional negotiating agenda, which appeared compatible with the multilateral talks. Subsequently, the Bush and Clinton administrations continued this approach and succeeded in concluding the Uruguay Round and integrating China into the WTO.

Eager to build on those results and integrate developing countries into the prosperous global economy, Presidents Clinton and George W. Bush pursued bilateral and regional free-trade initiatives, attempting 17 free-trade agreements (FTAs) with 47 countries. These agreements involved far more than trade; they also covered services, intellectual property, and investments. In effect, the movement for comprehensive bilateral and regional FTAs was intended to reach the original Reagan goal of promoting conditions in which private enterprise could flourish throughout the world economy.

During the Reagan years, world trade continued to grow more rapidly than world production, as it had since 1950. World exports of goods and services climbed 48.1 percent from 1981 to 1989, while world gross domestic product rose 29.7 percent. This expansion of trade brought both benefits and dislocations. Consumers gained from lower prices and a greater variety of merchandise. Imports surged as the United States recovered from the 1981–1982 recession, and as a result, the U.S. share of world imports rose three percentage points from 1980 to 1988. American consumers discovered that the low-cost shoes and apparel available in big-box stores, which previously came from domestic suppliers, now arrived from Hong Kong, Korea, Taiwan, and Singapore. These four countries boosted their share of world exports four percentage points.[15]

But the other side of Asian gains was the downward spiral of traditional American manufacturing—particularly the labor-intensive industries of apparel, footwear, steel, autos, electronics, and the like. Imports of manufactures rose 151 percent, with apparel up 234 percent and electrical equipment up 237 percent. Not surprisingly, many domestic producers and their workers found it difficult to compete with low-priced imports. The manufacturing sector lost more than 600,000 jobs net as companies closed plants and cut costs. While new service industries created some 15 million new positions and absorbed many dislocated workers, service jobs generally paid less than the jobs lost in the industrial sector.[16]

Widespread public concern about job losses and low-priced and sometimes low-quality imports during the mid-1980s prompted some retailers to experiment with patriotic marketing. Arkansas merchant Sam Walton decorated his Wal-Mart stores in red, white, and blue and made a public commitment to buy everything possible from domestic manufacturers. But after he died in 1992, his successors turned away from domestic sourcing and became more reliant on Chinese goods. They established Wal-Mart's global supply center in Shenzhen, China.[17]

As imports soared and manufacturing jobs disappeared, some political opponents criticized the Reagan administration for being too zealous and doctrinaire in pursuit of free trade and too supportive of Silicon Valley high tech and financial services. Certainly many in organized labor and import-competing and smokestack industries complained that the administration did too little to help traditional industries and their workers cope with surging imports. They wanted greater protection and even government industrial policies to restore the competitiveness of traditional American industries. Ironically, some free-trade enthusiasts seemed to overlook the significance of the structural trade deficit. They claimed that because the Reagan administration added trade barriers, it was the most protectionist since Herbert Hoover.[18]

In point of fact, Reagan was the first U.S. president since Grover Cleveland to endorse free trade enthusiastically. The Reagan administration used every opportunity to push for free trade and open markets. But it was not as doctrinaire as some critics claimed. In 1981, the administration persuaded Japan to impose voluntary restraint agreements on exports of Japanese cars to the United States, a step that benefited domestic automakers and honored Reagan's campaign pledge to autoworkers. The Harley-Davidson motorcycle case is another example. When the U.S. International Trade Commission, an independent fact-finding body, recommended in 1982 a high tariff to enable Harley to adapt to increased imports of large motorcycles from Japan, the administration reluctantly went along. After four years of tariff protection, Harley reported that it had developed new models and become export-competitive again. It asked for the tariffs to be removed. At that point, Reagan visited the Harley plant in York, Pennsylvania, revved up a Harley, and proudly asserted: "There are those in Congress who say our trade policies have not worked, but you . . . are living proof that our laws are working." In making a few pragmatic concessions, Reagan and his aides succeeded in maintaining congressional support for many market-opening initiatives. Students of contemporary politics know that some more philosophically rigid administrations have achieved far less, as long delays implementing FTAs negotiated by President George W. Bush with Colombia, Panama, and South Korea may suggest.[19]

Interestingly, some libertarians contend the Reagan administration was too protectionist, but that criticism overlooks a key fact. In the 1980s, the American market had the lowest average tariffs of any major market and was the favorite dumping ground for developing countries seeking to use export-led growth of manufactures for national development. From 1980 to 1988, the merchandise trade deficit soared, climbing from $25.5 billion to $127 billion. The rising trade deficit with Japan accounted for nearly $42 billion of this increase. Oil imports sharply declined from one-third of imports in 1980 to less than 10 percent in 1988, and manufactures rose from 54 percent of total imports to 82 percent.[20]

As the Reagan administration worked to knock down trade walls and open markets, it also took important steps to integrate financial markets and promote opportunities for private capital. Unlike trade, which had seen slow liberalization since World War II, financial markets generally remained segmented until the 1980s. Government exchange controls restricted private transactions. While the United States had removed its capital controls in 1974 and Britain would do so after Thatcher's election in 1979, governments elsewhere continued to regulate capital flows. During the 1980s, developed countries would remove many of these barriers, and the developing world would do so a decade later.

As part of the Reagan administration's market-oriented program, Treasury Secretary Donald Regan sought to expand private capital flows. He worked within the Paris-based Organization for Economic Cooperation and Development (OECD) to build consensus in support of reducing or eliminating barriers to direct investment. The administration sought a multilateral understanding to create an environment in which private direct investment could contribute to the development process and that would ensure fair and equitable treatment of foreign investors. The United States was particularly concerned about government restrictions on U.S. financial service providers—such as performance requirements—and sought a more open climate for investment.[21]

During Reagan's first term, high interest rates and the administration's desire to promote a strong dollar had the effect of increasing the dollar's value 56 percent on a trade-weighted basis, thus contributing to the trade deficit. But Reagan's economic policies attracted foreign investors. Over two terms, there was a 280 percent increase in inward foreign direct investment (FDI), as corporations—particularly Japanese firms—set up manufacturing operations in the United States. By 1988, Japan had emerged as the second leading supplier of FDI to the United States behind the United Kingdom. Japanese auto plants were springing up like mushrooms across the landscape of mid-America. Inward direct investment for equity investments ($168 billion) far exceeded U.S. direct investment abroad for equity investments ($17 billion) in the period 1982–1988, signaling rising foreign confidence in the American economy and its investment climate.[22]

Similarly, the Reagan administration sought to encourage deregulation of financial services, building on a phaseout of regulatory controls over interest rates late in the Carter administration. Donald Regan, a former Merrill Lynch executive and future White House chief of staff, enthusiastically embraced the Reagan administration's deregulatory agenda. He presented the administration's proposal in 1981 to repeal Glass-Steagall Act restrictions on banking that dated from the Great Depression. This law had separated commercial banking from investment banking. Regan suggested that bank holding companies be allowed to engage in a full range of financial activities, including underwriting, trading corporate securities, and offering insurance. Similarly, brokerage firms and insurance companies would be permitted to enter the banking business. These basic proposals, radical for the early 1980s, would eventually be adopted in 1999. While the Reagan administration did not achieve all its ambitions in the financial area, it succeeded in shaping political discourse on financial reform over the next 20 years and in preparing the way for integrated global financial markets.[23]

Some of Reagan's most important decisions in the financial area involved appointments to key positions. None of these was more important than the nomination of New York economist Alan Greenspan to succeed Paul Volcker as chairman of the Federal Reserve System in 1987. Volcker, an independent Democrat and experienced central banker, first appointed by President Carter at a time of spiraling inflation and then reappointed by Reagan in 1983, had succeeded in using tight interest rates to squeeze down inflation. But Volcker was cool to tax cuts and supply-side economics. The Reagan administration chose to appoint a successor more compatible with its philosophies. Greenspan, a business economist with libertarian instincts, subscribed to the belief that free markets operated efficiently without government oversight that might curtail risk taking. He backed the so-called Washington Consensus in behalf of free trade and open markets. He supported Reagan's deregulatory agenda and encouraged foreign governments to open their capital markets to Western banks. An enthusiastic critic of excessive government regulation, Greenspan urged repeal of the Glass-Steagall Act of 1933.[24]

At the operating level, the Reagan administration's push for deregulation, privatization, and tax cutting sometimes unsettled representatives of other governments in international agencies, where some governments favored socialism and parastatal enterprises. The administration sent Joe O. Rogers, a young economist and protégé of New York congressman Jack Kemp, to Manila to become ambassador to the Asian Development Bank (ADB). Depicted in the overseas media as a shoot-from-the-hip enfant terrible, the pugnacious Rogers had little success initially in shaking up the ADB and persuading the bank's controversial Japanese president to gear lending to market-oriented policies of recipient governments. Over time, however, the ADB and other regional banks would become more responsive to market realities.[25]

At the World Bank and International Monetary Fund, where the United States was the largest shareholder, there were similar conflicts but greater receptivity to the Reagan revolution. The U.S. Treasury directed U.S. executive directors to the Bank and Fund to give special attention to borrowing countries' use of tax policies to promote savings and investment, to liberalization of foreign trade regimes, and to support for the private sector. Traditionally, the U.S. government appointed the president of the World Bank, and Reagan replaced the retiring Robert S. McNamara, a former secretary of defense in the Kennedy and Johnson administrations, with A. W. Clausen, an experienced commercial banker from California. Clausen cleaned house and replaced McNamara's interventionist development economists with neoclassical trade economists, led by Anne Krueger of the University of Minnesota. The new staff members assigned higher priority to assisting private enterprise.[26]

A Worldwide Marketplace

A number of decisions taken during the Reagan administration would over a longer term facilitate integrating emerging countries into the global system. President Carter's enthusiasm for promoting human rights in non-Western societies, where the individual is often subordinated to the perceived good of society, had antagonized leaders in many developing world countries. Reagan administration officials approached human rights differently and focused on using private enterprise and expanding trade to help developing countries to grow, modernize, and become more democratic. In Brazil, China, India, and the Middle East, this approach improved working relationships. Indian Prime Minister Rajiv Gandhi followed the Reagan example and sought to liberate the private sector from onerous government regulations. The press dubbed him "Rajiv Reagan."[27]

Near the end of his presidency, Reagan reflected on how the world was turning away from state control of economies and returning to the marketplace: "From India to Argentina, from Africa to China, and even in the Soviet Union, the shackles of state economic domination are beginning to loosen." The movement to privatize state-owned enterprises had spread worldwide. In 1992, the World Bank found that 8,500 state-owned enterprises had been privatized. These included the national lottery in Malaysia, the zoo in Buenos Aires, and the Communist Party guest house in Czechoslovakia.[28]

Among the foreign leaders who embraced elements of Reagan and Thatcher's neoliberal agenda were neighbors and allies such as Japanese prime minister Yasuhiro Nakasone (1982–1987), Canadian prime minister Brian Mulroney (1984–1993), and Mexican president Miguel de la Madrid (1982–1988). Surprisingly, neoliberalism even appealed to some French socialists, such as European Commission president Jacques Delors and World Trade Organization director-general Pascal Lamy. It also won support from trade unionists, such as Australian prime minister Bob Hawke (1983–1991), and communists in Vietnam, China, and the Soviet Union, where the lure of free markets also produced long-term changes. Economist Milton Friedman made three trips to China and received a respectful hearing from Communist Party leaders for his neoliberal approach.[29]

Over eight years, Reagan, together with Thatcher, succeeded in knocking down many walls, particularly those segmenting the global economy. Their actions facilitated revolutionary developments in information processing and communications and accelerated the globalization process. As the president said in his 1989 Farewell Address: "We meant to change a nation, and instead, we changed a world. Countries across the globe are turning to free markets and free speech and turning away from the ideologies of the past."[30]

•   •   •

As scholars know, hindsight is twenty-twenty; foresight is not. In light of recent problems involving an increasingly volatile and underregulated financial markets sector and huge structural imbalances in the global economy, there could be debate about whether Reagan-era reforms went too far, too fast. Arguably, the contemporary pattern of budgetary and current-account deficits began on Reagan's watch. In his Farewell Address, President Reagan expressed regret at the widening budget deficit, which he blamed on congressional unwillingness to cut spending. But budget deficits in America long preceded Reagan, peaking during World War II and rising sharply during the Johnson administration. These deficits widened noticeably under Reagan's successors, particularly under George W. Bush and Barack Obama. The fiscal deficit was −3.1 percent of GDP near the end of his term in fiscal year 1988, compared with −2.7 percent under President Jimmy Carter (1980), −4.7 under President George H. W. Bush (1992), and −3.2 percent in the last year of George W. Bush's presidency (2008). During President Obama's first term the deficit averaged more than −8 percent of GDP. Only President Clinton left office with a budget surplus, arguably the result of good times and a conservative Republican Congress that held the line on spending increases.[31]

Under Presidents Clinton and George W. Bush, external imbalances would widen, particularly as the United States became more dependent on Chinese imports and lending. As a share of GDP, the current account deficit reached −3.4 percent in 1987. It surpassed that level (−4.3 percent) at the end of the Clinton administration and under George W. Bush (−6 percent) in 2006 and 2007. In the 1980s, President Reagan faced a similar situation, a closed Japanese home market and mercantilist trade practices that produced large trade deficits. His administration worked diligently to open the Japanese market to American trade and investments. Over time, the United States would succeed in pushing Japan's financial sector toward deregulation and in promoting greater export opportunities for American goods. The Japanese financial bubble burst in 1990 after Reagan left office, and today Japan's financial system is far more integrated into world markets as a result of initiatives pursued in the 1980s.[32]

To summarize, in global economic matters Ronald Reagan was a transformational president, one who left the presidency quite different than he found it and set the agenda for his successors. The presidencies of Bill Clinton and the two Bushes continued many of his initiatives in trade and finance. Not only did President Reagan push the Cold War to a triumphal end with his arms buildup and communications strategies but also he moved ambitiously to deregulate government and move activities into the private sector. His efforts gave impetus to a second great age of business expansion—which is ongoing, despite the volatility. Some of the most satisfying memorials to Reagan's efforts were erected in Eastern Europe, where he inspired people, encouraged economic change, and helped bring an end to Soviet-style dictatorship. In June 2011, Hungary honored Reagan with a full statue in Freedom Square, near the U.S. Embassy in Budapest. In Poland and the Czech Republic, there were other memorials and streets named to honor the fortieth president whose words and deeds broke down barriers and brought people and countries closer together.[33]

2

The "Great Expansion"

The Economic Legacy of Ronald Reagan

HENRY R. NAU

The recession that hit the U.S. and world economy in 2008 sparked renewed debates about economic policy and America's relative position in the world. Some pundits have used and continue to use the occasion to discredit the market-oriented policies of the past 30 years and revive predictions that America is in decline.[1]

Much of this debate is to be expected. It flares every time the business cycle dips.[2] And Democrats and Republicans have disagreed for decades about economic policy, with Republicans (by and large) advocating market-oriented incentives to stimulate growth and Democrats (generally) advocating government intervention policies to reduce inequality.

But this time the debate takes on added significance. Thirty years of consistent market-oriented economic policy have transformed the U.S. and world economy. From 1980 to 2010, a "Great Expansion" of both economic growth and, yes, income equality has created the contemporary world of globalization. Compared to the direction in which America and the world were heading in the 1970s, America today is a vastly more prosperous nation, and developing nations have become vastly more affluent and powerful. As Robert Samuelson writes:

> It is not true (although often asserted) that only the very wealthy have advanced materially. Since 1980, most households have experienced substantial income gains. Vast numbers of Americans enjoy gadgets and conveniences that didn't exist then or barely existed (computers, cell phones, flat-screen TVs). Homes got larger. Poverty rates fell. . . . The idea that typical living

standards have stagnated over any meaningful period (say, ten to fifteen years) is preposterous.[3]

Not only are the poor in America better off, but hundreds of millions of poor around the world have been pulled out of poverty. And the world economy is no longer run exclusively by the Group of Seven advanced industrial nations, as it was in 1980, but by the Group of Twenty that includes Brazil, Russia, India, China, and South Africa (BRICS for short) and other developing countries.

This Great Expansion of growth and equity was set on course in large part by the market-based economic policies of Ronald Reagan in the United States and Margaret Thatcher in Europe. Reagan reversed policy trends of the 1960s and 1970s toward greater government intervention. Across the board, he moved economic policies toward more market-oriented incentives in tax, monetary, regulatory, trade, and, most important, global financial policies. Other countries followed suit over the next two decades, initially France and Germany, then developing nations such as China, Mexico, and India, and finally the communist countries of Eastern Europe and the former Soviet Union. While we can rarely prove causality in the social sciences—the world is not only too complex, but, unlike physics, social science studies human beings who can change their minds—this worldwide shift of policies toward market rules, later labeled the "Washington Consensus," coincided with the Great Expansion. A plausible case can be made that the economic policies of Ronald Reagan are in good part responsible for these extraordinary results.

To be sure, Reagan (and Thatcher) made mistakes, and this chapter does not hesitate to point them out, nor does it hesitate to criticize, where necessary, both Republican (George H. W. Bush and George W. Bush) and Democratic (Barack Obama) presidents or credit appropriate policies pursued by Democratic presidents (Bill Clinton). Among the negatives under Reagan, the gap between skilled and unskilled workers grew wider (continuing under Clinton), deficits persisted (erased by Clinton), and debt piled up (less than under George W. Bush and Obama). The Great Expansion ultimately ended in today's so-called Great Recession. I address all of these matters with ample data and perspective.

Nonetheless, by most measures, the Great Recession, which is mischievously designated as such to recall the Great Depression, is an exaggeration. The recent recession is not as bad as the recession of the 1970s and early 1980s, which the interventionist policies of the 1970s produced.[4] Most of the gains of the past 30 years remain in place. Indeed, the biggest threat to these gains is not the recession of 2008–2009 but the recent return to interventionist policies eerily similar to the 1970s, which have contributed to the slowest recovery on record.

•   •   •

How did the Great Expansion happen, and what does it mean for the present and future debate about U.S. and global economic policy? Many details and supporting data appear in publications that I and others, including many contributors to this book, have written over the years.[5] In this abbreviated chapter, I focus on four aspects: (1) the growth record of the Great Expansion, (2) the economic policies of the 1970s that caused stagflation, (3) the Reagan policies that reversed stagflation and sparked the Great Expansion, and (4) the implications for the current economic debate.

Facts of the Great Expansion

By almost any measure, the previous 30 years from 1980 to 2010 witnessed unprecedented growth in economic prosperity and equity, reversing the stagflation of the 1970s and rivaling the "golden era" of global economic growth right after World War II during the 1950s and 1960s.

There are several facts about this period, often overlooked in the pessimism accompanying the recent financial crisis, worth mentioning.[6] From 1980 to 2007, world real gross domestic product grew by about 145 percent, roughly an average of 3.4 percent a year, a rate fully comparable to the 3.5 percent per year growth during the golden era from 1950 to 1973. Even if we include the downturn of the recent recession, the global growth numbers hold up. According to International Monetary Fund (IMF) numbers, after slowing to 2.7 percent in 2008 and then dipping by 0.4 percent in 2009, world growth rebounded by 5.2 percent in 2010, 3.9 percent in 2011, 3.2 percent in 2012, and 3.0 percent in 2013. It is expected to grow by 3.6 percent in 2014.[7]

None of this global growth came at the expense of growth in the United States. Taking into account two mild recessions in 1990–1991 and 2000–2001, the U.S. economy grew by 3 percent per year over this 30-year period and created more than 50 million new jobs, accommodating growing numbers of women and immigrants in the workforce. Per-capita income increased by 65 percent, and household income corrected for the number of people in a household (down from 3.14 to 2.57 persons) went up substantially. There are fewer middle-class households in the United States today, not because middle-class households have fallen into poverty but because they have moved into higher income categories. According to Stephen Rose of the Georgetown University Center on Education and the Workforce, fewer people live today in middle-class households with incomes between $30,000 and $100,000, but more live in households making more than $100,000, which has gone up from 12 percent to 24 percent, while the percentage of people living in households making less than $30,000 stayed the same.[8] Contrary to conventional wisdom, people in the United States moved up and out of the middle class, not down from it into lower income classes.

Even more important, this Great Expansion spread wealth from the rich to the poor countries, creating greater equality in global markets than ever before. Throughout this period, developing countries grew faster than developed countries—two and even three times as fast. As a result, the share of world GDP held by emerging markets increased from 13 to 22 percent, while the U.S. share, incidentally, stayed around the same at approximately 26 percent. Some 600 to 800 million people in China, India, Brazil, and other developing countries were lifted by the Great Expansion out of poverty and into the middle class. And on the list of the top 500 global firms compiled by the *Financial Times* in June 2011, the number of Chinese companies ranked fourth behind the United States, the United Kingdom, and Japan; China has 27 such companies, with another 18 in Hong Kong. India had 14 companies on the list, Brazil 12, and Russia 11, all up significantly in rank over the past five years.[9]

This unprecedented spread of global wealth and power over the past 30 years is largely ignored in the contemporary debate, recognized only in the lament that American power has relatively declined. But in fact it has happened, at least in considerable part, because of American power and intentions. The policies and leadership of the United States after World War II envisioned precisely this sort of global community, safe for freedom and open for entrepreneurship. Much commentary makes it seem as if globalization would have happened regardless of U.S. and world economic policies.[10] But to put the matter starkly, consider what globalization might have looked like, if it had existed at all, if the inflation and cartels of the 1970s had persisted or if the Soviet Union had won the Cold War.

Stagflation in the 1970s

So, *how* did this happen? Remember the 1970s. That was the decade of stag-flation, slow growth and accelerating prices. Here are a few facts about the economic conditions and policies that prevailed in the 1970s.[11]

•   •   •

From 1968 to 1980, average annual inflation rates around the world tripled in advanced countries, while average annual growth rates declined by 25 percent and average annual unemployment rates jumped by 50 percent, all of this in comparison to the previous golden era. Inflation rates in developing countries doubled, although growth rates increased by 15 percent, mostly due to oil.

What were the policies of this period that might plausibly account for this significant deterioration of economic performance? Here is what we see:

- Average annual fiscal deficits went up as a share of GDP in every country—in advanced countries by 25 percent and in developing countries by 300 percent. Budget deficits soared 10-fold in the United States and threefold throughout the other major economies.
- Taxes, too, went up dramatically as a share of GDP. In the advanced countries alone, from 30 to 46 percent of GDP. As former Council of Economic Advisers chair Michael Boskin notes, in the United States, "the federal government's role in this period was transformed from producer of goods and services to redistributor of income, taxing some people to provide benefit payments to others." A substantial productivity slowdown occurred. While the causes were complex, "a major reason . . . was the erosion of incentives to produce income and wealth . . . caused by high and fluctuating inflation and high and rising marginal tax rates, especially on investment income."[12]
- As a result, an eye-popping increase in the size of the government sector took place in domestic economies around the world. The average rate of growth of the public sector in the United States increased from 1.6 to 1.9 percent per year, while this same average in the other major industrial economies (France, Germany, Japan, and the United Kingdom) skyrocketed from −0.5 to 6 percent. As a result, within a single decade, the public sector in advanced countries grew from 35 to 45 percent of GDP.

- Monetary policy loosened everywhere—average annual growth of monetary aggregates, M1 and M2, shot up 20 to 40 percent in advanced countries and 30 to 70 percent in developing countries.
- Trade protectionism rose. From 1974 to 1980 alone, nonmarket controls on trade rose from 36.3 to 44.3 percent of traded goods. Cartels such as the Organization of Petroleum Exporting Countries (OPEC) sprang up, and the United Nations contemplated a New International Economic Order (NIEO) that made state intervention the model for the world economy.

Taken together, these policy developments clearly impacted economic performance. We cannot know precisely which ones or in what combination these developments caused the stagflation of the 1970s. Nonetheless, imagine if those policies had been continued and projected ahead into the 1980s and 1990s. Is it likely that we would have witnessed the Great Expansion? It seems doubtful.

Policy under the Great Expansion

In fact, none of these policies was continued over the next 30 years. Whether you agreed with Reagan's economic policies or not, Reagan addressed and reversed every one of these major policy trends, with the exception of fiscal deficits. He understood that there was no magic bullet to stir growth. The approach had to be comprehensive.[13] Each of Reagan's advisers preferred some parts of his economic program and rejected others. Supply-siders believed lower taxes and investment incentives mattered most and feared that tight monetary policy would subvert the program. Monetarists believed that inflation mattered most and, once tamed, would correct investment incentives automatically. Fiscal conservatives feared budget deficits most and, after spending was cut as much as possible, supported raising taxes or not cutting them so much.

Only Reagan put all the pieces together and deftly managed the interplay of the various parts. When aides complained about tight monetary policy, he stood firm.[14] When his budget director, David Stockman, attacked defense spending and budget deficits, Reagan took him to the woodshed.[15] When aides insisted he raise taxes, he resisted.[16] He compromised, for sure, but always around the edges, never at the center of his core priorities—such as (chief among them) reductions in marginal tax rates on income, where he never wavered. Reagan, critics alleged, never thought deeply about problems, but he did think broadly about them, and recent revelations suggest he thought more deeply than anyone realized.[17]

The United States and Great Britain led the way, but eventually all other countries followed suit and the world embraced the so-called Washington Consensus which called for *more* free-market-oriented domestic and international policies.[18] This consensus included the developing world, which never participated in the golden era of Bretton Woods, and the communist countries, which entered the world economy after the Cold War, some quicker than others.

Policy directions in the world economy shifted dramatically under the Washington Consensus. First, tax rates came down dramatically. While the average marginal income tax rate in the United States was reduced from 29.4 percent in 1981 to 21.8 percent in 1988, the top marginal tax rate was reduced from 70 to 28 percent. This takes into account the relatively small tax increases of subsequent years. In 1982, Reagan agreed to increase taxes by $1 for every $3 of expenditure cuts. But a Democratic House of Representatives reneged on the spending cuts. Reagan later called the agreement the worst mistake of his presidency.[19] Nevertheless, tax rates went down and stayed down, and despite that fact, tax revenues soared as a result of higher growth, rising from $599 billion in 1981 to $990 billion in 1989. Critics called the recovery a "consumption binge," an ironic complaint since most of the critics were Keynesians. But evidence then and today suggests that investment and productivity growth played a larger role.[20] Eventually tax-reduction policies spread to Europe and many developing and former communist countries.

Second, monetary policy tightened. Paul Volcker, the Federal Reserve chairman appointed by President Carter in October 1979, drove up the U.S. prime rate to 20.5 percent and the unemployment rate to 10.8 percent. Reagan complained not a single time about these policies despite disastrous losses by the Republicans in the congressional elections of 1982 (26 seats in the House). Indeed, he acknowledged privately that this was precisely the "bellyache" that the U.S. economy had to suffer in order to recover.[21]

•   •   •

Many analysts give Volcker primary credit for disinflation or equal credit to both Volcker and Reagan.[22] The argument is not convincing. Reagan's political role was far more important than Volcker's technical skills. When President Carter pressed for credit controls in the spring of 1980 to contain interest rates driven higher by the 1979 Fed policy changes, Volcker did what most Fed chairmen do under political pressure: he caved, and the economy went into a double-dip recession. Had Reagan been Carter, Volcker would have done the same. The difference was Reagan, not Volcker. As Milton Friedman pointed out, "No other president would have stood by and let Volcker push the economy into recession by restricting the money supply so sharply."[23] Thus, without Reagan—that is, with a reelected Carter—there likely would have been no monetary contraction. Without Volcker, Reagan would have simply found another inflation-fighting Fed chairman to administer the bellyache. In a private letter in February 1981, very early in his administration, Reagan wrote: "The goal is to have a steady and reasonable growth in the money supply instead of the rollercoaster we've had over the last several years with wild surges and then equally wild cutbacks."[24]

Other countries did complain about U.S. interest rates, sometimes personally and bitterly. German chancellor Helmut Schmidt lamented the "highest rates of interest . . . since the birth of Christ."[25] Eventually, however, Germany and other countries followed suit, and inflation rates around the world dropped sharply. France hit the wall in March 1983. Caught between Reagan's market program and his own radical socialist policies, French president François Mitterrand decided to stay in the European Monetary System and deflate the French economy rather than devalue the French franc. Not only advanced countries tightened monetary controls, but dozens of developing countries did as well, taking their central banks out of the control of finance ministries and running more independent and disciplined monetary policies.

Third, deregulation reversed the growth of the government sector. In the 1980s, the public sector as a percentage of GDP dropped by an average of 3 to 4 percent per decade in both advanced and developing countries. In the United States, the size of government relative to GDP did not grow at all from 1981 to 1989. Privatization took hold in one country after another, especially the newly liberated communist countries.

• • •

Here, too, Reagan's policies were pivotal. When the Professional Air Traffic Controllers Organization (PATCO) went on strike in August 1981, Reagan fired the members who failed to return to work by a deadline and ordered military air traffic controllers to fill in. PATCO demanded the kind of pay package that drove up wages and strangled growth in the 1970s, and Reagan was determined to break the pattern. Paul Volcker later called the Reagan firing of PATCO strikers "the single most important anti-inflationary step Reagan took."[26]

Fourth, the Reagan era launched new trade rounds to liberalize trade and roll back protectionism. In the deepest months of the recession, Reagan proposed a new multilateral trade round, a bold and unprecedented initiative under such circumstances. The initiative was initially rejected at the GATT (General Agreements on Tariffs and Trade) ministerial meeting in November 1982. But once growth resumed, GATT launched the Uruguay Round in 1986. While the multilateral talks lumbered along, Reagan signed bilateral free-trade accords with Canada and Mexico, agreements that culminated later in the North American Free Trade Agreement (NAFTA), signed by President Bill Clinton. Completed in 1992, the Uruguay Round transformed the GATT into the World Trade Organization (WTO) and dramatically expanded freer trade to include agriculture, commodities, and the new service sectors spawned by the information revolution. NAFTA went on to solidify Mexico's historic shift from economic autarky to membership in the global free-trading system.

Fifth, Reagan policies accelerated the bilateral liberalization of private financial markets, creating the global banking system that mobilized the massive savings of emerging markets such as China (which saves 40 percent of GDP) and applied them to fuel the industrial engines of the Great Expansion in the 1990s and 2000s. The Bretton Woods system of the golden era controlled private capital flows and funded international transactions largely through government accounts. An expanding global economy needed new and much larger sources of capital. Private commercial banks stepped in to recycle petrodollar flows in the 1970s, and the U.S. government began aggressively in the late 1970s and throughout the 1980s to sign bilateral financial agreements to free up all types of international capital transactions.

In the wake of the recent financial crisis, it is easy to forget how important these policies were. Without financial liberalization, savings from China, India, and other emerging markets could not have been mobilized to fuel the dramatic increase in the real economy of the world. Money flowed from developing countries to developed countries, financing the explosion of domestic and foreign investment that launched the information age. Manufacturing expanded in China, India, and elsewhere, while services, including financial services, became major centers of employment and profit in the advanced countries.

Deficits and Debt

True, imbalances emerged under Reagan. The domestic imbalances were most detrimental, especially the unprecedented boom in housing debt. But international imbalances also contributed. Ironically, large transfers of savings from emerging countries such as China were crucial for financing investment and imports in the advanced countries. International flows, however skewed, fueled growth—until domestic imbalances created a run on international accounts.

The Reagan era started the debt binge. Loose fiscal policy, coupled with tight money, produced the twin deficits: large budget and trade (current account) deficits. Or so it was argued. Budget deficits actually have little to do with trade deficits. Japan has run budget deficits for decades yet simultaneously has a trade surplus. It depends on the level of domestic savings. If these are large, as they are in Japan, they cover domestic debt and more, such that the country has excess capital to export. When domestic savings are low, as in the United States, budget deficits along with private debt have to be financed from abroad, resulting in capital inflows, which in turn finance import or trade deficits.

Nevertheless, although not the cause of trade deficits, the budget deficit was large and unprecedented, and in retrospect Reagan called his failure to cut federal spending and balance the budget "one of my biggest disappointments as president."[27] The administration missed its best chance to close the deficit following Reagan's landslide reelection in 1984, but it punted on both entitlement programs and waste in the military.[28]

That said, the budget and trade deficits in the 1980s were hardly the albatross dragging down growth that critics alleged. Indeed, they came down in the 1980s, in the case of the budget deficit from 6 percent in 1983 to 2.8 percent in Reagan's last budget. After a mild recession in 1990–1991 and relatively small tax increases in 1990 and 1993 (as in 1982–1983), growth continued robustly in the 1990s under the same basic policies. Neither George H. W. Bush nor Bill Clinton reversed Reagan's priorities. As leader of the opposing party, in fact, President Clinton did for Reagan economic policies what President Eisenhower did for Franklin Delano Roosevelt's New Deal. Clinton confirmed Reagan's free-market revolution by maintaining low taxes and low inflation, ending welfare programs such as Aid for Families with Dependent Children, declaring the end of the era of big government, deregulating financial markets (repealing Glass-Steagall), and promoting freer trade. To his credit, President Clinton passed NAFTA and the Uruguay Round over substantial opposition from labor unions within his own party and from Ross Perot, an independent political candidate. A huge stock market boom, fueled by free-market growth, filled the Treasury Department's tax vaults. By the end of the 1990s, the much-maligned budget deficits of the 1980s had completely disappeared.

What is more, Reagan's budget expenditures for defense eventually paid a huge peace dividend. The Cold War ended, and defense spending dropped dramatically in the 1990s. A revitalized American military patrolled peace and security in the new post–Cold War world. United Nations forces under American leadership expelled Saddam Hussein from Kuwait and signaled to the world that the expanding global economy—now including former communist countries—had a policeman that would preserve law and order. The world indeed became a single oyster opening for the first time in history to include all of the major developed and developing countries. And more than two decades after the Cold War, the United States continues to provide global security, in many cases with the same generation of weapons, now rapidly obsolescing, that the Reagan era generated.

Implications for Today

To be sure, the Great Expansion ended in 2008 with what some economists, many of whom seek to disparage market policies, now call the Great Recession. Debt finally exacted its costs. The Federal Reserve kept interest rates too low for too long, government housing agencies encouraged subprime home loans to families who could not afford them, and private banks, insurance companies, and bond-rating agencies securitized, sold, and insured loans without adequate capital reserves in case those loans could not be repaid. The excesses were not just in the United States; they were global. China's policies of an undervalued currency and export-led growth piled up massive current-account surpluses that were then lent to consumer-led countries such as the United States to pay for burgeoning imports. European and Japanese banks lent as aggressively as, if not more aggressively than, U.S. banks. Struggling with mountains of bad debt of sovereign nations, European banks faced the same precipice in 2011–2012 that American banks did in 2008.

However, the Great Recession, named thus to spark memories of the Great Depression and to justify massive stimulus spending, was nowhere near as serious as the Great Depression. Industrial production fell 32.4 percent in the Great Depression, twice as much as in the recent recession. In terms of unemployment and inflation, the 2008–2009 recession was not as severe as the recessions of 1973–1975 and 1981–1982, which the Ford and Reagan administrations confronted.[29] In addition, American industry is in much better shape today than it was in the 1970s. In 1982, business failures were 50 percent higher than in any other year since World War II, and they doubled again by 1984.[30] Today, business costs are under control, profits are recovering normally, and corporate balance sheets are flush with cash. Last, global growth, the legacy of freer market policies in both trade and financial markets during the Great Expansion, buffers the current recession, while oil crises disrupted global markets during the recessions of 1973–1975 and 1981–1982. China, India, and the emerging markets continue to grow today at robust, albeit somewhat lower, rates and sustain the global economy while the United States and other advanced countries recover from their financial excesses. Open global markets, often blamed for the present crisis, are in fact the principal factor softening the current downturn.

The current recovery, to be sure, is going very slowly. But the cause is only in part the unique characteristics of a financial crisis. As economists point out, financial crises take longer to resolve.[31] Banks and consumers have to reduce loans and expenditures, all of which prolongs slow growth. But the slow recovery may also be due to a return to some of the failed policies of the 1970s.[32]

Monetary policy has been excessively loose, with the Fed implementing in 2013 a third round of quantitative easing (manipulation of its balance sheet to lower long-term interest rates). While current inflation is still modest, it is hard to imagine that future inflation will not go up, perhaps very rapidly, once more normal lending and consumer spending resume.

Fiscal deficits and debts have simply gone off the charts. If Reagan's debts were a problem, the current ones are a catastrophe. George W. Bush is partly to blame. He cut taxes and, unlike Reagan, raised both defense *and* social spending. President Barack Obama piled on further deficits by massive spending to expand the public sector and, what is worse, by costly restrictions and class rhetoric ("fat cat bankers," "corporate jet owners," "millionaires and billionaires," "excess profits") to discredit the private sector. Perversely, government spending tries to stimulate a private sector that government interventionist policies increasingly throttle.

Regulatory policy is a case in point. Obama policies have tacked on new restrictions and costs for health care, energy emissions, bank lending, consumer protection, labor laws, environment, transportation, and a host of other business activities. Do these restrictions help growth? Probably not. As Nobel laureate Gary Becker writes, they do so only if government institutions involve fewer monopoly and other imperfections than private markets.[33] Most regulations are not efficient and reduce growth. Private industries hoard cash, at levels higher than at any time in 50 years, because they have no confidence whatsoever in a macroeconomic environment in which financial leaders are derided as "fat cats" and industry costs are rising.[34]

Trade policy is at a dead stop, if not in the early stages of a death spiral. Currency fluctuations increase to compensate for structural rigidities, and heads of state talk about their principal weapon being the defense of internal markets to expand domestic production and employment.[35] Obama was slow to move bilateral trade agreements through Congress and has said hardly a word about the comatose multilateral trade talks.

Financial markets are a new factor in the Reagan-inspired world economy. And a failure to regulate these markets in a timely and effective way contributed to the financial collapse of 2008. But this failure was shared by the Reagan, Clinton, and two Bush administrations. Robert Rubin and Larry Summers, treasury secretaries under Bill Clinton, debated the issues in 1998–1999 and decided that the private sector had better models to police risk than the government did. As one observer put it, "They did have more belief in the ability of the financial markets and financial institutions to police themselves than now seems to be warranted."[36] The George W. Bush administration made the same mistake, as did Alan Greenspan, the Fed chairman, who bridged the two administrations.[37] So it is hard to blame the financial collapse on Reagan-era policies alone.

What has not helped is the strident and populist overreaction of the Obama administration to financial markets. Some regulation is clearly warranted. Leverage ratios, the amount that capital-lending institutions retain to back up the loans and derivatives they underwrite, must be capped, and derivative markets must be made more transparent. But the Dodd-Frank legislation and new consumer protection regulations have burdened the lending sector with massive new costs. And the populist rhetoric against Wall Street has hamstrung already weak private-sector lending, disguising the equal responsibility of government agencies for the financial collapse. In the end, private-sector institutions will pay back practically every penny of bailout money they received from the government during the crisis, including the automobile companies the government rescued. But taxpayers paid out nearly $188 billion to bail out Fannie Mae and Freddie Mac, the two government-sponsored banks that alone accounted for $5 trillion of the housing market debt. Nearly $124 billion will still be owed in 2014.[38] No one has called the executives of these institutions "fat cats." But they, too, were paid handsomely and performed poorly. The Obama administration seems to be repeating some of the same mistakes of the 1970s, placing too much confidence in public-sector initiatives while making private-sector initiatives, which create the vast majority of jobs, more costly.

•   •   •

To sum up, Ronald Reagan came into office in 1981 after a decade in which major economic policies in the United States and other advanced countries had departed significantly from the free-market policies of the Bretton Woods golden era and arguably produced worldwide stagflation. His economic program addressed and reversed every one of these policy trends and correlated with, if not plausibly caused, the unparalleled economic recovery and expansion of the 30 years that followed. This Great Expansion not only equaled the growth performance of the golden era of the 1950s and 1960s but also spread the benefits more widely and equitably than ever before, lifting 600 to 800 million people in the developing world out of poverty and into the middle class.

It is still possible that the record of the Great Expansion was primarily caused by other factors, such as oil price increases in the 1970s and then oil price declines in the 1980s and 1990s, the policies of Deng Xiaoping in China and Mikhail Gorbachev in the Soviet Union that opened communist countries to capitalist markets, or the exogenous arrival of the information revolution. No doubt these factors contributed. Yet, if asked whether any or all of these factors would have had the same effect on economic growth if the Reagan policies had never existed, I feel quite comfortable with the conclusion that the Reagan policies were the most important cause of the Great Expansion. Moreover, given the recent reversion to policies of the 1970s, the ensuing "Slowest Recovery" on record may be not a result of Reagan-era free-market policies, but a departure from them.

3

"The Balancer"

Ronald Reagan, Party Politics, and U.S. Grand Strategy

PETER TRUBOWITZ

Each president holds the reins of power under different international and domestic conditions. The international environment can be security poor or security rich; the dangers posed by foreign powers can be great or small. What political parties expect of the presidents they back also varies greatly. Political parties may prefer "guns" to "butter," or the reverse. How much room for error or "slack" presidents have internationally, and how much they benefit from investing in guns as opposed to butter, goes far in determining how ambitious and expensive their foreign policies will be. Ronald Reagan's presidency was no exception to this rule. In foreign policy, geopolitics and partisan politics are the twin engines of American statecraft.

This chapter examines Reagan's foreign policy at the broadest level—the level known as grand strategy. By "grand strategy," I mean the purposeful and planned use of military, economic, and diplomatic means to achieve desired foreign policy ends, whether in peacetime or during wartime.[1] In contrast to many accounts that attribute Reagan's approach to statecraft to deeply held values and beliefs, I argue that the basic outlines of Reagan's foreign policy owed more to prevailing international and domestic conditions. This was as true of his strategy toward the Soviet Union as it was in general. I argue that, like other presidents who held office during the Cold War, Reagan had powerful geopolitical incentives to contain or balance against Soviet power. What distinguished Reagan's approach were equally powerful partisan incentives that he had to invest in military power.

This chapter is organized into three sections. I begin by briefly describing U.S. grand strategy during the Cold War and how the strategy known as containment varied across presidencies. I then examine the geopolitical and partisan incentives that Reagan had to pursue an assertive and expensive variant of containment—that is, to actively balance against Soviet power by investing heavily in national defense and power projection capabilities. I argue that Reagan's strategy toward Moscow cannot be fully understood without considering the powerful partisan and electoral incentives that he had to invest in such an assertive foreign policy. I conclude by considering some of the lessons of the Reagan presidency for how we should think about U.S. grand strategy.

Cold War Balancing

Balancing is one of statecraft's oldest grand strategies. Defensive in nature, balancing involves efforts by one state to prevent another state from upsetting the status quo—from increasing its share of power at the "defending" state's expense.[2] One form of balancing involves a leader's effort to build his or her state's military capabilities. International relations scholars call this "internal balancing" because a leader is relying on the state's own resources to deter a potential aggressor or to defend against the foreign aggressor should deterrence fail. A leader can also try to check a threatening state by pooling resources with other states in the form of alliances. This is called "external balancing."[3] Balancing against foreign threats frequently involves some combination of internal mobilization and resource pooling, though typically, leaders do attach greater weight to one strategy or the other.

America's leaders had little occasion to rely on balancing prior to World War II. Before the 1940s, the only president who could be classified clearly as a "balancer" is Woodrow Wilson (1913–1921), and in Wilson's case, this was true for a two-year span (1917–1918) of his presidency.[4] In the American context, the classic era of balancing was the Cold War, when president after president relied on costly efforts to defend the post–World War II status quo by checking Soviet (and for a time, Chinese) power.[5] The broad strategic principle that would guide U.S. grand strategy during the Cold War was part of U.S. strategic thinking as early as 1941, when Nicholas Spykman defined the central geopolitical goal of the United States as the preservation of a balance of power in Eurasia.[6] The objective was to prevent any state, or coalition of states, from gaining control over the Eurasian landmass, "where alone lay the resources and population levels which, if ever amalgamated, might overwhelm American might."[7] What eventually became known as the strategy of containment was an axiom of U.S. planning by 1945.[8]

It was the depth and durability of the commitment to containment, or internal balancing, that distinguished the country's foreign policy in this era from what had come before. Yet as John Lewis Gaddis points out, the Cold War consensus in favor of balancing against Soviet power was not a consensus over *how much* of the state's resources to invest in the effort.[9] On this, there was variation across administrations.

Some presidents like Reagan presided over large increases in U.S. military spending and constitute the starkest cases of internal balancing during the Cold War. Others relied heavily on external balancing, looking for ways to damp down arms spending and shift more of the security burden to allies.

Why did Reagan embrace an active balancing strategy when other presidents favored less expensive forms of containment? Explanations that emphasize the influence of his fiscal conservatism or anti-communist worldview are underdetermining. John Kennedy also presided over a sizable military buildup—he also actively balanced against Soviet power. However, Kennedy was no fiscal conservative. He embraced Keynesian ideas about economic growth and the role of government in promoting it.[10] Anti-communism is also underdetermining. Richard Nixon was a hard-core Cold Warrior, but his long-held anti-communist views did not prevent him from looking for ways to reduce the burdens of containment, including forging a "tacit alliance" with communist China against Soviet Russia.[11] Reagan himself proved to be more of a pragmatist in dealing with Moscow than many expected. In his second term, some conservative Republicans attacked him for supporting Soviet leader Mikhail Gorbachev's domestic reforms and for pursuing arms control agreements with the Soviet leader.[12]

To understand why Reagan opted to actively balance against Soviet power, one needs to consider his political circumstances. As I have shown elsewhere, presidents who hold office when the country faces an international challenger (a great power seeking to extend its geopolitical reach) have a strong incentive to check, contain, or diffuse the threat to reduce the risk of strategic failure and domestic blame.[13] Throughout the Cold War, worries about the domestic costs of international failure weighed heavily on America's leaders, sometimes inordinately so.[14] The risk of strategic failure (e.g., the possibility of a technological breakthrough that would tip the nuclear balance to the Soviets, the fall of a country to communism) led president after president to look for ways to hedge and limit their political exposure.

During the Cold War, security was scarce. Presidents could not afford to discount the risk of strategic failure because the danger of second-guessing by their domestic opponents was too great. Yet even during the Cold War, presidents had some choice over how actively to check Soviet ambitions and how intensely to invest the government's resources in the effort. That choice depended critically on how much it paid domestically for them to invest in military power: on how strongly their party preferred investing in guns over butter. Presidents like Reagan who led parties that stood to benefit electorally from investing in military power and national security more generally were more willing to invest in high-cost balancing strategies. For these presidents, partisan imperative *reinforced* geopolitical incentive.

The Reagan Revival

Foreign policy was a gut issue in the 1980 election campaign.[15] A string of international setbacks the previous year left the American people angry about the apparent loss of control over foreign affairs. More than 80 percent of the public believed that the country had sunk into "deep and serious trouble."[16] In his bid for the presidency, Reagan echoed these fears, repeatedly invoking the image of a weakening America in a world dangerously out of control, a world where hostile radical groups could take Americans hostage and where the nation's economic lifeline was increasingly vulnerable to blackmail. Starting from the premise that the erosion of American power was the result of misguided policies, Reagan blasted Jimmy Carter, blaming Carter and the Democrats for letting America's position in the world decline—for weakness and vacillation and for allowing Soviet military power to surpass that of the United States.

There were obvious political advantages in doing so. Carter's foreign policy misfortunes lent credence to the view that Republicans were better custodians of national security than the Democrats.[17] Meanwhile, Carter's preoccupation with foreign policy issues such as "human rights" and arms control fueled tensions within the Democratic Party. Many southern Democrats had grown disillusioned with the party's liberal foreign policy agenda—an agenda that left them vulnerable to Republican charges of "weakness" and "incompetence" on Election Day. Reagan could thus take a forceful principled stand in favor of greater American power, comfortable in the knowledge that such a stance would appeal to rock-ribbed Republicans while making it harder for southern Democratic lawmakers to align squarely behind Carter's reelection bid. As David Hoffman observes, Reagan was alert to the Democrats' weakness on national security and seized on the issue for "reasons of political tactics."[18]

The Republicans won big in the November election. Although Reagan received only 51 percent of the popular vote in a three-way race, he outpolled Carter by a full 10 percentage points. Moreover, Reagan won overwhelmingly in the Electoral College while the Republicans captured control of the Senate for the first time since the Eisenhower years.[19] The size of Reagan's Electoral College victory and Republican gains in the Senate gave the president an opportunity to redefine the nation's priorities and make good on his campaign promise to "Make America Great Again." Liberal observers who tried to console themselves by recalling that another Cold Warrior, Richard Nixon, had moved toward "the center" once in office found little comfort in the new president's rhetoric or actions. After a decade of strategic retrenchment in the 1970s, the United States under Reagan went on the "geostrategic offensive" in the 1980s.[20]

Nothing symbolized the shift in America's priorities more than the "Reagan buildup." The largest military buildup since the Korean War, Reagan's program was the linchpin in the Republicans' strategy to reassert American leadership abroad. Between 1981 and 1986, Reagan spent well over $1 trillion on national defense, a sum nearly equal to the total spent by Nixon, Ford, and Carter during the previous 12 years.[21] In 1986, the apex of the Reagan buildup in terms of outlays, the military consumed $273 billion, a 48 percent increase over 1980 in constant dollars. Significantly, research and development of new high-tech weapons systems (e.g., the "stealth" bomber, ballistic missile defense, precision-guided munitions) absorbed a large portion of the increase.[22]

The rapid expansion of American military capabilities under Reagan occurred in the context of expanding commitments. During the 1970s, the country's leaders had sought to narrow the nation's overseas interests and obligations. Despite important differences in emphasis and style, the Nixon, Ford, and Carter administrations all adopted strategies and policies that sought to minimize the costs of U.S. leadership and containing Soviet power. Sharper distinctions were drawn between "vital" and "peripheral" interests in the Third World. Various devices, ranging from Nixon's strategic opening to China to Carter's "three percent solution" (i.e., 3 percent of GDP) for NATO members, were used to shift some of the burden of containment to other countries (China, West Germany, and prerevolutionary Iran).

Reagan reversed course in all of these areas. Old commitments to allies and friends, neglected or downplayed in the 1970s, were renewed and strengthened during his presidency. At the same time, the Reagan administration sought to reassure both foreign and domestic audiences about American resolve in the post-Vietnam era by signaling its commitment to check unrest in regions deemed vital (the Persian Gulf, Central America, and southern Africa) and to make America's presence overseas more visible through offshore naval deployments, large-scale military maneuvers, and the funding of military proxies like the Nicaraguan contras, the Afghan rebels, and UNITA in Angola.

National security was the cornerstone of Reagan's foreign policy agenda. But the administration's strategy for restoring American power also called for a new approach to economics. Shortly after taking office, Reagan unveiled a comprehensive economic plan to "put the nation on a fundamentally different course."[23] Major shifts in federal budgetary, regulatory, and tax policy were advanced. Personal and corporate taxes were slashed, federal regulations on industry were rolled back, and federal spending on New Deal–style welfare programs was cut. In the area of foreign economic policy, trade restrictions put into place in the 1970s were rolled back, and exporters long dependent on financing from the federal government were encouraged to turn to the private sector.[24]

The magnitude of the changes initiated by Reagan sparked heated debate. Political commentators were sharply divided over the merits of the policy changes. Some stressed the benefits of putting the Soviets on the strategic defensive; others worried about the high costs of Reagan's program, which seemed to put the nation at risk of financial insolvency. Today, scholars and political analysts continue to debate the impact of Reagan's foreign policy. Did the Soviet Union collapse because of, or in spite of, the administration's foreign policies?[25] Was the Reagan administration's blend of "military Keynesianism" and "supply-side" economics responsible for disequilibrating international trade and monetary relations?[26] When viewed from the perspective of domestic politics, the significance of the Reagan Revolution is clear. For the first time in this century, "the national interest" was not defined in terms of the urban Northeast. In the 1980s, the foreign policies advanced by Reagan reflected the political imperatives of America's newest industrializing regions—the South and West.

Reagan's Sunbelt Alliance

Reagan's presidency marked the death of the coalition that had shaped the country's foreign policy since the 1930s.[27] For nearly three decades, the nation's foreign policy had been based on an alliance that spanned the Mason-Dixon Line—Franklin Delano Roosevelt's New Deal coalition. Forged in the shadows of depression and war, this liberal-internationalist alliance embraced the interests of big business, northern labor, and the "small town big men" who dominated southern society. The urban Northeast and the agrarian South were the domestic bases of political support for America's efforts to rebuild the world economy after World War II and isolate and contain the Soviet Union. These parts of the country were the earliest and largest beneficiaries of the policies of foreign aid, forward defense, and liberal trade that were aimed at promoting an open, interdependent world economy and at the Cold War isolation or "containment" of nations that threatened it. Because this coalition was rooted in the regional powerbase of the Democratic Party and the powerful eastern wing of the Republican Party, it provided the institutional framework for the bipartisan foreign policies of the Truman, Eisenhower, and Kennedy administrations. Politics did not stop at the water's edge during the Cold War years; rather, shared interests kept political divisiveness in check.

That bipartisan coalition lasted until the 1970s, when it began to fall apart under the combined weight of three developments: mounting social tensions triggered by the Civil Rights Movement and the Vietnam War, the economic decline of the industrial Northeast and the rise of the so-called Sunbelt states of the South and West, and the shift in the Republican Party's center of gravity from the Northeast to the Mountain West.[28] The first two drove North and South apart. The third created opportunities for coalition building between West and South. As the Republican Party aligned itself with the rapidly growing states of the Mountain West, it searched for allies in the country's other late developer, the South. Reagan was at the forefront of this Republican effort to turn the "power shift" in America's regional geography to the party's electoral advantage.

For years, the Northeast had been losing its long-standing lead in population, income, and jobs to the South and West. These regional disparities widened considerably during the 1970s as the big manufacturing states suffered huge job losses.[29] Plant shutdowns in the industrial Northeast were commonplace; so were small-business failures. While the number of manufacturing jobs declined in all parts of the country in the 1970s, most of the losses were concentrated in the traditional manufacturing belt. Between 1970 and 1980, the Northeast lost more than 567,000 manufacturing jobs, 311,486 of them in metals, electrical machinery, and transportation equipment. Many of these jobs were lost after 1975. Michigan, New Jersey, New York, Ohio, and Pennsylvania lost employment in every major manufacturing sector. In some areas, unemployment rates threatened to approach the record levels of the Great Depression.

By contrast, many state economies in the South and West prospered during the 1970s. Economic growth rates throughout the decade were substantially higher in the South and West than in the Northeast. Total capital formation, investments in manufacturing, and employment grew more rapidly outside the old industrial heartland. In 1980, there were, for the first time, as many manufacturing jobs outside the northern industrial core as in it. The headquarters of many Fortune 500 corporations relocated to the Sunbelt. And rates of migration from areas of low opportunity to faster-growing regions quickened. The big "winners" were the high-growth states in the South and especially the West. The big losers were the slow-growing states in the Middle Atlantic and Great Lakes areas.

Many factors contributed to this process of "regional restructuring": the diffusion of large-scale, high-tech production; lower transportation costs; and regional disparities in labor costs, energy prices, and local tax rates. No less important were the uneven consequences of the erosion of American commercial power in the international economy. While some sectors and regions reaped the benefits of expanding trade, others were net losers. Many semiskilled blue-collar workers who once enjoyed job security and good benefits were "displaced" by low-wage workers in Europe or Japan. So were many in the ranks of middle management. Sectors such as autos, steel, textiles, semiconductors, and consumer electronics experienced net job and capacity losses, while others such as aircraft, computers, movies, and finance boomed. Altogether, American industries lost 23 percent of their share of world exports in the 1970s. Areas hit hardest were those specializing in the production of nonmilitary capital goods and consumer durables—mostly the big cities in the manufacturing belt (e.g., Chicago, Milwaukee, Cleveland, Detroit). Because they were less dependent on the heavy industries that were taking a shellacking on international markets, Sunbelt cities did much better.

Spatial disparities in federal spending and federal tax policies also played a role in accelerating, if not encouraging, this regional shift in power. Federal expenditures and tax policies spurred the growth of Sunbelt cities such as Atlanta, Miami, Houston, and Phoenix while exacerbating economic difficulties in the older northeastern centers of Boston, Chicago, Detroit, and New York. The issue of federal bias in spending quickly emerged as a central one in Congress.[30] Federal spending trends associated with defense spending provoked the most controversy. Once concentrated in the Northeast, the pattern of military spending gradually shifted away from the Northeast and toward the South and West. During the early years of the Cold War, the Northeast received more than 60 percent of all prime military contracts.[31] By the Nixon years, the manufacturing belt's share of defense contracts had fallen to about 37 percent. Meanwhile, the Sunbelt received 54 percent.

This regional power shift created structural opportunities for an alliance between South and West; Republican political stratagems made it a reality.[32] In the 1970s, Republicans from the West aggressively pushed a foreign policy agenda that was now antithetical to the interests of the declining northern core. The party's long-standing commitment to anti-communism was grafted onto a "new" Republican foreign policy agenda that favored freer trade, a strong national defense, and "bolder, more assertive" international leadership. By playing on these and other issues (such as race), Republicans wrought havoc in the Democratic Party. Southerners left the party in droves. The Democrats' stronghold narrowed to the aging Northeast. No longer restrained by the demands of coalition building, the Democratic leadership adopted a foreign policy strategy that played well in the northern "Rust Belt": retrenchment. While most Democratic leaders continued to favor continued American participation in international institutions, they urged greater restraint in the use of military force, a smaller defense establishment, and a larger role for Congress in the foreign policymaking process.[33] Demands for "fairer trade," job retraining, and industrial policy became as obligatory in Democratic politics as demands for freer trade, "fast-track procedures," and "FTAs" (free-trade agreements) were in Republican circles.

As the domestic underpinnings of Cold War internationalism gave way, a new axis of regional competition over foreign policy emerged. Sectional competition within the United States found expression in conflicts between the Rust Belt and the Sunbelt. Democrats held on to their base in the industrial heartland; Republicans consolidated their hold on the West and established a powerful presence in the South. This shift was reflected in the declining number of Democratic seats in the House held by southerners. In 1947, southern Democrats held more than 60 percent of all Democratic seats. In 1980, the southern share of Democratic seats had fallen to below 40 percent—the lowest level since 1932. Meanwhile, changes in the regional bases of the Republican Party meant more and more northern seats, especially those in the big northeastern cities, were going to the Democrats. Long divided along East-West lines, the Republican Party swung decisively toward the West in the 1970s. The results of the process that began in the 1960s, with the Goldwater movement were manifest starkly: in Congress, a growing proportion of the Republicans' House seats were from western districts and increasingly, southern ones.

By the late 1970s, this process of regional restructuring had undermined the institutional and political bases of the internationalist house that Roosevelt built. In its place arose a new coalition, albeit an unsteady and not-fully-tested one, dedicated to the resurgence of American power in the international system. To be sure, this was not a classic power shift in which one clearly articulated coalition replaces another. In contrast to the New Deal realignment of the 1930s, when a new hegemonic bloc arose out of struggles set in motion by uneven growth, in the 1980s the sectional conflicts of the preceding decade simply intensified. Issues like defense spending, military intervention, and foreign aid continued to divide the country. Meanwhile, the "new sectionalism" that arose in the 1970s was sharpened over the course of the 1980s by the growing vulnerability of the manufacturing belt to international competition, and by the vigor and single-mindedness with which Reagan pursued his foreign policy agenda. Whatever promise Reagan's foreign policy held as "grand strategy," its mix of military Keynesianism and laissez-faire economics threatened the interests of the rustbelt states that formed the bedrock of the Democratic Party.[34]

Elected officials from the Northeast questioned the strategic merits of Reagan's military doctrines and programs. They also opposed the redistributive consequences of such large defense outlays and investments in high-tech weapons systems. Many lawmakers viewed the Reagan military buildup as a de facto regional development policy for the Sunbelt.[35] More fundamentally, they viewed the mix of military Keynesianism and laissez-faire economics that Reagan favored as a threat to the interests of the aging industries and metropolises they represented. Once at the cutting edge of international competition, the Northeast was now losing "market share" to foreign competitors and clamoring for federal relief. Lawmakers from the Northeast were no longer willing to pay the "overhead charges" of international leadership, which came in the form of heavy American defense military expenditures. By contrast, the West and the South, now the most internationally competitive parts of the country, were the strongest supporters of the kinds of military and defense policies that Reagan advocated. Since these regions stood to reap most of the benefits of an activist foreign policy, both in terms of its hoped-for effects on international commerce and its domestic spin-offs in the form of military procurement, southern and western lawmakers had a double incentive to back the Reagan administration's high-cost balancing strategies.[36]

For Republicans in the 1980s, foreign policy was a political weapon. It was an instrument for redistributing wealth from the northeastern "core" to the southern and western "periphery" and for expanding the Republican Party's electoral base in what was once the solidly Democratic South. Forced onto the political defensive, northern Democrats waged a rearguard battle, employing time-honored stratagems of obstruction and delay. Seen in this light, the fights between Republicans and Democrats over what America should do about Nicaragua's Sandinista regime, Russia's SS-18 nuclear missiles, or Japan's trade practices take on new meaning. They were battles in a larger, sectionally based political war for control of the federal government and its vast resources. Sometimes these sectional interests were laid out starkly; more often they were expressed in the lofty discourse of the Founding Fathers. The Republicans' foreign policy agenda, blending Hamiltonian realpolitik and Jeffersonian laissez-faire, was the Sunbelt's agenda. The liberal Democrats who now set the party's agenda were the guardians of the Rust Belt. They, too, invoked the Founders. They warned of the risks and costs of foreign crusades and centralized power—of concentrating too much political power in the executive branch and wasting resources sorely needed at home. America's role, they argued, should be to act as a model for—not a guarantor of—other peoples' quest for freedom from tyranny and repression.

In the 1980s, politicians from different parts of the country held fundamentally different views about how America should define its role in the world. They also held conflicting views about *who* should define it: the president or Congress. Yet in contrast to other periods in American history, when the Northeast dominated the executive, now southern and western interests had cornered the powers of the presidency, while the Northeast controlled most of the levers of congressional power. The result was regional deadlock: conflicts of regional interest were institutionalized as fights between two branches of government that were controlled by bitterly opposed political parties.

This helps explain why Reagan, despite his personal popularity, was unable to forge a consensus over foreign policy and why in some cases (Nicaragua) the White House resorted to secrecy while reversing course in others (arms control and human rights).[37] It also explains why George H. W. Bush, whose support in the South and West was never as solid as Reagan's, found it politically prudent to use the occasion of his Inaugural Address to call for a "new engagement" between the executive and Congress, a new spirit of bipartisanship.[38] Bush's peace offering was not, as some scholars would have it, just a natural swing of the pendulum between separate but equal powers. Nor can the rise of party conflict over foreign policy in the 1980s be understood in strictly ideological terms. Ideas cannot be so easily divorced from interests. In the 1980s, foreign policies that were deemed strategically imperative by "conservatives" were those that spoke to the interests in the rapidly growing Sunbelt: to its high-tech firms, export-oriented businesses, and military-industrial metropolises. "Liberals" who branded Republican policies reckless and destabilizing, and who called for more butter and fewer guns, were voicing the apprehensions and needs of the region suffering the brunt of foreign competition and what some even described as deindustrialization—the Northeast.

● ● ●

"I claim not to have controlled events," Abraham Lincoln wrote, "but confess plainly that events have controlled me." Lincoln was hardly a passive, disinterested president, but his admission reminds us that while presidents make grand strategy, they do not make it under circumstances of their own choosing. While Ronald Reagan's champions (and detractors) are quick to attribute his foreign policies to deeply held values and beliefs that he brought to the presidency, the basic outlines of Reagan's foreign policy owe more to prevailing international and domestic conditions. Like other presidents who held office during the Cold War, Reagan had a powerful incentive to balance against Soviet power. However, because Reagan's party also stood to benefit from investing in military power, actively balancing against Soviet power had the virtues of being both desirable and possible.

Throughout the Cold War, America's presidents as day-to-day reelection seekers thought about what geopolitics could do *for* them as well as about what it could do *to* them. Security was scarce and the risk of strategic failure was great—certainly far greater than it is today when the United States does not face a comparable geopolitical challenge. Today, America's leaders have a level of "geopolitical slack" that was inconceivable a few short decades ago. The challenge facing presidents who have geopolitical slack is to decide what to do with the room for maneuver that they enjoy. Should they seize the moment and look for ways to strengthen America's geopolitical position and, at the risk of antagonizing other states, seek to widen the nation's power advantages? Or should America's leaders be content to maintain the international status quo and focus more attention on solving problems at home?

Those who hope to find answers to these questions in Reagan's presidency should proceed with caution. This is not because the Reagan years have nothing to teach us. The reason is that Reagan's geopolitical circumstances were fundamentally different from those that face U.S. leaders today. What distinguishes our era of American statecraft from the Cold War is the wide scope of choice presidents have in defining the general thrust of grand strategy. How they make that choice will depend, as it always has, on their calculations about how to respond to domestic political incentives and geopolitical constraints (opportunity) in a way that is most likely to guarantee their own political success and that of the domestic coalitions they lead. In an era of unipolarity, when America enjoys preponderant power, the one strategy that presidents have little incentive to invoke is a strategy of balancing.

II

TRENDS IN GLOBAL DEMOCRACY

The Reagan Legacy

4

From Containment to Liberation

U.S. Strategy toward Eastern Europe

JEFFREY L. CHIDESTER

While the end of the Cold War was an event of global consequence, no region underwent a more dramatic—and more lasting—transformation than Eastern Europe. Shortly after the collapse of the region's communist regimes in the fall of 1989, the debate over what, and who, triggered the collapse began—a debate that endures to the present day. Ronald Reagan's role in particular has generated countless articles and tomes arguing the entire spectrum, from blaming him for extending the Cold War through his bellicosity to crediting him for single-handedly bringing Moscow to its knees—and everything in between. Like any complex geopolitical event, the truth likely lies somewhere near the mean.

The purpose of this chapter is not to relitigate Reagan's impact on the collapse of communism in Eastern Europe or to establish a causal connection between his policies and the present state of the region. Instead, it will examine Ronald Reagan in Eastern Europe today—the legacy of his eight years as president and his continued relevance in the region's civil discourse.

Reagan occupies a unique place in Eastern Europe. He is held in high regard by many on both ends of the spectrum for his steadfast commitment to freedom and his challenge to communist rule. Recent years have offered numerous junctures to reflect on his legacy—his death in June 2004, the twentieth anniversary of the fall of the Berlin Wall in November 2009, the centennial of his birth in February 2011. The verdict is often the same: without Reagan, communism would not have collapsed, or certainly not as soon as it did. More important, Reagan is frequently mentioned not only in retrospective analysis but also as a referential figure for *prospective* policy actions. A generation after leaving the Oval Office, his legacy is still living and breathing in the region.

Reagan's legacy has much to do with his decisive shift in American strategy toward Eastern Europe, and that is where this chapter begins—surveying U.S. policy from Franklin Delano Roosevelt to Jimmy Carter. Next, it examines Reagan's prepresidential outlook and presidential policies toward the region, each of which marked a clear shift in U.S. strategy. The chapter closes with a review of Reagan's legacy in Eastern Europe and his position as an exemplary figure today.

The Strategy

America's Cold War strategy toward Eastern Europe was forged in the crucible of the early postwar years, a period characterized by fear, ambiguity, and distrust between Washington and Moscow and the steady evolution from wartime cooperation to postwar confrontation. During the course of the war, as Soviet forces liberated the region from German control, governments friendly to Moscow were installed throughout Eastern Europe, and the foundations were laid for an active postwar role. Notwithstanding this wartime control, there was optimism about a less invasive postwar role for Moscow. Polls taken in 1944 and early 1945 indicated that the American public had little fear of Soviet communism or its expansion.[1] President Roosevelt was within this camp, hoping that Moscow would serve as one of the "Four Policemen" in maintaining global order. At the Yalta Conference in February 1945, he and Churchill extracted Soviet support for the Declaration of Liberated Europe, which committed the region to "the restoration of sovereign rights and self-government" and employing "democratic means" to solve internal challenges.[2] In a speech before Congress a month later, Roosevelt said the agreements made at Yalta "ought to spell the end of . . . the exclusive alliances, the spheres of influence, the balances of power" that existed before the war.[3]

Some were less sanguine than Roosevelt about Soviet intentions, even before the end of the war. Churchill, concerned about another dominant European power rising from the ashes of war, was particularly disturbed by Soviet actions in Poland and said prophetically that if Roosevelt failed to act, "Eastern Europe will be shown to be excluded from the terms of the Declaration on Liberated Europe, and you and we shall be excluded from any jot of influence in that area." At first, Roosevelt was comfortable giving personal assurances to Stalin that the United States would not seek an outcome in Poland "inimical to [Soviet] interest," but just prior to his death, he admitted watching "with anxiety and concern the development of the Soviet attitude since [Yalta]" and intimated to Churchill his desire to take a tougher line.[4] Cries of "Yalta" would eventually become the leitmotif for hawks throughout the remainder of the Cold War and a frequent refrain during the Reagan presidency.[5]

While Truman was more suspicious of Soviet activity than Roosevelt, he was still not eager to pick a fight with Moscow over Eastern Europe when U.S. priorities in other areas required Soviet cooperation. There was, in fact, still reason to be optimistic. Free elections had been held in Hungary and Czechoslovakia, providing the United States promising models for the region—independent nations, closely aligned with neither the United States nor the Soviet Union. In the months that followed, the Soviet Union offered a harbinger of things to come by interfering in political matters across the region, most notably after free elections in Hungary. Churchill's "Iron Curtain" speech of March 1946 was later described by Reagan as "a Paul Revere warning that tyranny was once more on the march."[6] Just two weeks earlier, George Kennan, who served as deputy head of the U.S. mission in Moscow, articulated a coherent framework from which to understand Soviet behavior; he argued that Moscow was "impervious to logic of reason" yet "highly sensitive to logic of force." The recalibrated approach, practiced throughout 1946 in different parts of the world, was most forcefully and publicly articulated on March 12, 1947, when Truman announced American support of Greece and Turkey against "outside pressures." Echoing Stalin's "two worlds" thesis from a year earlier, Truman said during his speech that "nearly every nation must choose between alternative ways of life."[7]

Containment policy took on a variety of forms across the globe, depending on America's national interests in each region. In Eastern Europe, the objective was twofold. To prevent communism from spreading to Western Europe was the first. According to National Security Council (NSC)-20/4,[8] Moscow was actively pursuing "the political conquest of Western Europe" as a principal element in its bid to "dominate the globe."[9] The possibility of communism spreading across Western Europe was very real; in early 1947, the Communist Party was a key member of the governing coalition in Italy and the largest party in the French National Assembly. A multibillion-dollar economic aid package known as the Marshall Plan was the primary component in America's strategy to stabilize the region, orient it toward the West, and solidify American leadership.

The second goal was to encourage the growth of independent nations in Eastern Europe. Stabilization of Western Europe was an antecedent to that strategy, according to Kennan, who contended that if this region could achieve economic stability and prosperity, "the communist regimes in Eastern Europe . . . would never be able to stand the comparison," and this would have "a disintegrating and eroding effect on the communist world."[10] To achieve this goal, the United States offered Marshall Plan aid to Eastern Europe and the Soviet Union. Moscow was apoplectic at the offer, rejecting it as an extension of the Truman Doctrine and an attempt to split Europe into two sides. Notwithstanding interest from Czechoslovakia and Poland, Eastern bloc rejection was de rigueur, and Moscow even urged communist parties in Western Europe to derail the plan. Truman's move—construed as provocative by Moscow—produced a shift in Soviet policy and a tightening of Soviet power in the region. Two months after the Paris Conference on the Marshall Plan, communist nations furthered the "two camps" paradigm with the creation of the Cominform.[11] Stalin fortified his "camp" in February 1948 by supporting a plan by Czechoslovak communists to stage a coup against the last remaining democracy in the region. The coup hastened the passage of the Marshall Plan, which, ironically, allowed the United States to cement its first goal while dashing hopes of the second.

Truman received a major break in June 1948, when Yugoslavia was expelled from the Cominform. Soon after, the United States initiated normal economic relations with Belgrade. The State Department was elated by this "break of the greatest significance." Others, however, were more circumspect, fearing that Tito's break would lead to another intensification of Soviet control. As CIA head Roscoe H. Hillenkoetter bluntly assessed, "The Communist regimes in Eastern Europe are firmly under Moscow control."[12] Even if others in the region were open to such overtures, the administration was limited in its ability to support independent-minded communists, as the American public did not grasp such nuance within the communist world.

Divisions continued to deepen between the two sides. Moscow's yearlong blockade of West Berlin provided another impetus behind the formation of the North Atlantic Treaty Organization (NATO) in April 1949, thereby fortifying the present spheres across Europe. Nonetheless, the Truman administration continued its plans to foment disunity within the communist world. In

August 1949, the Policy Planning Staff advocated going "on the offensive" to bring "the elimination or at least a reduction of predominant Soviet influence in the satellite states of Eastern Europe."[13] Four months later, Truman approved NSC-58/2 to "bring about the elimination of Soviet power from the satellite states."[14] This political strategy was fundamentally altered in April 1950 with the creation of NSC-68, which placed the onus of containment largely within the military realm. The document was noticeably quiet on strategies for Eastern Europe, beyond calling nationalism in the region a "vulnerability" for Moscow. While Congress continued to support economic aid to Yugoslavia, the administration's hopes for the spread of Titoism across the region had dampened.

There were signs that a Republican administration would chart a different course. The 1952 GOP platform, which railed against the "immoral policy of 'containment' which abandons countless human beings to a despotism and godless terrorism," prefigured Reagan's rhetoric, and future Secretary of State John Foster Dulles spoke often of "liberation." The Eisenhower administration, however, took a dim view of changes in the region in NSC-162, completed in October 1953, which stated that "the detachment of any major European satellite from the Soviet bloc does not now appear feasible except by Soviet acquiescence or by war."[15] NSC-162 merely formalized the administration's reaction four months earlier, when the Soviet military quelled a rebellion in East Germany. The policy was reaffirmed in the fall of 1956 when the United States, preoccupied with the emerging Suez Crisis, watched Moscow crush a nationwide uprising in Hungary. The uprisings in East Germany and Hungary demonstrated that the United States was not prepared to risk another war with the Soviet Union over Eastern Europe. For Dulles, that was simply too high a price to pay, for even if liberation policies "might result in the disintegration of the Soviet bloc, they would almost certainly cause the disintegration of the free world bloc . . . for our allies would never go along with such courses of action."[16] The administration was active in pursuing changes in the region through covert action and political rhetoric (such as the declaration of Captive Nations Week in 1953), yet despite the desires of Vice President Nixon and the Dulles brothers to keep incitement of revolution as an option, Eisenhower held that an "evolutionary" approach was "the right line."[17]

In his 1961 Inaugural Address, Kennedy pledged to "pay any price, bear any burden, meet any hardship, support any friend, oppose any foe" in defense of liberty. This said nothing, however, about changing the internal nature of existing communist states, and like his predecessor, little action was taken to

free the Warsaw Pact nations from Moscow's grip. Thoughts of exploiting fissures within the communist movement were considered. Director of Policy
Planning Walt Rostow saw opportunity in the Sino-Soviet split to "facilitate
the emergence of more independent and nationalistic Communist states, especially in Eastern Europe."[18] Support to Tito's Yugoslavia was continued, and
a small amount of economic aid was extended to Poland to gain favor in Warsaw,
but on the whole, interaction between the administration and Eastern Europe
was limited.[19] In a December 1961 meeting with Romania's new ambassador,
Kennedy noted that greater "political harmony" with the United States would
lead to increased trade.[20] In other words, liberalization was a prerequisite to
trade, not a desired result from trade. With the "loss" of China still fresh in
Americans' minds, the administration was careful about being viewed as
"soft on communism"—a charge that was particularly acute in Democratic
administrations.

Before the war in Vietnam escalated, Lyndon Johnson saw hope for a new
relationship with Eastern Europe. In March 1964, the CIA issued a special
report on Eastern Europe that described a "new and less rigid relationship"
with the Soviet Union, resulting both from Moscow's easing of control and
the growing willingness of Eastern European nations to insist on greater autonomy.[21] Two months later, Johnson announced his "bridge building" policy
of enhanced economic ties as a way of encouraging "peaceful cooperation" with
Eastern Europe and the Soviet Union.[22] Despite Johnson's public entreaties to
Congress to lower tariff barriers with the region, neither congressional opinion
nor public opinion was swayed, particularly as these nations supported communists in North Vietnam. Efforts to improve ties with individual nations
varied from little progress (Bulgaria, Czechoslovakia) to mild advances (Hungary, Romania), but relations with the region declined universally with the
Warsaw Pact invasion of Czechoslovakia in August 1968.[23] Military aid was
not an option, and in the end the administration simply expressed its opposition and watched as the reform movement was dismantled.[24] Despite the best
intentions, by summer 1968 the focus of the Johnson administration was squarely
on Southeast Asia.

While Nixon forged a new direction in America's national security strategy,
his administration's policy toward Eastern Europe was in many ways an extension of Johnson's focus on expanding economic ties. Little attention was
given to the region during Nixon's first term, as much of the focus remained
on Vietnam. But in National Security Study Memorandum (NSSM)-163,

drafted in October 1972, Nixon asked for a comprehensive policy review, with the goal of improved economic relations. In May of the following year, the administration approved National Security Decision Memorandum (NSDM)-212, which called for expanded economic ties with those demonstrating "satisfactory political conduct on international issues involving our interests."[25] Like Johnson, Nixon favored some regimes more than others. He developed particularly good relations with Romanian president Nicolae Ceaușescu, who had broken with Moscow over the Prague Spring, and with Yugoslavia's fiercely independent Tito. Nixon visited both nations and received both leaders in Washington during his tenure. Ceaușescu's visit in December 1973 marked the first official visit from a head of state in Eastern Europe (he visited again in June 1975). In June 1971, the administration undertook a national security study to examine possible developments in Yugoslavia in the wake of the aging Tito's death. A return to the Soviet orbit would represent an unacceptable loss, and all vehicles—political, economic, and military—were utilized to "strengthen Yugoslavia's internal and external positions and relations with Western countries."[26] Nixon also succeeded where Johnson had failed in liberalizing existing trade restrictions with Eastern Europe.

Ford largely continued the policy of the Nixon administration. A January 1975 State Department memorandum reaffirmed the policy to foster the "diminution of Soviet power" in the region and the expectation that good relations with the "favored trio" of Romania, Yugoslavia, and Poland would continue, while prospects remained low for the rest of the region ("the outsiders"). Opportunities were there to exploit, but they had to be "low-key, subtle and carefully calibrated to avoid arousing the suspicions of Moscow."[27] Ties with Romania and Yugoslavia thus remained strong. Trade with Bucharest reached an important threshold in April 1975, when Ford, by executive order, made Romania the first Eastern European nation to hold most-favored nation status. In Yugoslavia, concern about the post-Tito era remained, and in 1976, the administration agreed to sell the nation tube-launched, optically tracked, wire-guided (TOW) antitank missiles. Poland was increasingly courted during the Ford years as well, including reciprocal visits to Washington and Warsaw between Ford and Polish first secretary Edward Gierek in 1974 and 1975.[28]

A series of moves by the administration—both intentional and unintentional—made Eastern Europe a political liability for Ford. The first was the signing of the Helsinki Accords in August 1975, which made "inviolable" the postwar borders in Europe. This was met with outrage from hawks in both parties, including Reagan, as well as famed Soviet dissident Aleksandr Solzhenitsyn, who said Ford went to Helsinki "to sign the betrayal of Eastern Europe, to acknowledge officially its slavery forever."[29] Four months later, notes from a meeting between State Department counselor Helmut Sonnenfeldt and the European chiefs of mission were leaked to the press; Sonnenfeldt had conceded that "the historic challenge of the Soviet Union will not go away" and said the U.S. objective "should be the Finlandization of Eastern Europe."[30] Ford's perceived disregard for the plight of the region was further exacerbated during a presidential debate with Jimmy Carter where Ford contended there was "no Soviet domination" of Eastern Europe. In addition, anti-communists were outraged when Ford refused to meet with Solzhenitsyn when the dissident visited the United States.

The Nixon-Ford-Kissinger era ended abruptly with the inauguration of Carter, who rejected the realpolitik guiding the previous eight years and replaced it with a foreign policy built upon human rights and democratic values. He also rejected the bipolar Cold War paradigm and the politics this created, giving new emphasis to issues like transnational interdependence and North-South cooperation. In a 1977 speech at Notre Dame, for instance, Carter blamed the Vietnam War on America's "inordinate fear of communism." Yet, even with this philosophical shift, Carter's policy toward Eastern Europe was, in the main, similar to the Nixon-Ford years. In Presidential Directive (PD)-21, the Carter administration continued the strategy of working with Eastern European governments in an effort to "enhance their independence internationally and to increase their degree of internal liberalization." The administration treated each nation in the region on an individual basis, depending on that nation's relative internal liberalism and independence from Moscow. Poland, Romania, and Hungary continued to receive the "preferred treatment" of the Nixon-Ford era. In contrast, relations with Bulgaria, Czechoslovakia, and East Germany would only be improved after demonstrable changes in either of the two categories. Carter's ultimate objective, however, was "reconciliation," not liberation.[31] Stuart Eizenstat, Carter's domestic policy chief, aptly described the administration's resignation to Soviet power in Eastern Europe: "There are certain events over which you have limited control, Poland being a perfect example."[32] Reagan fundamentally rejected this position and would have the opportunity to reverse course early in his presidency.

The Shift

When Reagan took office in January 1981, a shift in policy toward Eastern Europe was predictable. Reagan's thoughts on the Eastern bloc had been well documented since the early days of the Cold War. In 1951, Reagan starred in and narrated a fund-raising video for the Crusade for Freedom, which supported the mission of Radio Free Europe to bring "a message of hope to millions trapped behind the iron curtain."[33] In his 1964 speech in support of Barry Goldwater, he condemned Johnson's "conspiracy of silence" against Soviet domination of Eastern Europe and accused him of selling out the region: "We cannot buy our security, our freedom from the threat of the bomb by committing an immorality so great as saying to a billion human beings now enslaved behind the Iron Curtain, 'Give up your dreams of freedom because to save our own skins, we're willing to make a deal with your slave masters.'"[34] As peace and cooperation with the Soviet Union gained new traction later in the decade, Reagan again wondered why we "speak of peace with no mention of freedom" for Eastern Europe: "Is it possible that while we are sorry for the captives, we do not want to offend the captors?"[35] While Reagan wished for freedom for both Eastern Europe and the Soviet Union, he clearly viewed the former as distinct from the Soviet Union in its role as "captives" to Moscow.

The signing of the Helsinki Accords in August 1975 was a defining moment in Reagan's break from the détente-era presidents. He joined the chorus of hard-liners in saying the accords "gave the Russians something they've wanted for 35 years. We in effect recognize Russia's right to hold captive the Eastern and Central European nations." On another occasion, he said the accords were good for nothing more than "wrapping garbage."[36] His most dramatic admonition came during a nationally televised address for the 1976 Republican nomination, when he charged Ford with putting America's "stamp of approval on Russia's enslavement of the captive nations":

> We gave away the freedom of millions of people—freedom that was not ours to give. . . . Now we learn that another high official of the State Department, Helmut Sonnenfeldt . . . has expressed the belief that, in effect, the captive nations should give up any claim of national sovereignty and simply become a part of the Soviet Union. He says, "their desire to break out of the Soviet straightjacket" threatens us with World War III. In other words, slaves should accept their fate.[37]

Reagan's beliefs were reaffirmed in the lead-up to the 1980 presidential campaign when he visited Europe. During a stop in Berlin, Reagan looked at the Berlin Wall and told adviser Richard Allen, "We have got to find a way to knock this thing down."[38] He continued to hammer away at this theme during the campaign. In a September 1980 campaign stop, he heralded Lech Wałesa, who directed Poland's Solidarity movement, as a model leader to the "captive nations."[39] In private letters as well, he expressed his commitment to "keep alive the idea that the conquered nations—the captive nations—of the Soviet Union must regain their freedom."[40] Just days after his victory over Carter, Reagan's national security team produced a report saying the United States "does not accept as a permanent historical fact the occupation or control by a power hostile to the United States of any territory beyond the borders of that power."[41]

When Reagan took office, he was eager to set a new tone with Moscow and reverse the course of U.S. policy toward the communist world. But as the administration was deliberating over its national security strategy, events were quickly escalating in Poland that required immediate attention. Rumblings against the communist regime in Warsaw had been taking place for years as Poland's economy, like many of its communist neighbors, continued to sour. Massive workers' strikes in Lublin and Świdnik in July 1980, and in Gdańsk a month later, led to the formation of the Solidarity trade union. Unlike Carter, Reagan saw opportunity in what was happening with the movement. Just weeks into his presidency, at a January 30, 1981, NSC meeting, Defense Secretary Caspar Weinberger recalled that "it was there that we decided the need to make a stand on Poland. Not only to prevent an invasion but to seek ways to undermine [Soviet] power."[42] For Reagan, it represented "the first major break in the Red dike."[43]

Both the United States and the Soviet Union recognized Poland's strategic importance to the future of communism in Eastern Europe. On September 15, Soviet general secretary Leonid Brezhnev said privately that "the very fate of socialism is at stake" and suggested that if Poland fails, "the preservation of the results of the Second World War" would be impossible.[44] The same day, the NSC met to discuss economic aid to Poland. Secretary of State Alexander Haig (who, unable to attend, asked his deputy, William Clark, to deliver his remarks) said Poland was the "first successful break in the Soviet model of Eastern European communism." He noted the potential "ripple effect" and said pointedly that if the West failed to provide assistance, it would be "the modern equivalent of Yalta, a historic act of indifference." National Security Adviser Richard Allen agreed, saying the United States could not (in classic Cold War language) afford to "lose" Poland.[45] But the situation required a delicate balance for Reagan: "This was what we had been waiting for since World War II. What was happening in Poland might spread like a contagion throughout Eastern Europe. But our options were limited."[46] Reagan did not want to give Solidarity false hope that his administration would support an uprising, as had happened in Hungary in 1956. At the same time, he was committed to preventing Solidarity from being crushed. A short-term aid package was extended to Warsaw.

On December 13, amid growing internal unrest, the Polish government—in accord with orders from Moscow—declared martial law, and Solidarity and its leaders were banned. According to Richard Pipes, the NSC's head of East European and Soviet policy, Reagan was "livid" and said, "We need to hit them hard and save Solidarity."[47] At an NSC meeting a week later, Haig asked whether the United States should be satisfied with the gains already achieved and use them as a "basis for a subsequent evolution toward further gains." Reagan then jumped in:

> This is the first time in 60 years that we have had this kind of opportunity. There may not be another in our lifetime. Can we afford not to go all out? I'm talking about a total quarantine on the Soviet Union. No détente! We know—and the world knows—that they are behind this. We have backed away so many times. After WWII we offered Poland the Marshall Plan: they accepted, but the Soviets said no. . . . [C]an we do less now than tell our Allies, "This is big Casino!" There may never be another chance! It is like the opening lines in our own declaration of independence: "When in the course of human events. . . ." This is exactly what [the Poles] are doing now. One other thing in addition to the Marshall Plan. The Soviets have violated the Helsinki Accords since the day it was signed. They have made mockery of it. We are not going to pretend it is not so.[48]

In overruling his secretary of state, Reagan displayed command of the history of U.S. Cold War strategy in Eastern Europe and forcefully declared his intent to break from tradition.

Strong support was given to Reagan's position, and soon thereafter the administration announced a series of sanctions against the Polish government. Many of these sanctions were imposed without support from America's Western allies. The United States also levied sanctions against the Soviet Union, with which the allies also refused to go along. Hard-liners in the administration were incensed at the feeble response of (in Reagan's words) "those chicken littles in Europe."[49] In June 1982, the United States broadened sanctions by banning equipment and technology needed by the Soviet Union to build the Siberian gas pipeline. This move outraged Western leaders, since it hurt Western European economies involved in the project.[50] The Reagan administration, against the unified advice of its allies, as well as Secretary Haig, took a hard line against Poland and the Soviet Union as the result of martial law—a point not lost on reformers within the Eastern bloc.

Poland was both a clarifying and a unifying force in determining the path forward vis-à-vis the Soviet Union. The Reagan administration's national security strategy was formalized in National Security Decision Directive (NSDD)-32, issued on May 20, 1982. NSDD-32 was a radical break from the prevailing U.S. national security strategy in that it not only continued the long-standing policy of containment but also restored the offensive element to roll back Soviet power. One of the key global objectives of NSDD-32 was to "contain and reverse the expansion of Soviet control and military presence throughout the world, and to increase the costs of Soviet support and use of proxy, terrorist, and subversive forces." According to Jeremi Suri, the "escalation of superpower tensions" became "explicit American policy."[51] In addition, the directive set out to "encourage long-term liberalizing and nationalist tendencies within the Soviet Union and allied countries."[52] One of the principal authors, William Clark, who became national security adviser in January 1982, said of NSDD-32, "Reagan made clear that the United States was not resigned to the status quo of Soviet domination of Eastern Europe. We attempted to forge a multipronged strategy to weaken Soviet influence and strengthen indigenous forces for freedom in the region. Poland offered a unique opportunity relative to other states."[53] In January 1983, a revised strategy toward the Soviet Union, NSDD-75, specifically noted the goal of "imposing costs on the Soviet Union for its behavior in Poland."[54] NSDD-75 went deeper than NSDD-32 in fleshing out the rollback strategy, and Poland was a central component.

Outside of Poland, however, the administration acknowledged the limits to American power in Eastern Europe based on the geopolitics of the time. At a July 21, 1982, NSC meeting on U.S. policy in the region, there was nothing resembling the liberation theme outlined in NSDD-32. New Secretary of State George Shultz said the United States should "encourage liberalization wherever possible" in the region; however, the bulk of the discussion was spent reaffirming the differentiation strategy and caution on East-West technology transfers.[55] Six weeks later, Reagan approved NSDD-54, a directive focused solely on policy toward Eastern Europe. "The primary long-term U.S. goal in Eastern Europe," read the document, "is to loosen the Soviet hold on the region and thereby facilitate its eventual reintegration into the European community of nations." His vision was the same across Eastern Europe, but like many previous presidents, this NSDD said the United States must tailor its policies to each country in the region. It conceded that Western influence in the region was "limited" and that this economic-based strategy may have a "marginal" impact. The directive was remarkably similar to that of its predecessors, even admitting in the text that it represented "a continuation of differentiation toward Eastern Europe which has been U.S. policy for nearly 20 years." While the "fundamental objectives of differentiation remain the same," it struck an even more tepid note in saying "its implementation will differ in that we will proceed more cautiously and with a clearer sense of our limitations, including budgetary ones."[56]

When viewed through the lens of Reagan's broader Soviet policy, this seeming contradiction in objectives is easier to understand. Where Reagan broke most dramatically from his predecessors was in his policy toward the Soviet Union. Scores of books and articles have been written demonstrating Reagan's intentions and efforts to defeat, rather than contain, Soviet communism; a full account is not necessary for this chapter. Long before he took the Oval Office, he had a simple view of the U.S.-Soviet struggle, made clear in his 1979 conversation with Richard Allen: "My theory of the Cold War is: we win and they lose."[57] His deeply held faith that the Soviet Union would ultimately end up on the "ash heap of history" and that America had a duty to hasten its collapse was unique among Cold War presidents. During his eight years in office, Reagan crafted and executed a broad policy framework—articulated first in NSDD-32—aimed at hastening the demise of the Soviet Union through economic pressure, rhetorical assaults, and overt and covert military assistance to anti-Soviet movements. What role these policies had in the eventual collapse of the Soviet Union is debatable, but Reagan's intent is inarguable.

Eastern Europe, then, was inextricably linked with the administration's broader crusade against the Soviet Union—and Reagan's larger goal of freedom throughout the entire Soviet bloc. Poland was the perfect vehicle for Reagan's broader goal, and in the ensuing years, U.S. actions against the Polish government would become a microcosm of the strategy outlined in NSDD-32.

The administration's assistance in keeping Solidarity afloat may have prevented the same tightening of Soviet power in the region as occurred after the uprisings in 1956 and 1968 and, judging from Politburo deliberations of 1980–1981, would likely have happened again had Solidarity been neutralized. As NSDD-54 clearly shows, if no other openings existed in Eastern Europe, Reagan's policy options would have been limited—even if his goals were far more ambitious than those of his predecessors—and he would have sought better targets of opportunity around the globe, such as Afghanistan, Angola, and Nicaragua. But an opening did occur in Poland through the imposition of martial law, and the administration's response fundamentally altered the trajectory of its policy throughout Eastern Europe, keeping alive a dissident movement in the heart of the Eastern bloc.

Following the plan outlined in NSDD-32, the Reagan administration facilitated substantial covert assistance from a complex and highly guarded network of allies, led by CIA chief William Casey, to sustain and advance Solidarity's cause. They found an unlikely partner in the AFL-CIO, with whom they worked closely to provide money and other equipment necessary to keep the movement strong. Of greater consequence was Reagan's "holy alliance" with the Catholic Church and its first Polish leader, Pope John Paul II. Reagan and John Paul agreed that if Poland were to become free, it would provide the spark to "free all of Eastern Europe." In the ensuing years, the Reagan administration worked hand in glove with the Vatican to coordinate assistance to Solidarity.[58] Also in line with NSDD-32, the administration utilized Radio Free Europe (RFE) to provide both news and moral support to the movement. In 1981, surveys indicated an average of 11 million listeners (42 percent of the population) in Poland each day, and roughly two-thirds listened during times of political crisis, despite strenuous effort by the government to jam broadcasts. The increased funding for RFE during the Reagan years ensured that more people in Poland, and across Eastern Europe, were receiving news from the West. Wałesa later said, "[RFE's importance] cannot even be described. Can you conceive the Earth without the sun?"[59]

Poland also provided an effective vehicle to exact significant economic pressure on the Soviet Union. The Reagan administration caused a row with its Western European allies by attempting to kill construction of the Siberian gas pipeline. The sanctions were lifted in November 1982, but the final pipeline was smaller than envisioned, and delays in construction prevented billions of dollars in desperately needed hard currency from reaching Moscow. The NSC also worked behind the scenes to tighten credit in Eastern Europe as a way to place further strain on the Soviet economy. Western bankers were quietly discouraged from extending the short-term loans Warsaw needed to make its debt payments, forcing Moscow to choose between providing the credits itself or severely damaging the credit rating of the Soviet Union and the Eastern bloc. Moscow chose not to step in, causing much-needed loans to dry up throughout the region. Soviet central banker Vladimir Kutinov later lamented that the United States had "forced our hand in Poland" and proved that "the emperor had no clothes."[60] In accordance with NSDD-32, the administration was indeed "forcing the USSR to bear the brunt of [the Soviet alliance's] economic shortcomings."

The Reagan administration did not eschew entirely its predecessors' policy toward Eastern Europe. Despite criticism during the 1980 campaign, it continued to participate in the Conference on Security and Cooperation in Europe and, in an ironic twist, found the Helsinki process to be a useful channel to criticize human rights violations in Eastern Europe and the Soviet Union.[61] It preferred to work with more liberal and independent nations and continued to support Yugoslavia, which was, according to NSDD-133, "a useful reminder to countries in Eastern Europe of the advantages of independence from Moscow and of the benefits of friendly relations with the West."[62] Vice President Bush paid visits to Hungary, Romania, and Yugoslavia in 1983, affirming—in both word and deed—the strategy outlined in NSDD-54. During his trip, Bush made a veiled reference to the Polish model of U.S. policy by saying the United States "does not seek to destabilize or undermine any government, but . . . we support and will encourage all movement toward the social, humanitarian and democratic ideals."[63]

However, as Solidarity survived and Moscow slowly released its grip on Eastern Europe, the Reagan administration looked to exploit new opportunities more aggressively than any administration since the early days of the Cold War. After a January 1985 meeting with Hungary's foreign minister, Reagan wrote in his diary, "Hungary is a target for friendly efforts to woo them a little away from the Soviets. They don't seem too unwilling."[64] The CIA would later provide aid to Hungarian émigré groups in hopes of opening channels into the nation's internal politics. In 1986, on the 30th anniversary of the Hungarian uprising, a letter signed by 122 of the most notable dissidents in Eastern Europe was released, calling for united action against Soviet domination; the NSC sent $25,000 to the group drafting the letter. Covert support was also given to other dissident movements in the region, including in Czechoslovakia.[65] According to Shultz, administration hawks opposed increasing cooperation with Eastern Europe to encourage liberalization, but they were overruled, and Deputy Secretary of State John Whitehead was placed in charge of regional policy in the summer of 1986. During a February 1987 tour of the region, Whitehead reported "things are changing." Shultz noticed reformers were "taking a longer and longer lead off first base," and the administration increased its offers of economic incentives in an effort to prod along the forces of history. Thus, while the Reagan administration initiated new strategies to mitigate Soviet power in Eastern Europe, its parallel use of "carrots," even in Poland during Reagan's second term, continued one of the tactics used by previous administrations and outlined in NSDD-54.[66]

Perhaps the greatest point of departure was the administration's use of rhetoric. As John Lewis Gaddis has written, by 1980 the world had come to accept the bipolar order of the Cold War. Reagan used "drama to shatter the constraints of conventional wisdom" and cast the Soviet Union as a temporary power. In this, "his preferred weapon was public oratory."[67] He used the bully pulpit time and again to attack Soviet control of Eastern Europe. Reagan decried "the division of Europe into spheres of influence" and said that "passively accepting the permanent subjugation of the people of Eastern Europe is not . . . acceptable." In a speech before the United Nations, he singled out Soviet violations of the Yalta agreements, which led to "ruthless repression" in Poland and the "domination of Eastern Europe."[68] Other senior administration officials followed the same line on Yalta. Shultz said the United States "does not recognize the legitimacy of the artificially imposed division of Europe," and Bush called Moscow's violation of Yalta "the primary root of East-West tensions today."[69] Even when the administration began to take a relatively softer line vis-à-vis the Soviet Union in the second term, the rhetoric on Eastern Europe remained the same. These verbal assaults were often dismissed as simplistic or criticized as bellicose by Reagan's opponents, yet they found a receptive audience behind the Iron Curtain.

When Reagan left office in January 1989, few predicted the pace and breadth of change that would sweep Eastern Europe in the coming year. It was, appropriately, Solidarity that led the way, winning concessions in April to semifree parliamentary elections that ultimately brought the first noncommunist government in Eastern Europe. For his part, Gorbachev unwittingly hastened collapse on July 7 when he announced: "Any interference in internal affairs, any attempts to limit the sovereignty of states—whether of friends and allies or anybody else—are inadmissible."[70] The collapse of the Eastern bloc reached its dramatic climax four months later in Berlin, and on December 4, in Malta, Bush and Gorbachev officially ended the Cold War. Gorbachev resigned from the presidency of the Soviet Union on Christmas Day, 1991.

The Legacy

According to Irving Kristol, "Leaders who had one very big idea and one very big commitment—this permitted them to create something. Those are the ones who leave a legacy." From the time the Cold War began, Ronald Reagan's "one very big idea" was to rid the world of communism, and this left a powerful legacy across Eastern Europe. Historical figures tend to recede into the collective memory with the passage of time. Yet, a generation after leaving the White House, Reagan's legacy in Eastern Europe persists and has gained new meaning over time.

To be sure, Reagan does not pervade the daily political conversation in Eastern Europe today; to suggest otherwise would be misleading. But he still occupies space in the public square, and taken as a whole, allusions to Reagan today reveal two distinct and equally potent legacies. The first observes Reagan's policies during his presidency and the extent to which these policies impacted events within the region. This—the most common of political legacies—is purely *retrospective* in nature. The second relates to what Reagan symbolizes in the political dialogue of Eastern Europe today. He is a referential figure for ideas he espoused during his presidency and to which people still subscribe today. This second type of legacy is decidedly *prospective* in nature.

Visit any Eastern European capital, and you are bound to run into some sort of monument to Ronald Reagan. While American presidents have a long history of such honorifics on foreign soil, Reagan's tokens of immortality in Eastern Europe far exceed the average. In July 2007, Poland became the first nation in the region to honor Reagan with a statue—a 10-foot structure across from the U.S. embassy. The country followed it up with an 11.5-foot statue in November 2011. This was in addition to the three Ronald Reagan Squares already in existence in Warsaw. In June 2011, a seven-foot statue of Reagan was placed in Budapest's Freedom Square, marking Reagan's second statue in the Hungarian capital. A month later, officials in Prague renamed a street in Reagan's honor. And there is an ongoing debate between conservatives and the governing Social Democrat/Left Party coalition in Berlin over the best way to commemorate Reagan's legacy in eastern Germany.[71] More monuments can be expected in the region in the months and years to come.

These monuments bear tribute to Reagan's role as *a* principal figure in the collapse of communism in Eastern Europe and the end of the Cold War—a sentiment that broadly reflects his legacy throughout the region. There are critics, to be sure. But the vast majority view Reagan, along with other leaders and social forces, as a consequential figure in these events. For instance, Bence Stagel, a member of the Hungarian Diet, said Reagan's policies were indirect but crucial to his nation's freedom, and former Czech prime minister Václav Klaus called Reagan a "key factor" in the fall of communism—a sentiment shared by Václav Havel. Ruprecht Polenz, foreign policy spokesman for Germany's Christian Democrats, said Reagan's "persistence in deed and clarity in speech" were a critical factor in the region's changes. Hungarian Deputy Prime Minister Zsolt Semjen said it was a matter of consensus "by all normal political forces in Hungary" that Reagan, Pope John Paul II, and Mikhail Gorbachev were responsible for Hungary's freedom—with Reagan deserving the lion's share of credit. Albanian Prime Minister Sali Berisha cited Reagan first, along with Gorbachev, John Paul, Helmut Kohl, and George H. W. Bush, as the "architects" in the fall of the Berlin Wall and subsequent collapse of the Eastern bloc. Czech Ambassador to the United States Petr Gandalovic credited Reagan's honesty about the nature of the Soviet Union with inspiring people to fight against the communist regime in Prague. Czech Prime Minister Petr Necas echoed this point, saying Reagan's bluntness in describing the Soviet Union as an "evil empire" made him one of the leaders who contributed most to Czech freedom. He spoke for the millions of people aspiring for freedom behind the Iron Curtain.[72] Recognizing the multitude of forces at play, Reagan is placed in the pantheon of leaders who brought to conclusion 45 years of East-West conflict.

Some go even further, arguing that Reagan was *the* decisive force in defeating Soviet communism. In November 2011, Lech Wałesa asked "whether today's Poland, Europe, and world could look the same without President Reagan. As a participant in those events, I must say that it's inconceivable." Hungarian Prime Minister Viktor Orban described Reagan as "the leader who changed, who renewed this world and created in it a new world for us in Central Europe." Foreign Minister Karel Schwarzenberg argued, "If he had not believed that the empire of evil, as he called it, must be fought with, not lived with, we would probably still live in the Warsaw Pact." And Roman Joch, director of Prague's Civic Institute and adviser to Prime Minister Petr Necas, said plainly: "Reagan won the Cold War. For those of us who suffered under communism, he was our liberator."[73] This is a debate never to be fully resolved, yet these testimonies are indicative of Reagan's impact and continuing popularity in a region to which he devoted so much attention. It is this opinion that serves as the foundation for Reagan's legacy as a referential figure today.

The Symbolic Ronald Reagan

Because of his hallowed memory among much of the region's electorate, associating with Reagan is often good politics for Eastern European politicians. Sometimes it can be whimsical, as when Jozefina Topalli, vice president of the Albanian Democratic Party and speaker of parliament, was asked about the possibility of succeeding the 65-year-old prime minister, Sali Berisha, and noted that Reagan became president at 69 and was reelected at 73. It can likewise be misguided, as when the Czech conservative group D.O.S.T. invoked Reagan's name to lodge a complaint against the Prague Pride gay festival. Or policymakers may distort Reagan's policies to make a case. In June 2007, former Slovak prime minister Jan Carnogursky invoked Reagan in speaking out against the proposed antimissile shield in Poland and the Czech Republic.[74]

The vast majority of Reagan references, however, coalesce around one of two images: first, as a bold advocate for freedom and, second, as the standard-bearer for the set of economic policies known colloquially as "Reaganomics."

Reagan's legacy as a champion of liberty has been applied in a wide spectrum of cases. In April 2010, for example, Gao Zhisheng, a Chinese lawyer and dissident known for challenging human rights abuses in his country, disappeared. Leaders around the world called on the Beijing government, suspected of detaining Gao, to release him. In his meetings and correspondence with senior Soviet officials, Reagan relentlessly pursued the release of religious leaders and political dissidents. Roman Joch, an adviser to the Czech prime minister, said the West needed to find a new Ronald Reagan to change China in the same way he confronted and changed the Soviet Union.[75]

Hungarian deputy prime minister Zsolt Semjen found Reagan's policy toward Moscow instructive when dealing with Beijing, albeit for different reasons than in the case of Gao Zhisheng. Semjen was in agreement that China's human rights record was unsatisfactory and reforms were needed. However, he looked to Reagan for a model on balancing human rights interests with economic interests. In July 2011, Semjen advocated dialogue with Chinese leaders on human rights issues while continuing to conduct business: "This is what U.S. President Ronald Reagan did: he defeated the Soviet Union, yet kept the dialogue running with Gorbachev."[76]

Following the December 2010 election in Belarus, President Alyaksandr Lukashenka took harsh measures against his political opponents. European Union (EU) leaders responded by imposing travel bans and freezing certain assets of Lukashenka and his allies, but the group remained divided on sanctions, with Italy, Greece, Latvia, and others opposing more severe measures out of fear they would only hurt ordinary citizens in Belarus. In response, Slovak foreign minister Mikulas Dzurinda, who served as an opposition figure in Czechoslovakia during the Cold War, recalled the impact of the "very tough, very clear position" Reagan took against communist regimes in Eastern Europe during the 1980s and argued that a "tough, strong, principled position" would embolden the Belarussian people and increase the prospect for change.[77] Speaking more broadly on the need for Reagan's boldness, Czech senate deputy chairman Premysl Sobotka castigated the present American and European leaders, accusing them of appeasing opponents of liberty and democracy.[78]

In January 2012, Eastern European libertarians invoked Reagan in their opposition to the Anti-Counterfeiting Trade Agreement (ACTA), the European version of the Stop Online Piracy Act, which was shelved in the United States in January 2012. Fierce opposition was mobilized to challenge both ACTA and SOPA, yet EU leaders succeeded in passing ACTA in January 2012. In Poland, Janusz Palikot, leader of the libertarian Palikot's Movement, was irate at the U.S. Embassy in Poland's inquiry into Sejm activity regarding ACTA. Said Palikot, "Ronald Reagan, who was a symbol of fight for freedom . . . would be now ashamed of the U.S. embassy, which acts more like the then Soviet embassy. . . . We have not quit the Warsaw Pact just to allow the U.S. to replace Russia in the role it had played in this Pact."[79]

Eastern European references to Reagan's defense of liberty are too numerous to list here, but the examples given illustrate the range encompassed. Reagan is at once a model for freedom of political conscience, freedom from authoritarian rule, freedom against bureaucratic overreach, and the strategy of linking economic cooperation to internal reforms. This struggle for political freedom is something with which Eastern Europeans have a long history and a remarkable record of success in recent decades, as evinced by Freedom House's annual measurement of political rights and civil liberties. In Freedom House's 1990 study, the region scored an average of 4.0 in political rights and 3.8 in civil liberties on a scale of 1 to 7, with 1 representing the highest degree of freedom. For the past several years, the region has held steady at 1.7 in both categories. Even more remarkable is how quickly these former communist nations joined the Western military alliance, fighting alongside American soldiers in Afghanistan, Iraq, and other theaters with the mission of expanding freedom, beginning with the 1990–1991 Gulf War.[80] Moreover, Poland and the Czech Republic went so far as to join the United States in a joint missile defense program.

The growth in economic freedom has followed a similar trajectory, according to the *Index of Economic Freedom,* an annual study conducted by the Heritage Foundation and the *Wall Street Journal* to measure "the march of economic freedom around the world." During the first year of the study, which was several years into the postcommunist transition, six of the eight former Eastern bloc nations (excluding East Germany and Yugoslavia) scored an average of 53.7, on the low end of the "mostly unfree" category. In the 2012 *Index,* these nations earned an average score of 66.0—higher than some of their Western European neighbors such as France, Italy, and Portugal. East Germany and Yugoslavia are less straightforward for their own reasons, but the trend is similar.[81] Eastern Europeans also enjoy, on average, much lower corporate and income tax rates than their neighbors to the west.

Reaganomics is not the desired track for many policymakers in the region, but for those who support the philosophy of lower taxes and smaller government, Reagan frequently serves as the model. The EU constitution, first approved by European leaders in Rome in October 2004, was rejected by referenda in France and the Netherlands in 2005, forcing a "period of reflection." In 2007, officials in the Czech Republic's governing Civic Democratic Party were leery of the revised constitution under consideration, and they invoked Reagan to build their case. Foreign Minister Karel Schwarzenberg said the bureaucratic complexities would have to be dramatically streamlined to earn Czech support. To illustrate his point, Schwarzenberg said, "We need a great European deregulation, similar to what Reagan did in the U.S." As Schwarzenberg and his European counterparts continued to hammer away at revisions, Czech leaders remained unsatisfied. In May 2007, Schwarzenberg again pointed to Reagan, this time emphasizing the economic benefits generated by streamlining the bureaucracy: "Europe needs Ronald Reagan.

Reagan was someone who by deregulation paved the path to a new economic upswing."[82]

Reagan was not always used as the foil to Western European policymaking. Czech leaders had grown increasingly concerned with America's economic response to the global financial crisis and the degree to which American officials looked to government intervention to get the economy growing again. Czech prime minister Mirek Topolanek, worried about possible contagion from a flailing American economy, warned President Barack Obama on the day of his inaugural, "It is true what Reagan said: governments do not resolve anything, they themselves are part of the problem." Topolanek got himself into trouble two months later by characterizing Obama's stimulus package as a "way to hell."[83] In April 2009, Czech president Václav Klaus made a similar observation about his "exceptional fear" of the return to Keynesian policies to resolve the ailing global economy and urged a return to "the revolution of Ronald Reagan and Margaret Thatcher."[84] What the global economy needed, Klaus, Topolanek, and others from the Civic Democratic Party argued, was a return to the market-oriented economic policies embodied in Reaganomics.

Later in the year, German federal economics minister Rainer Bruederle urged tax cuts as a means to increasing economic growth. Bruederle was asked how, in a time of rising budget deficits, one could justify reducing government revenue through tax cuts. In response, Bruederle cited Reagan and the U.S. economy throughout the 1980s and 1990s: "Ronald Reagan reduced taxes, giving a boost to growth in the process. His successor Clinton then presented a balanced budget. What this shows is this: you can only sort out the budget if you have previously produced growth."[85]

In addition to advocating Reagan-era economic policy, many leaders across the region implemented such policies themselves. In a speech before the Israel Council on Foreign Relations, Albanian prime minister Sali Berisha credited Reagan in November 2011 with the economic philosophy that guided his nation's economy to success while the rest of the global economy struggled:

> I learned a great lesson from one of the most admired personalities of the world, Ronald Reagan—and that was the importance of low taxes. . . . Reagan wrote that money in the accounts of private people is worth more than in the public coffers. So I have ensured that my country has the lowest possible fiscal burden, and with predictable results. Albania enjoys double-digit growth. Despite the very serious global financial crisis around us, Albania did not feel the recent recession.[86]

Here, too, these samples illustrate how Reagan represents the suite of policies within the conservative economic philosophy: lower taxes, deregulation, reduction of the public sector, and trust in the power of markets. The most recent global economic downturn has intensified the divisions between fiscal conservatives and social democrats, giving the principles of Reaganomics renewed meaning and influence.

The symbolic Ronald Reagan, then, is utilized for a wide range of policies, but at the most basic level he represents two ideas: political and economic liberty. When Reagan took office, he set out to achieve a small list of big goals—restore American power, reduce the size and scope of government, unleash markets, confront the Soviet Union, expand global democracy. Reagan's symbolic legacy today is a reflection of the goals he set, and largely achieved, during his presidency. Not coincidentally, he represents the same ideas in the United States, Europe, and other parts of the world. While Reagan's legacy in Eastern Europe will always retain a parochial component due to his specific policies in the region, Reagan's symbolism today is as a standard-bearer of the global center-right.

• • •

Ronald Reagan fundamentally altered the prevailing U.S. strategy toward the Soviet Union, and in so doing, he left an enduring imprint on the nations of the former Eastern bloc. A generation after his presidency, he is regarded at once as a principal actor in the collapse of communism in Eastern Europe and a referential figure for conservative policymakers today. The first legacy is likely to stand the test of time. The second legacy will only last so long as the ideas embodied by Reagan bear fruit and resonate with the Eastern European public and the people safeguard the freedom to pursue them in the public square.

5

Reagan's "March of Freedom" in a Changing World

PAUL KENGOR

How has the world transformed since the Reagan years? The answers, of course, are many and varied. But among them, nothing dominated the international stage in the Reagan era quite like the Cold War division and competition between the two superpowers. For more than 40 years, the rivalry between the United States and the Soviet Union, the West and the East, free-market democracies versus communist/totalitarian regimes, pervaded and threatened the global scene. In 1989, the year that ended Ronald Reagan's stay in the White House, that Cold War peacefully ended, with the likewise peaceful end of the Soviet Union coming shortly thereafter.

Today's world is markedly different, so much so than anyone born after 1989 cannot even imagine the world that has since passed. The global stage was again transformed with the advent of September 11, 2001, and what President George W. Bush subsequently called the War on Terror, which resulted in major wars in Afghanistan and Iraq, both of which Bush's successor, President Barack Obama, has dealt with, and which future presidents henceforth will continue to face. At the time of the writing of this chapter, Reagan's presidency ended two and a half decades ago, and half the years since then have been dominated by the aftermath of September 11. To some degree, at least in American eyes, radical Islamic terrorism has replaced global communism as the primary international threat.

But here is where that new world, that world transformed, gets particularly interesting, in light of where and how Ronald Reagan has had an ongoing influence on the international scene.

George W. Bush gave many reasons for sending troops first into Afghanistan and then Iraq. His reasons for invading Afghanistan were understandable to most Americans, given that Afghanistan was the location that harbored Osama Bin Laden and his conspirators. The vast majority of Americans supported Bush's move into Afghanistan. Bush's reasons for going into Iraq, however, were not accepted as easily or widely.[1] Bush pointed to Saddam Hussein's past and suspected continued pursuit of terrorism and weapons of mass destruction (WMDs)—and, most crucial, the perceived inability of the world to stop those pursuits. But Bush also pointed to something else: he claimed that removing Saddam might enable democracy in Iraq, sowing the seeds for further democratization in the Middle East. He argued the same about removing the Taliban. Such democratization, Bush and certain advisers hoped, might ultimately produce a long-lasting "democratic peace" in the region.[2] And here, alas, on this essential matter of spreading democracy and freedom, George W. Bush invoked the thinking and vision of Ronald Reagan—a remarkable gesture on Bush's part, and one that was missed by not only the wider general public but by pundits and even by Reagan scholars.

Ronald Reagan had spoken glowingly and inspiringly of a natural, historical "March of Freedom." He had hoped to advance and extend that march to what he believed was its next natural, historical destination: the Soviet bloc countries of Eastern Europe (i.e., those aforementioned communist/totalitarian states). He wanted to help liberate that region, to bring democracy and freedom there, to bring "pluralism" (a word his administration used in formal directives). That goal, detailed at length in this chapter, is noteworthy enough. It clearly speaks to this volume's thesis of a world transformed. But did the march end in Europe? That is, has the march and the transformation stopped?

Well, it is critical to understand that a recent president, George W. Bush, sought to pick up that torch—or at least what Bush perceived as the torch. In comments neither widely heard nor understood, and scarcely reported on or picked up by scholars, Bush boldly stated his own intention to further Reagan's March of Freedom. He claimed he would extend the march into the one region where political freedom (post–Cold War) remains most absent: the Middle East. Bush directly invoked Reagan's march, vowing to extend it far beyond the former Iron Curtain. It would be an extremely difficult and controversial undertaking.

The goal of this chapter is not to evaluate the success of that Bush objective, especially at this point in history. Likewise, the goal is not to attempt to resolve the pros and cons of Bush's objective, though I will acknowledge the disagreement and dispute with Bush's appropriation and application of Reagan's thinking. Among those most offended were, ironically, Reagan conservatives. For the record, I personally have reservations and reasons to think that Bush's objective will fail to come to fruition in the Middle East, though I could also make a case (persuasive or not) for its merits. The main objective of this chapter, however, is to illuminate this crucial Reagan concept; to underscore its broader Cold War context, motivations, and ambitions; and to then highlight its sudden resurrection and ramifications in recent times—resurrected by the person of George W. Bush.

Indeed, with Bush believing as he did and doing what he did, other presidents likewise will be dealing with the legacy of this modern projection of Reagan's vision. Whether President Obama and his successors realize it or not, they walk in the footsteps of Reagan's March of Freedom not merely in Eastern Europe but (because of George W. Bush) in the Middle East as well.

Reagan's Vision for Eastern Europe

First, we must consider what Ronald Reagan meant by the "March of Freedom," how he envisioned it and intended it, and how that freedom march played out in Eastern Europe.

In assessing Ronald Reagan's impact, few regions are as instructive as the one he endeavored to most transform: Eastern Europe. This was from the outset one of the more universally laudatory areas of Reagan involvement, in that supporting Eastern Europe's liberation did not require allying with or reluctantly supporting questionable or rogue regimes, as was sometimes the case with Reagan's anti-communist policies in Latin America (El Salvador in particular).[3] In Eastern Europe, Reagan policy embraced genuine good guys that Americans and freedom-lovers everywhere could accept and respect, such as the Solidarity labor union and Charter 77 movement, such as Lech Wałesa and Václav Havel. In Eastern Europe, Reagan did not need to hold his nose and grudgingly do business with tyrannical governments; quite the contrary, he could genuinely say, without dispute, that he was allying against tyranny. No one questioned whether Solidarity or Charter 77, unlike the contras in Nicaragua or mujahedin in Afghanistan, was comprised of genuine "freedom fighters."[4] Liberal intellectuals in the United States liked Lech Wałesa (a union leader) and liked Václav Havel (a poet and playwright) and what they represented. And so, the advancement of the Reagan "freedom" mission in Eastern Europe was, fortunately for the president, not tainted or hampered like the advancement of Reagan's anti-communist policies elsewhere. The president had a much easier time winning domestic support for his liberation policy in Eastern Europe than in Latin America or elsewhere.[5]

As to that policy of liberation, a lengthy track record of Reagan writings and statements, even prior to his presidency, as well as attestation by Reagan advisers and official White House directives, reveal that a transformation of Eastern Europe had been precisely Ronald Reagan's longtime intent.[6] During the presidency, this is particularly evident in formal National Security Council (NSC) policy directives—officially known as National Security Decision Directives (NSDDs). Among them, NSDD-75, authorized by Reagan in January 1983, stated that U.S. policy "should seek wherever possible to encourage Soviet allies to distance themselves from Moscow in foreign policy and to move toward democratization domestically." Chief among these allies, of course, was Eastern Europe. "The primary U.S. objective in Eastern Europe," NSDD-75 made clear, "is to loosen Moscow's hold on the region," while also promoting civil liberties in the region. The Reagan team believed it could advance this objective by "carefully discriminating" in favor of countries that "show relative independence" from the Soviet Union in their foreign policy or that show "a greater degree of internal liberalization."[7]

Significantly, this meant changing not just Eastern Europe but also the Soviet Union itself, both its reach into Europe and its political and economic system. NSDD-75 sought: (1) "To contain and over time reverse Soviet expansionism. . . . This will remain the primary focus of U.S. policy toward the USSR"; (2) "To promote, within the narrow limits available to us, the process of change in the Soviet Union toward a more pluralistic political and economic system in which the power of the privileged ruling elite is gradually reduced."

This was an extraordinary ambition. To repeat: the Reagan administration was seeking a "process of change" in the Soviet Union toward greater political and economic pluralism. It was hoping to reduce the monopoly on power by the "ruling elite" (read: Communist Party leadership in the Kremlin). At this point in history, very few were so optimistic.

Partly based on previous NSDDs like 32, 45, 54, and 66, NSDD-75 was tamely titled "U.S. Relations with the USSR." Written by Richard Pipes, the Harvard Sovietologist who spent 1981 and 1982 as the top adviser on Eastern Europe at Reagan's NSC, NSDD-75 was shepherded by close Reagan aide and confidant William P. Clark, who had been hired as Reagan's national security adviser on January 1, 1982. In a short but extremely productive tenure from January 1982 through mid-October 1983, Clark oversaw the execution of more than 100 Reagan NSDDs—all pursuing and maintaining a cohesive set of policy beliefs and goals.[8]

When the Soviets learned of the contents of NSDD-75, they were apoplectic.[9] They realized the directive was aimed at extending freedom and democracy and thus reversing communism throughout the Soviet empire, from East Berlin to eastern Siberia. One article in the Soviet press apocalyptically warned that the "New Directive" "Threatens History." It stated, "Directive 75 speaks of changing the Soviet Union's domestic policy. In other words, the powers that be in Washington are threatening the course of world history, neither more nor less."[10]

A dispatch by TASS, the official Soviet news agency, decried the grand ambitions of Ronald Reagan and his band of freedom "crusaders." Making reference to the previous summer of 1982, TASS reminded Soviet citizens that Reagan had devised a "strategy" that constituted a "'crusade' against communism," a "'roll-back communism' policy."[11]

Here, TASS was pointing to a goal that Reagan had declared in June 1982—his March of Freedom declaration at Westminster in London.

April–May 1982: Readying for Westminster

Before stepping back to June 1982, we should first consider just a few of the notable moves made by Reagan and his administration in advance of the Westminster Address, most of which have long since receded into news archives.

Reagan gave several significant public speeches in April and May heralding what he insisted was the coming triumph of freedom and democracy over communism.[12] Martial law had been declared in Poland the previous December, and Reagan, though outraged, felt that the ugliness that was martial law afforded beautiful possibilities to begin breaking the Soviet stranglehold on Eastern Europe.[13] Among these speeches, Reagan spoke at his alma mater, Eureka College, on May 9, 1982, where he made some emphatic statements. He insisted that the "course" Soviet leaders had chosen would "undermine the foundations of the Soviet system."[14]

When Reagan said such things, many observers, particularly academic Sovietologists, thought the Soviet system was *not* faltering. Reagan, however, believed that the Soviet system *had* to be failing because it was a communist system, and communism, he was convinced, simply did not work. He also contended that the Soviet Union's overextension in foreign policy would be a loss in the long run and that the world was now witnessing the terminal phase of that long run. He insisted that the West do nothing to spare the Soviet Union from final termination.

Reagan said that President Harry Truman was right when he said of the Soviets: "When you try to conquer other people or extend yourself over vast areas, you cannot win in the long run." He told his alma mater that the Soviet elite held power so tightly because, "as we have seen in Poland," they "fear what might happen if even the smallest amount of control slips from their grasp. They fear the infectiousness of even a little freedom."

Within a week and a half of this speech, Bill Clark's National Security Council produced another crucial NSDD. Called "U.S. National Security Strategy," NSDD-32 was signed on May 20, 1982.[15] It stands as a further demonstration that the Reagan team early on intended something historically monumental that indeed would transpire within just a few years.

NSDD-32 began by stating that Reagan national security strategy "requires development and integration of a set of strategies, including diplomatic, informational, economic/political, and military components." It then listed 10 bullet points laying out the "global objectives" of Reagan administration policy. The objectives included this one on the first page: "To contain and reverse the expansion of Soviet control and military presence throughout the world, and to increase the costs of Soviet support and use of proxy, terrorist, and subversive forces." This was reiterated on page four of the directive, almost as if to ensure there was no mistaking the bold intention: the American objective, repeated NSDD-32, was "to contain and reverse the expansion of Soviet influence worldwide." This was not a matter of picking one or two spots the administration hoped to try to contain; the Reagan White House was seeking *reversal* of Soviet "influence" on a *"worldwide"* scale.

NSDD-32 wanted to not merely contain the Soviet Union, but go beyond containment to reverse or roll back positions and territory it already controlled—meaning Eastern Europe and numerous other spots around the world. "Increasing the costs of Soviet support" meant U.S. support of counter-Soviet forces like the mujahedin rebels in Afghanistan and Solidarity in Poland, among others.

As to the latter, NSDD-32 authorized clandestine support for Poland's Solidarity movement. It called for secret financial, intelligence, and logistical support to ensure the survival of the independent trade union as an explosive force within the heart of the Soviet empire.

This bold objective was easier said than done. There was considerable internal debate within the White House over aiding Solidarity, but the detractors were vetoed by Reagan.[16] Richard Pipes recalled: "The president talked about . . . how we had to do everything possible to help these people in Solidarity who were struggling for freedom."[17] Reagan instructed Bill Casey, director of central intelligence (DCI), to draw up a covert plan; the DCI enthusiastically complied. In fact, Casey had moved to prepare plans for aiding Solidarity as early as April 1981, half a year before martial law.[18]

One of those intimately involved in devising NSDD-32 was Tom Reed, an NSC staffer close to Bill Clark. Reed dubbed this particular directive "the plan to prevail" and "the roadmap for winning the Cold War." The "bottom line" of NSDD-32, said Reed plainly, was "to seek the dissolution of the Soviet empire."[19] Even then, stressed Reed, NSDD-32 was just the beginning.[20] It was one component of a broader framework.

The Soviets were gravely aware of what NSDD-32 constituted. Writing in *Pravda*, Yuri Zhukov warned that the aim of the directive was to place "massive pressure" on the Soviet Union, with an intent to "bring about internal reforms" in the country.[21] Professor Vitaly Zhurkin stated on Moscow's widely watched *Studio 9* television program that NSDD-32 "said plainly that the United States puts to itself the task of weakening the system of alliances of the Soviet Union."[22] Another article in *Pravda* derided NSDD-32 as "adventuristic," "insane," and the "administration's bible." *Pravda* directly attributed the directive to Reagan himself, noting that the president "personally put forward his observations" on each section.[23] *Pravda* grasped NSDD-32's importance as a reflection of Reagan personally and as a potential barometer of the Soviet Union's rocky road ahead.[24]

These actions set the tone and context for Reagan's extremely important trip to Europe in June 1982.

June 1982: From the Vatican to Westminster

In June 1982, President Reagan made a high-profile trip to Europe, a consequential stop in his audacious attempt to alter the course of the Cold War. The highlights were a meeting with Pope John Paul II on June 7, followed by the Westminster Address on June 8, and both very much interrelated.

Reagan and the pope met at the Vatican. It had been a little over a year since assassination attempts were made against both men.[25] The pope had received a cable from Reagan the day he was shot, in which the president expressed his shock and prayers.[26] Since then, the staffs of the two men had worked to arrange a meeting to seek areas of collaboration against Soviet communism in Europe. "It was always assumed the president would meet with the Holy Father as soon as feasible," said Bill Clark, who traveled with the president to the Vatican, "especially after they both took shots in the chest only a few weeks apart. . . . Because of their mutual interests . . . the two men would come together and form some sort of collaboration."[27]

Reagan had long coveted such an idea. As early as June 1979, when John Paul II made a historic visit to his native Poland, Reagan (not yet president) was convinced that the new pope was key to Poland's fate.[28] Among the earliest goals he set as president was to officially recognize the Vatican "and make them an ally."[29]

On June 7, 1982, the two men talked alone for 50 minutes in the Vatican Library. The shootings were raised right away. Cardinal Pio Laghi, apostolic delegate to the United States, said that Reagan told the pope: "Look how the evil forces were put in our way and how Providence intervened." John Paul II agreed with that interpretation. Bill Clark said both men discussed the "miraculous" fact that they had survived.[30]

The Protestant and Catholic, said Clark, shared a "unity" in spiritual views and in their "vision on the Soviet empire," namely, "that right or correctness would ultimately prevail in the divine plan." That day, each shared their view that they had been given "a spiritual mission—a special role in the divine plan of life." Both expressed concern for "the terrible oppression of atheistic communism," as Clark put it, and agreed that "atheistic communism lived a lie that, when fully understood, must ultimately fail."[31]

Carl Bernstein, in a major 1992 cover story for *Time* magazine, reported that Reagan and the pope then and there, that June 7, quietly joined forces not only to shore up Solidarity and pressure Warsaw "but to free all of Eastern Europe." In that first meeting, wrote Bernstein, they consented to undertake a clandestine campaign "to hasten the dissolution of the communist empire." The two men "were convinced that Poland could be broken out of the Soviet orbit if the Vatican and the U.S. committed the resources to destabilizing the Polish government and keeping the outlawed Solidarity movement alive after the declaration of martial law in 1981."[32]

Reagan told the pope: "Hope remains in Poland. We, working together, can keep it alive."[33]

Both leaders were convinced that a free, noncommunist Poland would be, in Bernstein's words, "a dagger to the heart of the Soviet empire." They were certain that if Poland became democratic, other Eastern European states would follow.[34] Bernstein's conclusion is fully confirmed by Reagan's own words and those who served him.[35]

A cardinal who was one of John Paul II's closest aides put it this way: "Nobody believed the collapse of communism would happen this fast or on this timetable. But in their first meeting, the Holy Father and the president committed themselves and the institutions of the Church and America to such a goal. And from that day, the focus was to bring it about in Poland."[36]

Bear in mind that this meeting occurred only two and a half weeks after NSDD-32, which had formally established such aims and committed to seeking such alliances.

The Westminster Address

Thus, when Ronald Reagan arrived in London the next day, June 8, 1982, he had been inspired in a most atypical way. There, he delivered the Westminster Address. He confidently stated:

> In an ironic sense, Karl Marx was right. We are witnessing today a great revolutionary crisis. . . . But the crisis is happening not in the free, non-Marxist West, but in the home of Marxism-Leninism, the Soviet Union. It is the Soviet Union that runs against the tide of history by denying freedom and human dignity to its citizens.

Reagan then spoke of not merely a long-term "hope" for freedom, democracy, and the defeat of Soviet communism, but a "plan":

> What I am describing now is a plan and a hope for the long term—the march of freedom and democracy which will leave Marxism-Leninism on the ash heap of history as it has left other tyrannies which stifle the freedom and muzzle the self-expression of the people. . . . For the ultimate determinant in the struggle now going on for the world will not be bombs and rockets, but a test of wills and ideas—a trial of spiritual resolve: the values we hold, the beliefs we cherish, the ideals to which we are dedicated. . . . What kind of people do we think we are? . . . Free people, worthy of freedom and determined not only to remain so, but to help others gain their freedom as

well. . . . Let us now begin a major effort to secure the best—a crusade for freedom that will engage the faith and fortitude of the next generation. For the sake of peace and justice, let us move toward a world in which all people are at last free to determine their own destiny.

Note Reagan's belief that a people "worthy of freedom" should help others gain freedom. They should be willing to embark upon an "effort," upon a "crusade for freedom," to help "*all* people" secure their "own destiny" of freedom. This was a pronouncement and a plan, and even an exhortation.

The initial draft of the address was prepared by speechwriter Tony Dolan, whereupon it was heavily edited by Reagan. Dolan insists he merely used words Reagan himself had been using for decades.[37] Reagan biographer Lou Cannon agreed: "Reagan's message had been much the same when Dolan was a toddler and Reagan was writing his own speeches on three-by-five cards."[38] An examination of the draft of the speech (available at the Reagan Library) shows this. Reagan's handwriting appears on every page, with entire sections crossed out, rewritten, and inserted.

And as with most of his speeches, Reagan had to fight White House "pragmatists," as well as the State Department, from gutting the speech of the very features that made it meaningful and memorable, including the section that he personally penciled into page 14 of the May 24 version of the draft: "What I am describing now is a policy and a hope for the long term—the march of freedom and democracy which will leave Marxism-Leninism on the ash-heap of history."

The word "policy," on top of "hope," cannot be understated. The final draft used the word "plan." Both "policy" and "plan" are remarkably revealing words, with "policy" even stronger in relaying intentions. Either way, this was not just rhetoric. Reagan was proposing a plan of action, literal *policy*.

There was much more to the speech. Reagan made clear why he was so sure of a coming Soviet calamity. He asserted that the Soviet Union was undergoing a "deep economic" "failure," the "dimensions" of which were "astounding." As evidence of the Soviet crisis, Reagan's speech borrowed material he had used in his self-written 1970s radio addresses, including this passage:

Were it not for the tiny private sector tolerated in Soviet agriculture, the country might be on the brink of famine. These private plots occupy a bare three percent of the arable land but account for nearly one-quarter of Soviet farm output and nearly one-third of meat products and vegetables.

Overcentralized, with little or no incentives, year after year, the Soviet system pours its best resources into the making of instruments of destruction. The constant shrinkage of economic growth combined with the growth of military production is putting a heavy strain on the Soviet people. . . .

The decay of the Soviet experiment should come as no surprise to us. Wherever the comparisons have been made between free and closed societies—West Germany and East Germany, Austria and Czechoslovakia, Malaysia and Vietnam—it is the democratic countries that are prosperous and responsive to the needs of the their people.

Here was foreknowledge of the disaster bearing down upon the Soviet Union. And, in fact, as Reagan called attention to economic failures that were abounding and getting worse, he and his team were working to exacerbate Soviet problems through a comprehensive collection of economic-warfare efforts.[39] Yes, the Soviet system might be faltering, but Reagan believed that those internal contradictions needed to be exploited and exacerbated to the breaking point.

Returning to his broader goals of spreading democracy and reversing communism, Reagan also invoked the language of universal "inalienable" rights:

We must not hesitate to declare our ultimate objectives and to take concrete actions to move toward them. We must be staunch in our conviction that freedom is not the sole prerogative of a lucky few but the inalienable and universal right of all human beings. The objective I propose is quite simple to state: To foster the infrastructure of democracy—the system of a free press, unions, political parties, universities—which allows a people to choose their own way. . . .

It is time that we committed ourselves as a nation—in both the public and private sectors—to assisting democratic development. I do not wish to sound overly optimistic, yet the Soviet Union is not immune from the reality of what is going on in the world.

The speech envisioned the extension of freedom and democracy into that part of the world that most needed it: Eastern Europe, the Soviet empire, "the heart of darkness," as Reagan had once called it. Reagan would not merely predict such a change, but make it official administration policy. He would try to reverse the Soviet hold on the region and thereby reverse the Soviet empire, reverse the Cold War, and reverse the course of history.

Grandiose as this was, it had long been Reagan's thinking. In the 1950s, as a 40-something actor in Hollywood (and a Democrat), he had signed on to General Lucius Clay's Crusade for Freedom;[40] now, as president of the United

States in the 1980s, he was spearheading his own crusade for freedom.[41] "Let us move toward a world in which all people are at last free to determine their own destiny," he urged at Westminster. "This is precisely our mission today: to preserve freedom as well as peace. It may not be easy to see, but I believe we live now at the turning point."

Reagan evoked a historic crossroads—a "turning point," a "forward strategy for freedom." This was the vision laid out at Westminster.

It is easy to forget that Reagan's optimism was hardly the consensus at the time. There in London, Andrew Alexander, a *Daily Mail* columnist, protested: "To be invited to defend ourselves against communism is one thing. To be asked to join a crusade for the overthrow of communism is quite another."[42] Lou Cannon, the *Washington Post*'s White House correspondent, recalled that the Western press derided the Westminster Address as "wishful thinking, bordering on delusional."[43] And yet, argued Cannon years later, the address "stands the test of time" as Reagan's most "farsighted" speech, "predictive of the events that would occur in Eastern Europe."

As for the Soviets, they portrayed Reagan as delusional, though clearly the speech sent them reeling. In *Pravda,* V. Bolshakov informed Russians that in London the American president had declared a "global 'crusade' against communism." He commented:

> [Reagan] advocated not competition but confrontation . . . especially [with] the USSR and Poland, in order to change their existing system. The president left no one in any doubt on this score, calling the "crusade" against communism declared by him a "march for freedom and democracy," as a result of which "Marxism-Leninism will be consigned to the garbage heap of history."[44]

Pravda did not like this American bravado and responded with some swagger of its own. Bolshakov taunted the Reagan team: "If the U.S. administration supposes that by means of force and ideological sabotage it will succeed in 'changing history,' let it remember that its numerous predecessors in the sphere of organizing 'crusades' against communism finished up in the very place where Washington resolved to dispatch Marxism-Leninism—the garbage heap of history." History waited in anxious anticipation. Who would find vindication: Ronald Reagan or *Pravda?*

Freedom's Tide

History's verdict came down on the side of the March of Freedom and quicker than anyone thought possible. Ronald Reagan left the presidency in January 1989. By the end of that year, Solidarity candidates swept 99 of 100 seats in a free and fair election in communist Poland, the Berlin Wall crashed in a soon-to-be reunified Germany, Václav Havel peered at the presidency of Czechoslovakia rather than prison walls, and the continent's worst dictator, Romania's Nicolae Ceauşescu, was executed. Two years later, the Soviet Union itself ceased to exist, as Mikhail Gorbachev on December 25, 1991, formally resigned as its head and thus turned out the lights on what Reagan had dubbed an "Evil Empire." The Cold War was over.

The world could not have imagined this in June 1982 when Reagan made that speech in London. In the 1970s, before he won the White House, Reagan frequently cited data from Freedom House marking the number of free and unfree nations in the world.[45] When he did so, he bemoaned the lack of freedom. As president, he dedicated himself to improving those numbers. By the early 1990s, we could cite that same source to demonstrate the turnaround: in 1980, there were 56 democracies in the world; by 1990, there were 76. The numbers continued an upward trajectory, hitting 91 in 1991, 99 in 1992, 108 in 1993, and 114 in 1994, a doubling since Reagan entered the Oval Office. By 1994, 60 percent of the world's nations were democracies. By contrast, when Reagan lamented the lack of freedom in the mid-1970s, the number was under 30 percent. In his time from president-elect to ex-president, the number of democracies increased from less than a third to a strong majority.

By the end of the violent century, which saw more than 50 million perish in two world wars and more than 100 million murdered by communist governments,[46] 120 of the world's 192 nations were democracies. Outside of Western Europe, 90 percent of Latin American and Caribbean nations were considered democracies, 91 percent of Pacific Island states, and 93 percent of the nations of East Central Europe and the Baltic area—the former Soviet region.

A "March of Freedom" was indeed what Ronald Reagan both sought and got. And it is critical to understand that he also got it with the indispensable help of friends: Mikhail Gorbachev, Boris Yeltsin, Pope John Paul II, Margaret Thatcher, Lech Wałesa, and Václav Havel, not to mention entire Eastern European movements like Solidarity, Charter 77, and the blood, sweat, and tears of millions of ordinary citizens. Ronald Reagan did not do it alone—a fact that Reagan conservatives must accept. Likewise, Mikhail Gorbachev did not do it alone—a fact that Western liberals stingy to Reagan must accept.

Gorbachev himself set that record straight. "In my view," he wrote in his memoirs, "the 40th president of the United States will go down in history for his rare perception."[47] In an interview for a PBS documentary, Gorbachev added: "He [Reagan] is really a very big person—a very great political leader."[48] At a dinner in Cambridge, England, in 2001, a British academic dismissed Reagan as "rather an intellectual lightweight." Gorbachev did not tolerate the slight of his old partner, reprimanding his host: "You are wrong. President Reagan was a man of real insight, sound political judgment, and courage."[49] In 2002, Gorbachev called Reagan "a major individual" and added: "If at that time someone else had been in his place, I don't know whether what happened would've happened."[50]

It is hard to imagine any of what happened occurring without Reagan, Gorbachev, and the cast of others. For instance, though Reagan pushed and prodded and poked the Soviets—pursuing everything from the Strategic Defense Initiative (SDI) to economic warfare to Stingers for the Afghan rebels, just for starters—only Gorbachev could have repudiated Article 6 of the Soviet Constitution in February 1990, thereby stripping the Soviet Communist Party of its constitutional monopoly on political power. Sure, Reagan called for political pluralism in the Soviet Union, well before Gorbachev came to power, but it took Gorbachev to enact the change and make it a reality. This epic transformation of Europe was a group effort, even as no one loudly trumpeted the ambition quite like Reagan.

Václav Havel, the Czech playwright-turned-president, said of Reagan: "He was a man with firm positions, with which he undoubtedly contributed to the fall of communism." Václav Klaus, Havel's successor, added: "He was certainly one of the greatest statesmen of the recent era. I think that without him, the end of the communist regime would not have been so fast and even would not have been so calm as it really was."[51]

Even more effusive is Lech Wałesa, first president of a post–Cold War, free Poland and Nobel Peace Prize winner. Wałesa was grateful for Reagan's "very strong backing" of Solidarity. He praised Reagan's devotion to "a few simple rules: human rights, democracy, freedom of speech" and his "conviction that it is not the people who are there for the sake of the state, but that the state is there for the sake of the citizens."[52] Given a chance to thank Reagan directly, Wałesa said to the president: "We stood on the two sides of the artificially erected wall. Solidarity broke down this wall from the Eastern side and on the Western side it was you."[53] Poles had needed a friend, said Wałesa, "and such was Ronald Reagan." He said that Reagan had "emboldened" and "encouraged" him.[54] "We owe so much to Ronald Reagan," concluded Wałesa. "We Poles owe him freedom."[55]

Tangible signs of Reagan's transformation in Europe include not only a fallen Berlin Wall but the literal statues erected to Reagan from Warsaw to Budapest to Prague. Poles created a Ronald Reagan Legacy Committee tasked with naming town squares and train stations and other sites after the American president. Reagan is an honorary citizen of Gdansk and Kraków. It is fascinating to watch Eastern Europeans eagerly and voluntarily build monuments to an American president where statues of Lenin, Stalin, and various regional despots were once cemented at the tip of a bayonet. These are visible manifestations of the success of Reagan's March of Freedom.

Overall, the 1980s saw the launch of an explosion in freedom worldwide. This splendid development was a momentous one that Ronald Reagan desired and pursued. Few presidents got so much of what they wanted.

George W. Bush and Freedom's Dungeon

There was, however, a part of the world that seemed immune to this wave, to freedom's march: the Middle East. A decade after the Cold War, the Middle East was the least democratic region on the planet. A 1999–2000 survey by Freedom House, done, tellingly, before September 11, 2001, found that while 63 percent of the world's nations were technically democracies, an astonishing zero of the 16 Arab countries in the Middle East were democratic. Such were the final Freedom House figures to close out the last century.

Then came September 11, 2001, which, as another Republican president, George W. Bush, put it, "changed everything." It was the first year of a new century, but it was much more. September 11 came 10 years after the end of the Soviet Union. This 10-year hiatus was characterized by Bush in his Second Inaugural Address as "years of repose, years of sabbatical" between the "shipwreck of communism" and the "day of fire."

And now, this new Republican president would attempt to extend Ronald Reagan's March of Freedom to that one area on earth that has been most resistant. He would seek to lay the groundwork in the two most unlikely places: the Taliban's Afghanistan and Saddam Hussein's Iraq.

Bush's thinking stemmed (in part) from a "democratic peace" perspective. September 11 desperately showed Americans that the pathology of Middle East violence had to be squelched; it had violently entered the once-safe confines of the United States. How to mend the Middle East? Bush concluded that hope lay in political and economic freedom. To the extent that the hostile Middle East might became more democratic, it might become more peaceful.

George W. Bush thus sought to sow the seeds for such a transformation in the Middle East's two most repressive states. After removing the Taliban in the fall of 2001, he ordered U.S. troops into Iraq, where they removed Saddam Hussein's regime in the spring of 2003.

It goes without saying that Bush hit a buzz saw in Iraq, not during the initial 2003 invasion, which went extraordinarily well from a military operational standpoint, but in the extremely difficult (and deadly) occupation from 2004–2006, prior to the so-called surge successfully implemented by General David Petraeus. As the body bags piled up in Iraq, Bush's popularity plummeted not only among Democrats but even Republicans. Americans bitterly questioned their president's leadership. A 2007 Gallup/*USA Today* poll judged Bush the most unsuccessful modern president. By contrast, the president judged most successful in that poll was Ronald Reagan. And it was, ironically, Reagan's mantle from Westminster that George W. Bush picked up.

Speaking on November 6, 2003, Bush gave arguably the most far-reaching address of his presidency, promising to move Reagan's "March of Freedom" into the Middle East. He spoke to the National Endowment for Democracy, a group created by Ronald Reagan and rooted specifically in the 1982 Westminster Address.

"The roots of our democracy can be traced to England and to its Parliament and so can the roots of this organization," Bush began his speech. "In June of 1982, President Ronald Reagan spoke at Westminster Palace and declared the turning point had arrived in history. . . . President Reagan said that the day of Soviet tyranny was passing, that freedom had a momentum that would not be halted. He gave this organization its mandate: to add to the momentum of freedom across the world." That mandate, said Bush, was as important 20 years ago as today. He noted that observers on both sides of the Atlantic pronounced Reagan's speech "simplistic and naïve and even dangerous." "In fact," said Bush, "Ronald Reagan's words were courageous and optimistic and entirely correct."

Like Reagan, Bush cited data from Freedom House. He said that in the early 1970s there were only 40 democracies in the world. As the twentieth century ended, there were 120. "And I can assure you," Bush promised, "more are on the way." He immediately followed with: "Ronald Reagan would be pleased, and he would not be surprised."

Bush said the world had just witnessed, in little over a generation, the swiftest advance of freedom in history. Historians will search for explanations for this occurrence, but, argued the president, the world already knows some of the reasons they will cite. Among them, he maintained, "It is no accident that the rise of so many democracies took place in a time when the world's most influential nation [America] was itself a democracy." After World War II, reported Bush, the United States made military and moral commitments in Europe and Asia that protected free nations from aggression and created conditions for new democracies to flourish. Now, in the Middle East, under his administration, America would do so again.

That progression of liberty, said Bush, is "a powerful trend" that, if not defended, could be lost. "The success of freedom," he said, "rests upon the choices and the courage of free peoples, and upon their willingness to sacrifice." Because the United States and its allies were steadfast, noted the 43rd president, Germany and Japan became democratic nations that no longer threatened the world. Bush then explicitly affirmed his faith in democratic peace: "Every nation has learned, or should have learned, an important lesson: Freedom is worth fighting for, dying for, and standing for—and the advance of freedom leads to peace." "And now," thinking of the Middle East—and, like Reagan, speaking of a "turning point"—Bush continued: "we must apply that lesson in our own time. We've reached another great turning point—and the resolve we show will shape the next stage of the world democratic movement." Bush stated:

> In many nations of the Middle East—countries of great strategic importance—democracy has not yet taken root. And the questions arise: Are the peoples of the Middle East somehow beyond the reach of liberty? Are millions of men and women and children condemned by history or culture to live in despotism? . . . I, for one, do not believe it. I believe every person has the ability and the right to be free.
>
> Some skeptics of democracy assert that the traditions of Islam are inhospitable to representative government. This "cultural condescension," as Ronald Reagan termed it, has a long history. After the Japanese surrender in 1945, a so-called Japan expert asserted that democracy in that former empire would "never work." Another observer declared the prospects for democracy in post-Hitler Germany are, and I quote, "most uncertain at

best." . . . Seventy-four years ago, the *Sunday London Times* declared nine-tenths of the population of India to be "illiterates not caring a fig for politics." . . . Time after time, observers have questioned whether this country, or that people, or this group, are "ready" for democracy—as if freedom were a prize you win for meeting our own Western standards of progress.

Seeing the Islamic nations of the Middle East as no exception, Bush contended that "in every region of the world, the advance of freedom leads to peace." The "freedom deficit" in the Middle East had to be changed. "Therefore," said Bush, "the United States has adopted a new policy: a forward strategy of freedom." This phrase was Ronald Reagan's, offered in London in June 1982 and also in Los Angeles in August 1987.[56] Bush insisted: "This strategy requires the same persistence and energy and idealism we have shown before. And it will yield the same results. As in Europe, as in Asia, as in every region of the world, the advance of freedom leads to peace." This advance of freedom was "the calling of our time; it is the calling of our country."

In a jolt to liberals and conservatives alike, Bush echoed the unlikely progressive-conservative presidential troika of Woodrow Wilson, Franklin Delano Roosevelt, and Reagan: "From the Fourteen Points to the Four Freedoms, to the speech at Westminster, America has put our power at the service of principle." What principle was that? Bush wrapped up with a signature statement for his presidency, or (at least) the hope of his presidency: "We believe that liberty is the design of nature; we believe that liberty is the direction of history. . . . And we believe that freedom—the freedom we prize—is not for us alone, it is the right and the capacity of all mankind." Bush concluded: "This is, above all, the age of liberty."

It was as if Ronald Reagan had entered that room, at least in spirit. "With all my heart," Reagan had said in an October 1988 speech at Georgetown University, "I believe that this is the age of freedom."

Bush, Reagan, and the Liberty Legacy—and Questions

For George W. Bush, like Reagan before him, this was a grandiose vision. His plans and ideas for the world likewise endeavored to be utterly transformative. Like Reagan, did he think this reinvigorated freedom tide would swell during his lifetime? And what pitfalls might befall his thinking? Might the world witness a "march" toward Middle East democracy or, quite the contrary, toward *theocracy?* What if democratic elections in the Middle East, in places like

Afghanistan and Iraq, produced only one legitimate election one time? The Bush White House hoped not for the likes of Hamas but for modern Middle East versions of Hamilton and Madison and Jefferson, for movements more like Solidarity than the Muslim Brotherhood.

The democracy project in the Middle East is a perilous one that certainly has not witnessed the immediate positive transformation that Reagan saw in Eastern Europe the final year of his presidency. Who in Iran has penned a Muslim version of Havel's Charter 77? Where is the Saudi Andrey Sakharov or Aleksandr Solzhenitsyn? Is there a Middle East equivalent to the fall of the Berlin Wall? In Bush's final year in office, were similar such winds blowing? Was the Arab Spring just that, or a giant mirage? Is it really what so many in the West hoped for? Have democratic advances in the Arab world—those that are potentially real and lasting—been prompted or aided by U.S. military intervention, or were they strictly the result of spontaneous aspirations and actions of ordinary Arab people? Is democracy about elections or, more substantially, about a deeper implementation of democratic institutions, rule of law, and a wider culture more hospitable to long-term democratization?

How have and will George W. Bush's Oval Office successors view all of this? Will they be committed at all or in part to some of these same hopeful ideas? Do they view his ideas as noble or naive, as prescient or shortsighted, as bold or dangerous, as promising or perilous?

These are not merely sticky current policy questions but huge historical unknowns yet to be played out. In the last several years, the people of the Middle East—comprised of all sorts of factions—have demanded that long-entrenched autocrats and despots step down or be forcibly removed, from Hosni Mubarak in Egypt to Muammar Gaddafi in Libya. But what has replaced them? Was the Muslim Brotherhood the "wind of change" the world had hoped for in Egypt, akin to the Solidarity sweep that took political power in Poland in June 1989? What about Iraq and Afghanistan? They are not being run by Middle East equivalents of Wałesa and Havel. What about Syria? A brutal civil war that has threatened to drag in the world's major powers seems to present the Syrian people with a bad choice between an entrenched dictator and Islamists advocating Sharia law, some in concert with Islamists in Iraq. In Syria, as in modern Egypt and Iraq, non-Muslim religious believers, particularly ancient Christian minorities, have fled under brute persecution, as their churches and communities and lives are destroyed.

If this is a new age of freedom in the Middle East, prompted by U.S. action, it does not look good. Is this Ronald Reagan's March of Freedom, as George W. Bush had conceived extending it?

Ironically, those most offended by the very thought of such promising Bush-Reagan foreign-policy comparisons—and by Bush's appropriation of Reagan—seem to be Reagan conservatives. They angrily castigate Bush for the debts and dead left by two wars in the Middle East. A common criticism of Bush from the right is the charge that Islam is not compatible with democracy, an assertion that Bush himself disagreed with emphatically. Many Bush detractors looked upon the Middle East and saw a future of theocracy rather than democracy. Some observers considered the prospects of heightened theocratic repression in Iraq and a Shiite axis among Shiite majorities in Iraq and Iran.[57] Religious conservatives (including many orthodox Roman Catholics) foresaw violent attacks on Christian minorities in Iraq, which have indeed occurred, sparking an exodus of believers fleeing the country.[58]

There were influential conservatives who questioned the Iraq war from the outset, from the likes of Pat Buchanan to Jeane Kirkpatrick to Boston University professor Andrew Bacevich to even William F. Buckley Jr.[59] Many conservatives questioned the feasibility of democracy-building in Afghanistan and Iraq and the Middle East generally. They saw Bush's vision as quixotic neo-Wilsonian internationalism. Conservatives have never been fans of Woodrow Wilson, and they judged Bush's attempts to make the Middle East safe for democracy idealistic nonsense that would only cause grief.[60] Among many segments of the right, the "neocons" who backed Bush's Middle East policies are considered pariahs; "paleoconservatives" and isolationist Republicans lash out at the neocons as nothing short of dangerous.[61] One conservative colleague consulted for this chapter, an expert on the intellectual history of the conservative movement (who asked not to be identified), simply said that "the Iraq war was an enormous mistake. Let's move on." Many conservatives who admire Reagan deem Bush a terrible failure and insist that Bush's actions in the Middle East bear no legitimate comparison whatsoever with Reagan's actions during the Cold War.[62]

Reagan's plan for liberating Eastern Europe never included military intervention. He did not invade Poland when martial law was declared. Margaret Thatcher famously contended that Reagan "won the Cold War without firing a shot." That might be hyperbole, but he certainly fired far fewer shots than did George W. Bush. Reagan was extremely judicious about using military force, doing so only in Grenada in October 1983 and via a quick military strike against Libya in April 1986; in both cases, the force he used was brief and successful, without great risks.[63] Reagan most certainly supported strong military action against the Soviets in Afghanistan, but did so via (significant) American military aid to the Afghan rebels, not through direct deployment of U.S. soldiers engaging Red Army troops. Whether Ronald Reagan would have invaded Iraq after September 11 is something we cannot know, though his track record in Eastern Europe was one that fully eschewed military force. Reagan provided covert support to democratic elements, like Solidarity, to advance the March of Freedom; Bush pursued a military option.

The Bush disapproval among many conservatives also held for many Republicans generally and, of course, for the wider general public and stood in stark contrast to the long-held approval of Ronald Reagan. Going into the final year of his presidency, Bush posted the worst approval ratings (according to Gallup) of any president since Harry Truman, surpassing even Richard Nixon and Jimmy Carter. With an approval reduced to only about 20 percent, Bush was not even getting the support of many Republicans. A November 2011 CBS News poll found that half of Republicans believed the Iraq War was "not worth it," and 67 percent of the public at large said the war "was not worth the loss of American life and other costs associated with the war."[64]

Nonetheless, like Reagan, Bush believed that freedom is "contagious," a God-given right belonging to *all* human beings of all religions and regions—Muslims of the Middle East being no exception. In October 2005, Bush spoke at the Reagan Library. He wistfully noted that Reagan believed that "freedom is the right of every man, woman, and child on Earth" and that freedom is (here he directly quoted Reagan) "one of the deepest and noblest aspirations of the human spirit."[65] He commended Reagan for recognizing (in Bush's words) "that America has always prevailed by standing firmly on principles and never backing down in the face of evil." He said that Reagan understood that the struggles America faces are "a test of wills and ideas, a trial of spiritual resolve." "And like the ideology of communism," claimed Bush, "Islamic radicalism is doomed to fail." Prevailing, Bush insisted, would require following Reagan's example of leadership, strategy, vision, and "resolve to stay in the fight until the fight [is] won."

Unlike Reagan, Bush's response to what he perceived as the enemy of the century—an enemy he likewise called "evil"—would not win him accolades in his time. In 2004, Bush won reelection by only a few percentage points; in

1984, Reagan was returned to office by sweeping 49 of 50 states. In 1989, the year he left Washington, Reagan could turn on his television and happily observe a Europe transformed—just as he had wanted. Bush will wait much longer to see any similar legacy, if ever at all. Right now, it seems unimaginable that conservatives (and Americans generally) could one day look back at George W. Bush as fondly as they do Ronald Reagan.

And even though he should have more postpresidential years ahead of him than Reagan did, Bush avers that his full impact will not be known until he has left this earth. Perhaps he was a bit envious when he said in a tribute to Reagan on his birthday, "America knows you came here 20 years ago and changed the world."

• • •

For better or worse, fittingly or not, Ronald Reagan's vision has dramatically inspired the broader vision and actions of at least one post–Cold War president. George W. Bush took Reagan's ambition in significant new directions, or perhaps diversions. For that reason alone, Reagan's March of Freedom has legs beyond Europe.

Undeniably, Reagan likewise spoke of the "freedom" movement in universal terms. If that march is real, and on the move in the Middle East right now, recommended under the tattered, troubled presidency of George W. Bush, will it be prodded and sustained (or perhaps even invoked) by Bush's Oval Office successors? It has most assuredly not been invoked by Barack Obama. President Obama's actions in Afghanistan, Iraq, Egypt, Libya, Syria, and elsewhere have involved various shades of intervention and nonintervention and moments at the brink, but they most certainly have not involved an incorporation of Bush's rhetoric about a March of Freedom. Will other presidents after Obama be sympathetic to Bush's thinking?

Either way, today's president and those who follow deal with major Middle East changes made by President George W. Bush—changes inspired, rightly or wrongly, by Ronald Reagan's vision. And that is another definite, lasting Reagan impact upon a wider world that continues to be transformed.

A NEW NATIONAL STRATEGY

Reagan's Defense Policy Revisited

6

The Beginning of a New U.S. Grand Strategy

Policy on Terror during the Reagan Era

KIRON K. SKINNER

Reports of the unrelenting bureaucratic infighting among Reagan administration foreign policy principals overshadowed Washington's policies on global terror in the 1980s. Those policies were similarly eclipsed by the Iran-Contra affair, in which White House efforts to achieve an opening with Iran and freedom for American hostages in Lebanon were linked to U.S. aid to the Nicaraguan resistance movement against what the administration described as a tyrannical regime in Managua.

Looking beneath the high drama of bureaucratic politics and the worst political scandal of the Reagan administration, however, scholars and other analysts have found evidence that administration officials engaged in an impressive amount of activity in law enforcement, intelligence gathering, international law, and interagency coordination in combating global terror.[1] The administration's strategic doctrine on terrorism that developed alongside these areas has received less attention. This lacuna is addressed herein. Furthermore, it will be posited that, in establishing the intellectual and institutional building blocks for combating new threats of global terror, the Reagan administration began to develop a grand strategy that was distinctly different from the overarching Cold War policy of containment. In all, these changes left a marked legacy not only beyond the Reagan years but into the post-9/11 battle against international terrorism.

President Ronald Reagan's strategy was based on building up previously underdeveloped political and military arrangements and introducing new approaches for combating terror while reserving the use of force as a last resort.

President Reagan's lasting legacy in U.S. terrorism policy is the set of laws, institutions, national security directives, and cautious military policies that he put in place. Though he was often characterized as a military hawk, his policies on terrorism suggest otherwise. The president was much more of a practical policy planner, responding to the growing threat of terrorism through the legislative process and new institutional arrangements such as the creation of U.S. Central Command (USCENTCOM) and U.S. Special Operations Command (USSOCOM). His most forceful use of military power in response to acts of terror against U.S. citizens abroad included the brief air war against Libya in 1986 and military maneuvers such as Operation Earnest Will and Operation Prime Chance, which will be discussed later in the chapter. These maneuvers were designed to help end the Iran-Iraq War, not only a regional crisis but a conflict at the heart of terrorism directed against the United States in the 1980s.

•   •   •

President Reagan's reticence to use military responses was likely influenced by the loss of American lives at the Marine barracks in Beirut, Lebanon, in 1983. As one writer has observed, the attack "was a seminal moment in the growing collision between American power and jihadi terror."[2] He avoided military activity for reasons that led to the Iran-Contra scandal. When the focus of international relations is most directly people rather than bombs, bullets, trade, or commerce, the consequences of conflict are sobering. Factoring people, as opposed to impersonal nation-states or international institutions or regimes, into theories of international relations is intrinsically complicated.[3] It is even more onerous in practice. The importance of securing the freedom of U.S. hostages in Lebanon made it impossible for President Reagan to abide completely by his declared policy against negotiating with terrorists. Selling arms to Iranians, the benefactors of Hezbollah, was as close as he could go to the edge of that policy.

This chapter shows that the institutional and policy responses to terrorism the fortieth president grappled with remain a central doctrinal struggle for U.S. presidents. Part of the legacy of the Reagan administration's policies on terrorism is the inherent difficulty of creating a cohesive and consistent strategy against forces that defy the precepts of doctrines U.S. leaders have developed around nation-state conflicts.

The 1980s: An Era Marked by Terrorism

At the dawn of the 1980s, the United States faced its most significant terrorist event abroad when 66 Americans were taken hostage in the U.S. embassy in Tehran on November 4, 1979. In response to the transformative geopolitical events of 1979, the Iranian revolution, the hostage crisis, and the Soviet invasion of Afghanistan, President Jimmy Carter enunciated a far-reaching set of institutional responses. These actions included the creation of the Rapid Deployment Force, a precursor to USCENTCOM, which would come into existence during the Reagan presidency. He also issued a warning about violations of U.S. national security in the Persian Gulf. Speaking to a joint session of the U.S. Congress on January 23, 1980, President Carter cautioned: "An attempt by any outside force to gain control of the Persian Gulf region will be regarded as an assault on the vital interests of the United States of America, and such an assault will be repelled by any means necessary, including military force."[4]

In retaliation for the U.S. citizens taken hostage, President Carter imposed an oil embargo against Iran, and on April 7, 1980, he severed U.S.-Iran diplomatic ties.[5] On April 24, the United States launched a rescue mission, the failure of which was confirmed by President Carter the following day. Three of eight helicopters malfunctioned and one crashed as the mission was being abandoned. Eight members of the 90-plus team were killed.[6]

President Carter could not avoid these issues during the 1980 presidential race. During his first weeks in the Oval Office, he had an approval rating of 66 percent that climbed to 75 percent in March 1977. Yet, at the end of 1980, only 34 percent of Americans polled approved of the president's job performance.[7] The economy, in particular, was important on Election Day, but having Americans in captivity in Iran contributed to the sense among voters that President Carter was an ineffective leader.[8]

The specter of Senator Edward M. Kennedy entering the presidential race loomed for months. Unfortunately for President Carter, the senator made his presidential campaign official on November 7, three days after the hostage crisis began.[9] President Carter ultimately garnered 3 million more votes than the senator in the heated primary contest.[10] On top of the hostage crisis, however, the unrelenting challenge from Senator Kennedy and his liberal base added a sense of foreboding about the likelihood that President Carter would win in 1980. In fact, Senator Kennedy took his campaign fight all the way to the Democratic

National Convention in New York City. He finally conceded to President Carter and endorsed him during his convention speech on August 12.[11]

President Carter then turned to his next challenger, Ronald Reagan. The former California governor had a spectacular showing in the primaries, receiving nearly 5 million more votes than George H. W. Bush, his main opponent.[12] On July 17, at the Republican National Convention in Detroit, Governor Reagan accepted his party's presidential nomination with great enthusiasm.[13]

Along with Congressman John Anderson, a third-party candidate, President Carter and Governor Reagan went into the fall campaign battling on major issues such as the economy, energy policy, social policy, defense spending, and national readiness. Due to the sensitivities of the private negotiations and channels surrounding the White House's attempt to have the hostages released from captivity, Iran was not always in the foreground during the presidential campaign.[14] It was a factor, however. Throughout the presidential race, it was always just below the surface; critics of the president, including those seeking to unseat him, sometimes pointed to the hostage crisis as a failure of U.S. leadership in the world.

In his televised campaign address on October 19, Governor Reagan stated that "in Iran, terrorism has been elevated to the level of national policy in the assault on the U.S. Embassy and the year-long captivity of our fellow-citizens."[15] During the only presidential debate between the president and the governor, Reagan shied away from a direct rebuke of President Carter, but he made known his concerns:

> Once they [the hostages] are safely here with their families and that tragedy is over—and we've endured this humiliation for just lacking 1 week of a year now—then, I think, it is time for us to have a complete investigation as to the diplomatic efforts that were made in the beginning, why they have been there so long . . . what did we have to do in order to bring that about, what arrangements were made? And I would suggest that Congress should hold such an investigation.

Later, the governor suggested that the Carter administration had not sufficiently protected U.S. personnel in Tehran: "We had adequate warning that there was a threat to our Embassy, and we could have done what other Embassies did— either strengthen our security there or remove our personnel before the kidnap and takeover took place."[16]

President Carter spoke of the wider threat of terrorism, not just the crisis in Tehran:

> The most serious terrorist threat is if one of those radical nations, who believe in terrorism as a policy, should have atomic weapons. Both I and all my predecessors have had a deep commitment to controlling the proliferation of nuclear weapons in countries like Libya or Iraq. We have even alienated some of our closest trade partners, because we have insisted upon the control of the spread of nuclear weapons to those potentially terrorist countries.[17]

"I know that tonight the fate of America's 52 hostages is very much on the minds of all of us," Governor Reagan declared in his major address on the eve of the election. He continued, "Like you, there is nothing I want more than their safe return—that they be reunited with their families after this long year of imprisonment."[18]

During the weeks before the election, the Carter administration was engaged in negotiations with Iranian leaders to free the hostages. The demands were "not acceptable," the president wrote in his diary on November 2. He added: "They've got words like 'confiscate the shah's property' and demand that the U.S. government remove all private claims against Iranian assets. These are things we cannot do under our law, and they're not right anyway."[19] A Gallup Poll analysis suggests that what appeared to be intractable Iranian positions for freeing the hostage as the presidential election approached were "seen by many observers to have clearly worked in GOP candidate Ronald Reagan's favor. Public discouragement and frustration rose after it became obvious that these demands would be difficult to meet."[20]

The state of the economy, including high inflation and stubborn unemployment, and the defense posture of the nation were on voters' minds on November 4. The hostage crisis also mattered as voters weighed whether to end the Carter presidency. President Carter made this assessment of the gloomy days before the election: "It was increasingly clear to me and my advisors that if we could not secure the release of the hostages before the election—an unlikely prospect at best—our chances of beating Reagan were slim."[21]

•   •   •

Radical Islamic students released some hostages, but 52 were held in captivity for 444 days. They were released on January 20, 1981, in the wake of Ronald

Reagan being sworn in as president. That was "a final humiliation" for the Carter administration, according to Vice President Walter Mondale.[22]

While the Iranian hostage crisis was headed toward its one-year anniversary, another Middle East explosion happened. On September 22, Iraq invaded Iran in a quest for control over the Shatt al Arab waterway, along with other regional issues. This long and bloody war would not end until the final year of Ronald Reagan's presidency. This conflict added further complications to U.S. policy in the region, as the official U.S. stance was to remain neutral, and in the context of the presidential campaign, there was a heightened sense among informed voters that the United States had few good options in the Middle East.[23]

President Carter was defeated by Governor Reagan on November 4. The Californian won nearly 51 percent of the popular vote, the president 41 percent. President Carter was the first elected White House occupant to lose office since President Herbert Hoover's defeat in 1932.[24]

Reviewing the intersection of the Iranian hostage crisis with U.S. presidential politics places in context the domestic and geopolitical landscape that President Reagan was inheriting. While he was at the podium being sworn in as president, U.S. citizens who had been held in captivity were boarding planes for the United States. Terrorism, born of both Iranian politics and other radical Islamic forms, was the first major foreign policy issue President Reagan had to face. Iran and terrorism would have a major impact on his presidency, especially the doctrinal and institutional choices he would oversee in the national security arena.

President Reagan and Terrorism

On May 6, 1981, President Reagan expelled Libyan government officials from the United States and ended that country's diplomatic presence in Washington in response to reports indicating that U.S. diplomats in Paris and Rome were being targeted for assassination by President Mu'ammar Gaddhafi. In the months that followed, U.S. Navy jets and the Libyan Air Force exchanged fire near the Libyan coast and the navy shot down two Libyan warplanes.[25]

On July 19, 1982, in the midst of the civil war among the Christian Phalange, Druze, and Shiites in Lebanon, as well as the occupation of Syrian and Israeli troops, David Dodge became one of the first of several U.S. citizens to be taken hostage in Lebanon in the 1980s.[26] While some hostages escaped or were released, other Americans would be captured or killed, with the hostage crisis continuing until 1992.[27]

Tragedy struck the U.S. embassy in Beirut, Lebanon, on April 18, 1983, when a suicide bomber drove a truck of explosives into the complex. Of the 63 people killed, 17 were U.S. citizens. The Reagan administration placed blame for the attack on Hezbollah (the Shiite Muslim "Party of God"), a radical Islamic organization that had recently formed.[28] Yet the administration, which believed that Iran and Syria were providing Hezbollah with financial support and armaments, undertook no major military retaliation. The Reagan administration issued National Security Decision Directive (NSDD) 138 a year later, which authorized enhanced use of force and intelligence gathering to combat terrorism. John Fass Morton writes that "NSDD-138 provided authority for preemptive and retaliatory military operations against terrorists."[29] As a result, U.S. military responses would be developed in line with the evolving strategic doctrine of President Reagan's national security team and the institutional changes that the doctrine mandated.

The United States suffered an even greater tragedy in Beirut on October 23, 1983, when another suicide bomber drove a truck of explosives into the U.S. Marine barracks at Beirut International Airport. Shortly thereafter, a suicide bomber struck a building used by French officers; 241 Americans and nearly 60 French servicemen were killed.[30] Great Britain and Italy joined the United States and France as part of the Multinational Force (MNF) deployed to separate the warring parties in Lebanon and help stabilize the country, torn by civil war. A few months later, President Reagan withdrew U.S. forces, and by April 1984, all members of the MNF had left Lebanon.

In December 1983, the U.S. embassy in Kuwait and other buildings in a neighborhood inhabited by employees of the U.S. company Raytheon were bombed. The suicide bomber and several others were killed in the attack. The Reagan administration did not mount a military retaliation against Al Dawa, the Shiite group thought to be responsible for the atrocity.[31]

As noted earlier, from 1982 until the end of the hostage crisis in 1992, numerous other Americans would be taken hostage in Lebanon. On March 16, 1984, William Buckley, the Central Intelligence Agency's station chief in Lebanon, was abducted. Treated harshly by his captors, Buckley died in captivity.[32] In response to the expanding crisis, the Reagan administration undertook a campaign to free the hostages. The effort involved engagement with states that the United States believed to be sponsors of terrorism through organizations like Hezbollah.

The multifaceted U.S. campaign was not limited to the hostage crisis. Dominated by Sunni Muslims, Saddam Hussein's government was concerned about Ayatollah Ruhollah Khomeini's 1979 return to Iran and rise to power and the implications for Iraq's Shiite majority. The Iraqi leader also coveted the Shatt al Arab waterway, controlled by Iran. Tensions rose, and border skirmishes resulted in Iraq's invasion of Iran on September 22. For eight years, the two countries were locked in a bloody war that reportedly claimed more than a million lives. Despite the U.S. stance of neutrality in the war, the Reagan administration became involved with both countries. In November 1984, diplomatic relations between the United States and Iraq were resumed after a 17-year disruption. President Reagan endorsed starting a political dialogue with Iran, which resulted in the authorization of Israel to sell U.S.-originated arms to Iran.[33] This exchange began in the summer of 1985 "despite an existing U.S. embargo."[34]

As Kiron Skinner, Annelise Anderson, and Martin Anderson have reported, Secretary of State George P. Shultz and Secretary of Defense Caspar Weinberger opposed the Iranian initiative. National Security Adviser Robert "Bud" McFarlane and his team supported the initiative and managed the sale of tube-launched, optically tracked, wireless-guided (TOW) missiles to Iran through Israel in the summer of 1985, followed by HAWK missiles a few months later. McFarlane resigned in December and was replaced by Admiral John Poindexter, who continued the operation, along with Lieutenant Colonel Oliver North, deputy director for political-military affairs at the National Security Council (NSC). The project continued during the next year.[35]

The Iranian initiative soon became an arms-for-hostages deal. The Reagan administration had identified Iran as the source of Hezbollah's resources, and those in charge of the operation at the NSC believed Iran was the key to freeing U.S. hostages in Lebanon. The Iranian initiative was revealed in *Al Shiraa*, a Lebanese magazine, on November 3, 1986, and President Reagan addressed the American people on national television on November 13, saying:

> For 18 months now we have had under way a secret diplomatic initiative to Iran. That initiative was undertaken for the simplest and best reasons: to renew a relationship with the nation of Iran, to bring an honorable end to the bloody 6-year war between Iran and Iraq, to eliminate state-sponsored terrorism and subversion, and to effect the safe return of all hostages. . . .

The charge has been made that the United States has shipped weapons to Iran as ransom payment for the release of American hostages in Lebanon, that the United States undercut its allies and secretly violated American policy against trafficking with terrorists. Those charges are utterly false. The United States has not made concessions to those who hold our people captive in Lebanon. And we will not. . . .

Our government has a firm policy not to capitulate to terrorist demands. . . . No concessions policy remains in force, in spite of the wildly speculative and false stories about arms for hostages and alleged ransom payments. We did not—repeat—did not trade weapons or anything else for hostages, nor will we.[36]

The crisis expanded when Attorney General Edwin Meese III publicly stated that revenues of between $10 million and $30 million from the arms sales to Iran were being used to support the Nicaraguan contras.[37] President Reagan disavowed any knowledge of the contra initiative, which violated the spirit, if not the letter, of the Boland Amendments on U.S. aid to Central America. An independent counsel was appointed, and it would indict North, Poindexter, and Weinberger; McFarlane accepted misdemeanor charges. All of these men were pardoned, had their charges dismissed, or had their conviction vacated.[38] Their actions, however, contributed to the most severe scandal of the Reagan administration and underscored the difficulty of effectively carrying out the policies on terrorism.

In addition to the hostage crisis, more attacks were carried out against Americans in Lebanon. On September 20, 1984, a truck bomb targeted a U.S. embassy annex outside of Beirut. Two U.S. military officers were among those killed. United States foreign policy leaders discussed plans to respond through the use of covert operations. Reportedly because of other terrorist activities in the country, however, those plans were rejected, and the United States took no major steps to respond militarily.[39]

Nor was there a significant U.S. military response when Kuwait Airways Flight 221, en route to Pakistan, was hijacked and diverted to Tehran on December 3, 1984. A couple of U.S. government officials on the flight were killed. Hezbollah was reportedly linked to the hijacking, and the U.S. Department of State offered a financial reward "for information leading to the arrests of those involved in the hijacking."[40]

Six months later, TWA Flight 847 was hijacked. On its way from Athens to Rome, the flight was diverted to Beirut, with the hijackers demanding the release of Shiite Muslims imprisoned in Israel and Kuwait.[41] Growing impatient when their demands went unanswered, the hijackers shot and killed U.S. Navy officer Robert Dean Stethem and threw his body on the tarmac. Subsequently, Israel, which denied that it was capitulating to terrorists, released some Shiites from prison. A German court convicted Mohammed Ali Hamadei, who was reportedly involved in the hijacking, and sentenced him to life in prison, but years later he was released. Imad Mughniyah, a founder of Hezbollah, eluded capture but remained on the FBI's Most Wanted List until he was killed in 2008 by a car bomb in Damascus, Syria.[42]

The Palestine Liberation Front was blamed for the October 7, 1985, hijacking of the *Achille Lauro*, an Italian cruise ship, near Alexandria, Egypt. The U.S. government also had evidence indicating that Libya was involved. In an act reminiscent of the TWA Flight 847 tragedy, the hijackers killed Leon Klinghoffer, a U.S. citizen, when the United States would not grant their demands. The four hijackers left the ship and boarded a flight out of Egypt. In addition to the hijackers, Mohammad Abbas, considered the plot leader, was on the plane. United States fighter jets intercepted the Egyptian airliner, forcing it to land at a North Atlantic Treaty Organization (NATO) base in Italy. Italian authorities sent Abbas to Rome. He traveled to Yugoslavia and eventually made his way to Iraq. Abbas was captured by U.S. officials in Iraq following the 2003 invasion of that country. He died in U.S. custody.[43]

• • •

On December 27, five U.S. citizens were among those killed in bombings at the Rome and Vienna airports. The Libyan leader proclaimed the attacks "heroic," and U.S. officials believed that Abu Nidal was involved, receiving aid from Gaddhafi.[44] The Reagan administration responded by severing economic ties with Libya on January 7, 1986. Soon U.S. naval exercises in the Gulf of Sidra followed. On March 24, Libya fired a missile at U.S. military aircraft as the naval exercises were taking place in the Gulf of Sidra. Then, on April 5, a discotheque in West Berlin was bombed. Intelligence reports linked Libya to the attack, in which approximately 200 people, including Americans, were wounded and three people died. Nine days later, President Reagan announced that U.S. air and naval power were being used against Gaddhafi's headquarters and various military installations. The Reagan administration hoped its military strike would destabilize the Libyan government and lead to the removal of Gaddhafi, who was reportedly injured in the attacks.[45]

But on December 21, 1988, Libyan-backed terrorism was in full force. In transit from London to New York, Pan Am Flight 103 exploded over Lockerbie, Scotland, killing the nearly 270 people on board and on the ground.[46] The State Department later reported that the U.S. and British governments had firm evidence that Libya was involved in the Lockerbie bombing.[47] In April 1999, Gaddhafi's regime turned over the two Libyan suspects in the attack, who were brought to trial in the Netherlands. Al Amin Khalifq Fhimah was acquitted, but in February 2001, Abdelbaset Ali Mohmed al-Megrahi was found guilty and given a life sentence. Released from prison on humanitarian grounds in 2009 because of poor health, he died on May 20, 2012.[48] In 2003, Gaddhafi's government accepted responsibility for the attack and agreed to pay the victims.[49]

The Iranian hostage crisis dominated the hours before Ronald Reagan was sworn in as president in January 1981; the airplane bombing over Lockerbie took place one month before he completed his second term as president. President Reagan's diary entries for January 12 and 17, 1989, reveal a president thinking about the broad implications of the Lockerbie attack and Libyan aggression.[50] There were other terrorist activities during the 1980s, but this review underscores the deadliness and unrelenting nature of the threats that emerged from radical Islam during Ronald Reagan's White House tenure. This section also has highlighted some of the Reagan administration's military and nonmilitary responses to terrorism.

The following sections include a review of the institutional and doctrinal responses of the Reagan administration.

Reagan Administration Perspectives on Terrorism

A careful look into the positions taken by a number of President Reagan's foreign policy advisers reveals the genesis of terrorism policies that emerged during the 1980s. Though not necessarily cohesive, these positions provided a body of analysis of the problems associated with combating global terror that heretofore had not been a core aspect of U.S. strategic doctrine. President Reagan established a high bar for his administration's counterterrorism policy, which held that U.S. government officials would not negotiate with terrorists. Nor would the president condone assassination as a means of dissuading terrorists from targeting Americans. President Reagan reviewed his policy in his memoirs, stating:

We couldn't negotiate with kidnappers. That would simply encourage terrorists to take more hostages. And as a nation we placed limits on how far we could go to counter terrorism. A few people within the administration wanted to follow Menachem Begin's slogan of "an eye for an eye" and assassinate leaders of the most bloodthirsty groups that had committed terrorism against the United States and its citizens—but this was a game that America couldn't and didn't play. Early in my administration, I signed an order prohibiting direct or indirect involvement in murder during covert operations. This was one reason why the CIA had difficulty infiltrating terrorist groups—many of which required new members, as a show of loyalty, to assassinate an enemy of the organization.[51]

The U.S. leader also required that military and intelligence responses to terrorism be organized around the protection of human life. He said:

> Often, during our searches for terrorists, as after the marine barracks bombing in Beirut, we collected information that gave our experts reasonable confidence—but not absolute certainty—that they knew where the terrorists were located. I vetoed proposals to attack several of these sites. I just didn't want to take the chance that we'd kill innocents. George Shultz and Cap Weinberger concurred in this position.[52]

The president's strategy for combating terrorism included addressing the fundamental problems in the Middle East:

> The key to achieving a permanent peace in the Middle East and ending the strife that had led to the taking of the hostages was to get other moderate Arab countries, in addition to Egypt, to help us work out an agreement that provided for the acceptance of Israel's right to exist together with a land-for-peace concession that gave territory and autonomy to the Palestinians. The problems wouldn't go away until we solved the problems of the Palestinians and until the security of Israel was ensured with adequate safeguards.[53]

Improving relations with moderate Arab leaders, which President Reagan accomplished in state visits by King Fahd, King Hussein, and President Hosni Mubarak, was an important component of his Middle East and terrorism policy. For instance, against opposition from some congressional leaders and concern among Israeli leaders and their supporters in the United States, President Reagan prevailed in his first year in office in winning congressional approval for selling Airborne Warning and Control System surveillance planes. Alexander Haig, President Reagan's first secretary of state, defended the sale on the grounds that "our friendship with Saudi Arabia is not based solely on its role as an oil supplier. Saudi Arabia is proving itself an essential partner in our broader interests."[54]

Secretary Haig sought to establish a strong connection between terrorism and Soviet policy. However, a special National Intelligence Estimate, produced during the first few months of Reagan's presidency, "did not give Haig what he wanted, namely the evidence of the existence of a worldwide terrorist network supported by (and alive only because of) the Soviet Union."[55] Instead, the document included the key judgments that "the USSR pursues different policies toward different types of revolutionary groups that conduct terrorist activities. . . . [And] there is conclusive evidence that the USSR directly or indirectly supports a large number of national insurgencies and some separatist-irredentist groups." However, "with respect to Soviet policy toward nihilistic, purely terrorist groups, available evidence remains thin and in some respects contradictory, even though the human intelligence collection programs of the United States and its friends have been giving this problem close scrutiny for some years."[56]

In 1984, Secretary Shultz outlined a counterterrorism policy that focused less on possible Soviet connections to terrorists and more on how to establish strategies of preemption, prevention, and retaliation. The policy he outlined was not primarily tied to Soviet policies and international behavior. Speaking at a meeting of the Trilateral Commission on April 3 in Washington, D.C., he revealed, without going into detail, his thinking on preemption as part of the Reagan administration's counterterrorism policy:

> State-sponsored terrorism is really a form of warfare. Motivated by ideology and political hostility, it is a weapon of unconventional war against democratic societies, taking advantage of the openness of these societies. How do we combat this challenge? Certainly we must take security precautions to protect our people and our facilities; certainly we must strengthen our intelligence capabilities to alert ourselves to the threats. But it is increasingly doubtful that a purely passive strategy can even begin to cope with the problem. This raises a host of questions for a free society: in what circumstances—and how—should we respond? When—and how—should we take preventive or preemptive action against known terrorist groups? What evidence do we insist upon before taking such steps?
>
> As the threat mounts—and as the involvement of such countries as Iran, Syria, Libya, and North Korea has become more and more evident—then it is more and more appropriate that the nations of the West face up to the need for active defense against terrorism.[57]

The secretary's most comprehensive statement on preemption and terrorism was made in his address before the Park Avenue Synagogue in New York City on October 25:

> We must reach a consensus in this country that our responses should go beyond passive defense to consider means of active prevention, preemption, and retaliation. Our goal must be to prevent and deter future terrorist acts, and experience has taught us over the years that one of the best deterrents to terrorism is the certainty that swift and sure measures will be taken against those who engage in it. We should take steps toward carrying out such measures. There should be no moral confusion on this issue. Our aim is not to seek revenge but to put an end to violent attacks against innocent people, to make the world a safer place to live for all of us. Clearly, the democracies have a moral right, indeed a duty, to defend themselves.[58]

Shultz's ideas about preemption did not become the overarching operational military doctrine during the Reagan years. However, they did represent a doctrinal shift away from the reactive approach to terrorism of the era. Shultz made an effort to place preemption and strong defense on terrorism in the larger context of U.S. Cold War strategy. He said, "We are on the way to being well prepared to deter an all-out war or a Soviet attack on our principal allies. . . . We have worked hard to deter large-scale aggression by strengthening our strategic and conventional defenses."[59] By placing counterterrorism efforts in the context of overall U.S. strategic doctrine, Secretary Shultz was able to make the case that preemption and strong defense were consistent with current U.S. strategy, as well as with the American way of war in general.

At a Defense Department and National Defense University conference on low-intensity warfare on January 15, 1986, Secretary Shultz continued to place the growing terror threat in terms of U.S.-Soviet geopolitical competition. He declared that "terrorists and communist guerillas" as well as "Soviet-backed insurgencies" posed profound threats to American security. He was also sober about the use of American power, particularly in response to terrorists:

> We are right to be reluctant to unsheath our sword. But we cannot let the ambiguities of the terrorist threat reduce us to total impotence. A policy filled with so many qualifications and conditions that they all could never be met would amount to a policy of paralysis. It would amount to an admission that, with all our weaponry and power, we are helpless to defend our citizens, our interests, and our values. This I simply do not accept.[60]

The secretary of state continued to advocate preemption and prevention:

> The time to act, to help our friends by adding our strength to the equation, is not when the threat is at the doorstep, when the stakes are highest and the needed resources enormous. We must be prepared to commit our political, economic, and, if necessary, military power when the threat is still manageable and when its prudent use can prevent the threat from growing.[61]

The secretary of defense offered a different approach to U.S. security challenges. A month after Secretary Shultz's remarks on terrorism in New York, Secretary Weinberger articulated his requirements for the use of U.S. military power. Speaking at the National Press Club in Washington, D.C., he listed the following major tests to be used when considering the use of American military force abroad:

1. Military force should be used only in conflicts that are "deemed vital to our national interest or that of our allies."
2. If U.S. interests are at stake in a conflict and combat troops are to enter the conflict, the United States intends to win. This entails using a force of the size "necessary to achieve our objectives."
3. Political and military objectives should be clearly articulated before entering a conflict.
4. "The relationship between our objectives and the forces we have committed . . . must be continually reassessed."
5. The support of the American people and the U.S. Congress must be in place prior to entering hostilities.
6. "The commitment of US forces to combat should be a last resort."[62]

Secretary Weinberger has been criticized for putting forth a set of requirements that constituted a bureaucratic block to using force of any sort.[63] While he was concerned about the implications and the legacy of U.S. failure in the Vietnam War, Weinberger also was assessing U.S. involvement in conflicts in Lebanon and Grenada. He has written that the U.S. invasion of Grenada was carried out to help restore political stability to the island nation and safely bring home Americans studying in the country.[64] He was troubled, however, by U.S. military involvement in Lebanon.

As reviewed earlier, France, Italy, and the United States formed a Multinational Force, a peacekeeping unit, following Israel's invasion of Lebanon on

June 6, 1982. The MNF was to separate the warring parties, help stabilize the country in the midst of a complicated civil war, and facilitate the Palestine Liberation Organization's (PLO) exit. On September 10, following the PLO's departure, the MNF withdrew from Lebanon. Its reentry soon thereafter was a response to the massacre of hundreds of Palestinian refugees at the Sabra and Shatila camps, as well as to the murder of the president-elect. But what was the objective?

By the end of August 1983, for the first time in the conflict, the MNF was returning fire in response to mortar and rocket attacks. In backing the Lebanese army, the MNF and their governments were seen as siding with the Lebanese government, dominated by Christians, against the Shia, Druze, and others. Matters were not helped by the Lebanese army's attack on the Shia area of West Beirut on August 31. By September 19, Navy battleships were providing gun support for the Lebanese army, and the USS *New Jersey* arrived a few days later. Weinberger writes, "The result was that the scattered elements of the second MNF basically came to be viewed by many of the warring factions as simply a prop for an unpopular Lebanese government."[65] In this context, the secretary of defense was laying out requirements that meant tailoring means to ends, and having clear ends.

It is here that the Weinberger Doctrine actually meets the Shultz Doctrine, and both were consistent with President Reagan's thinking. Inadvertently harming innocent lives while involved in a low-intensity conflict and putting U.S. servicemen in harm's way were of utmost concern to Reagan, Shultz, and Weinberger. While Shultz appeared more forward leaning in his strategy of preemption and his strong advocacy of U.S. involvement in Lebanon in 1982–1984, he was mindful of the risks of becoming involved in a country in the midst of civil war that was also an occupation zone (Israel and Syria were there) and in which many Americans remained in captivity. The statesmen suggested different strategies but their assessments of the risks and the increasingly complicated problem of terrorism were not as divergent as has been portrayed. Weinberger did not oppose preemption on principle. Rather, he argued for a more rigorous and continuous evaluation of means and ends.

Institutionalizing the U.S. Response

In the absence of institutionalizing their ideas and public pronouncements, leaders' speeches and statements on terrorism could provide guidance to the current administration but would not be binding upon the next president, nor would they necessarily help lay the foundation for future policymaking. As previously asserted, however, the policy on terror that evolved in the Reagan administration did provide the building blocks for the terrorism policies of future administrations, as evidenced by public statements that reflected national security directives and laws the president and his foreign policy advisers championed.

For instance, National Security Decision Directives 138 and 179, the creation of new military commands, a few military operations in the Persian Gulf area, and several pieces of legislation on terrorism that President Reagan asked the U.S. Congress to consider, are authoritative examples of institutional mechanisms for creating a national security policy on terrorism that was distinct from the Cold War strategy of containment.[66]

• • •

More than 250 Americans were killed in 1983 by Islamic radicals using the tactics of terrorism such as suicide bombs and the indiscriminate bombing of public places.[67] And there was no end in sight. It was in this context of escalating attacks on Americans, especially in the Middle East, that President Reagan signed NSDD 138 on April 3, 1984.

The directive was declassified a few years ago. It outlined a bold initiative "to prevent, counter, and combat terrorism." It espoused preemption as part of the overall strategy for addressing terrorism: "Whenever we have evidence that a state is mounting or intends to conduct an act of terrorism against us, we have a responsibility to take measures to protect our citizens, property, and interests."[68] Legislative measures, bilateral and multilateral diplomacy and coordination, economic sanctions on terrorist organizations and their state supporters, and enhanced intelligence and military operations were among the other strategies outlined in NSDD 138.

In addition to the directive itself, the substance of the presidential action is reflected in statements and speeches by officials of the Reagan administration in which they described aspects of the directive. Noel C. Koch, deputy assistant secretary of defense, said that NSDD 138 "represents a quantum leap in countering terrorism, from the reactive mode to recognition that pro-active steps are needed."[69] Secretary Shultz's April 3, 1984, speech at a meeting of the Trilateral Commission asked, "When—and how—should we take preventive and preemptive action against known terrorist groups? What evidence do we insist upon before taking such steps?"[70] National Security Adviser Robert McFarlane also discussed the directive:

> First of all, the practice of terrorism by any person or group in any cause is a threat to our national security. The practice of international terrorism must be resisted by all legal means. State-sponsored terrorist acts or threats are hostile acts and the perpetrators or sponsors must be held accountable. Fourth, whenever we obtain evidence that an act of terrorism is about to be mounted against us, we have a responsibility to take measures to protect our citizens, property, and interests. The very threat of terrorism represents aggression and warrants acts of self-defense.[71]

National Security Decision Directive 138 was followed by four bills on terrorism, which the White House transmitted to Congress on April 26, 1984. The Act for the Prevention and Punishment of the Crime of Hostage-Taking was the administration's attempt to put into practice the International Convention against the Taking of Hostages, adopted by the United Nations on December 17, 1979, and signed by President Reagan in September 1981. The bill "would amend the Federal kidnapping statute to provide for Federal jurisdiction over any kidnapping in which a threat is made to kill, injure, or continue to detain a victim in order to compel a third party to do or to abstain from doing something."[72] The bill was incorporated into the Comprehensive Crime Control Act of 1984, which was included in HJ Res 648, signed into law on October 12, 1984.[73]

The main premise of the Aircraft Sabotage Act was that there were gaps in U.S. laws on hijacking and the sabotage of airplanes. The act sought to strengthen U.S. adherence to the Montreal Convention, which it had signed in 1972, that instructed participating states to outline jurisdiction related to offenses against civil aviation.[74] Like the Act for the Prevention and Punishment of the Crime of Hostage-Taking, the Aircraft Sabotage Act was incorporated into HJ Res 648.

The Act for Rewards for Information Concerning Terrorist Acts was incorporated into the 1984 Act to Combat International Terrorism. President Reagan declared that the bill, signed into law on October 19, was designed to "provide resources and authorities essential in countering the insidious threat terrorism poses." He added that the bill was "an important step in our multi-year effort to counter the pervasive threat international terrorism poses to our diplomatic personnel and facilities overseas."[75]

The Prohibition against the Training or Support of Terrorist Organizations Act of 1984 was never signed into law.[76] However, the Reagan administration had an impressive record of spearheading new legislative measures on terrorism policy during its first term.

Ideas about preemption, prevention, and retaliation outlined in NSDD 138 and articulated by Secretary Shultz were difficult to translate into a cohesive policy of counterterrorism, as evidenced after members of Hezbollah hijacked TWA Flight 847 on June 14, 1985. The crisis pointed to the "sluggish bureaucracies" in Washington, as well as "indecision among U.S. allies."[77] A month later, NSDD 179 was signed by President Reagan.[78]

The new directive called for a task force on counterterrorism to be headed by Vice President George H. W. Bush. The duties of the task force included reviewing "national priorities currently assigned to effectively combat terrorism."[79] The assessment was completed by the end of the year, and in February 1986 the *Public Report of the Vice President's Task Force on Combating Terrorism* was released to the public. The report recommended a major overhaul of how the U.S. government addressed terrorism, including improved coordination among government agencies on intelligence gathering, law enforcement, and the range of options for responding to terrorist attacks. It also called upon Congress and the executive branch of government to work closely on additional legislation to close loopholes and gaps that impede U.S. efforts to combat terror.[80]

Two months before the Reagan presidency ended, Vice President Bush released a report that examined terrorist activities throughout the world. In his letter of transmittal, he wrote that the recommendations of his 1986 report "became the cornerstone of U.S. counterterrorism policy," and he declared that the administration's counterterrorism policy was "the toughest in the Free World."[81] This claim may be disputed, but the Reagan administration did establish policies and institutional arrangements to combat terror that blazed a path for subsequent administrations to follow.

During the Reagan administration, military institutions were created that had as their core mission the prevention of terrorist attacks. On January 1, 1983, the U.S. Central Command (USCENTCOM) was established. It grew out of President Carter's Rapid Deployment Joint Task Force, which was started in March 1980 in response to the Soviet invasion of Afghanistan and growing crises throughout the region. USCENTCOM was responsible for protecting U.S. interests in the broader Middle East. United States Special Operations

Command (USSOCOM) became operational on April 16, 1987. Its work entails covert missions and unconventional warfare activities.[82]

Two military operations are worth noting. Operation Earnest Will, which began on July 24, 1987, and ended on September 26, 1988, was a maneuver in what has been called the Tanker War. The Tanker War was the phase of the Iran-Iraq War in which the United States helped create an international coalition to block Iranian menacing of Kuwaiti oil tankers attempting to pass through the Persian Gulf. In August 1987, Operation Prime Chance was undertaken. The USSOCOM mission of protecting non-American oil tankers that the United States reflagged as they passed through the Persian Gulf ended in June 1989.[83]

In support of these missions, the Reagan administration helped create an international coalition. It is particularly noteworthy because, despite opposition from some conservatives in the United States, President Reagan and Secretary Shultz recruited the Soviet Union to join this coalition of primarily Western democracies. It is significant that the Reagan administration's view of Iran's aggression in the Persian Gulf as acts of terrorism was taking place as the last chapter of the Cold War was being written.[84]

Institutional and Doctrinal Legacy

During the Clinton administration, NSDD 138 was succeeded by Presidential Decision Directive (PDD) 62 on combating terrorism. As one writer notes, "PDD 62 was more expansive in its coverage than NSDD 138 and addressed a broad range of unconventional threats, to include attacks on critical infrastructure, terrorist acts, and the threat of the use of weapons of mass destruction. . . . PDD 62 created the position of National Coordinator for Security, Infrastructure Protection, and Counter-terrorism, which would coordinate program management through the Office of the National Security Advisor."[85]

On January 23, 1995, President Bill Clinton issued Executive Order 12947, which focused on "Prohibiting Transactions with Terrorists Who Threaten to Disrupt the Middle East Peace Process."[86] It built upon President Reagan's NSDD 138, which advocated imposing tight sanctions against "organizations or states which support or export terrorism."[87]

• • •

On August 7, 1998, radical Islamists attacked two U.S. embassies in East Africa. Thousands were wounded, and 12 Americans were among the more than

220 people killed. President Clinton responded on August 20, 1998, by issuing Executive Order 13099, which listed Osama bin Laden and al Qaeda among the terror targets for U.S. sanctions and reinforced the earlier presidential decree.[88]

Also on August 20, President Clinton undertook Operation Infinite Reach. This military retaliation used cruise missiles to strike terrorist targets and al Qaeda leaders in Afghanistan and a pharmaceutical plant in Sudan that some members of President Clinton's administration suspected of being used to make chemical weapons.[89] These directed strikes were similar to measured military strikes against radical Islamists by the Reagan administration.

While members of President Reagan's national security team expressed ideas about preemption, President George W. Bush elevated the concept into a key element of his strategic doctrine for addressing global terror. At the U.S. Military Academy at West Point on June 1, 2002, he declared: "Our security will require all Americans to be forward-looking and resolute, to be ready for preemptive action when necessary to defend our liberty and to defend our lives." Preemption was further articulated in the president's National Security Strategy of September 2002: "While the United States will constantly strive to enlist the support of the international community, we will not hesitate to act alone, if necessary, to exercise our right of self-defense by acting preemptively against such terrorists, to prevent them from doing harm against our people and our country."[90] These words led to a firestorm of criticism that President Bush had made a major departure in strategic doctrine. As John Gaddis has shown, however, preemption has long been part of U.S. strategic thinking, planning, and execution.[91]

•   •   •

President Bush's strategy of preemption was at odds with the Weinberger Doctrine, however. President Reagan's secretary of defense had cautioned against any use of force in response to terrorist attacks or other forms of aggression without clearly stated means and ends, as well as firm support from the American public. Bush's policy was brash in that it did not meet these criteria. The president declared the country to be in a long war that had to be waged not for political expediency but for moral reasons related to preserving and enhancing freedom worldwide. In his 2002 West Point speech he said: "Because the war on terror will require resolve and patience, it will also require firm moral purpose." As one military analyst has noted, "The NSS assumes that the war on terrorism is necessary and, by its nature, necessarily protracted, so rather than mold the doctrine to address American tolerances, as do Weinberger and Powell, it crafts the strategies necessary to win the war and then tries to sell that strategy to the public."[92]

President Bush also built upon the institutional legacy of the Reagan era by undertaking the most significant overhaul of the national security apparatus since the National Security Act of 1947, which created the Defense Department and the National Security Council. Following the killing of nearly 3,000 Americans through multiple acts of terror on September 11, 2001, President Bush created or reorganized numerous agencies to address domestic and international terrorism. These agencies include the Department of Homeland Security, which merged 22 government entities in an effort to protect the American homeland against attack; the Director of National Intelligence, which was to unify the numerous intelligence agencies; and the Federal Bureau of Investigation and the Department of Justice, which were reorganized to better participate in combating terrorism.[93] The Patriot Act was signed by President Bush in an effort to allow intelligence and law enforcement agencies to work together on terrorist threats.[94] On the military front, the U.S. Northern Command, designed to protect the American homeland, and the U.S. Strategic Command, with its mission of preventing long-range attacks, were created during George W. Bush's presidency.[95]

President Barack Obama's approach to the threat of terrorism has not been radically different from that of his predecessors. While he has dispensed with the phrase "global war on terror," which came into common use during the George W. Bush administration, he has continued many of Bush's policies. The intelligence, military, and political institutions Bush created have grown in size and importance during the Obama administration. The use of drone strikes against enemy targets in Pakistan, Yemen, and countries where the United States has enemy targets engaged in terrorism has its roots in Bush administration policies and is reminiscent of President Reagan's attempt to use military force in a directed and narrow way when dealing with terrorism.[96] Furthermore, USCENTCOM and USSOCOM, established by President Reagan, are among the most important military and intelligence assets at the heart of President Obama's success in taking down Osama bin Laden and weakening the al Qaeda network.

Observers have tended to view Reagan's policies on Middle East terrorism through the prism of Iran-Contra, but there is much more to the story. Reagan's strategies for combating terrorism typically were intellectually nuanced and less militaristic than has been reported. The president cared deeply about American values and struggled to develop strategies that were consistent with them and with the values of a democratic society more generally. Policy on terrorism during the Reagan years offered nothing short of the beginning of a new U.S. grand strategy that redounds today, having charted a path through laws and directives that have strongly influenced, and at times even helped guide, future administrations.

7

Ronald Reagan and American Defense

ELIOT A. COHEN

Even Ronald Reagan's severest critics would admit that he was a man of conviction—terrifying convictions, some thought, but sincerely held. In no area was this truer than defense and, to a lesser extent, the use of force, which are not quite the same thing.

Reagan was, as he often told admiring audiences, an American exceptionalist. But he was also "a democratic internationalist," in Lou Cannon's words, who believed that "the blessings of freedom and material prosperity" were due to others, as well as Americans.[1] Yet the possibility of the spread of these freedoms was constrained by the threat of modern totalitarianism. An unambiguous anti-communist, he believed in the necessity of confronting Soviet expansionism wherever it appeared. He saw the United States as, in the words of the Puritans of 350 years earlier, "a city on a hill" and unambiguously a force for good in the world. He took a long view of the struggle for liberty, a universal aspiration destined to triumph. Indeed, his faith in the special beneficence that had placed the United States between two "shining seas," as he often put it, made him confident that in the long run, history would flow along an American course, if Americans were wise enough to adhere to what he took to be the basic principles of the American founding.

Given Reagan's belief in the essential goodness of America, in the universality of the principles of individual liberty, and his unremittingly dark view of the Soviet Union, it is unsurprising that the first principle of his foreign policy was, very simply, strength. "Peace is *made* by the fact of strength—economic, military, and strategic. Peace is *lost* when such strength disappears or—just as bad—is seen by an adversary as disappearing."[2] Reagan could not conceive that American strength might produce misjudgments or errors, nor did he ever seem particularly concerned about wasted or diverted resources. "I've known four wars in my lifetime. None of them came about because we were too strong."[3] The key to Reagan's defense policy may be found in those words. He believed in preserving American strength and was convinced that to be strong enough was virtually to guarantee that that strength would not need to be used. He painted himself as a conservative who believed in maintaining the strategy put in place at the outset of the Cold War, deterrence. "'Deterrence' means simply this: making sure any adversary who thinks about attacking the United States, or our allies, or our vital interests, concludes that the risks to him outweigh any potential gains. Once he understands that, he won't attack. We maintain the peace through our strength; weakness only invites aggression."[4]

Reagan's belief that adequate strength in and of itself would guarantee peace was one of his legacies to the Republican Party in the decades that followed his presidency. While other postwar Republican presidents believed in robust defense spending, neither had quite Reagan's faith that the mere existence of overwhelming American military strength would have beneficent effects. Eisenhower, for example, thought sound strategic doctrine as important as strength and feared that there could be too much of a good thing, hence his warnings of a military industrial complex; Nixon thought in terms of manifestations of will to use such power (think of the Christmas bombings, a massive eleven-day air campaign on North Vietnam that took place between December 18 and 29, 1972). Reagan's views were simpler and starker.

Reagan's views of military power were shaped chiefly by two wars: World War II, during which he served stateside, and the Vietnam War, which so nearly tore apart the America of his late middle age. His conceptions of military prowess, courage, and sacrifice were those of 1941–1945, and some of his most powerful speeches—the Normandy speech on the fortieth anniversary of D-Day, above all—evoked a thoroughly heroic picture of the war. "These are the boys of Pointe du Hoc," he said, pointing to the D-Day veterans at the dedication of the monument to the U.S. Army Rangers there. "These are the men who took the cliffs. These are the champions who helped free a continent. These are the heroes who helped end a war."[5] Reagan's own participation in that conflict was minor—he was a reservist who made training films, although as he often pointed out, his eyesight would have disqualified him from active service—but he felt keenly the sentiments of that generation and represented them, as he understood them, to their children and grandchildren.

Vietnam was something very different. "The only immorality of the Vietnam War was that our government asked young men to die in a war that the government had no intention of winning," he once wrote.[6] "The cause was a just and noble one," he told a Vietnam veteran in 1982, but the failure of the government was that it was a cause "the government was afraid to let them [the military] win."[7] Reagan was also appalled by the American public's failure to recognize the sacrifice of American servicemen, and as president he acted to reverse that. In February 1981, barely a month after assuming office, he decided to take charge of the ceremony that belatedly awarded Master Sergeant Roy P. Benadvidez the Congressional Medal of Honor for conspicuous gallantry demonstrated under fire in Vietnam in 1968. The president, not the secretary of defense, read the citation at the Pentagon event.[8] Part of Reagan's conception of his responsibility as president was to undo the damage done to the military by the Vietnam War and to avoid anything like it in the future.

Both understandings were, of course, oversimplified in the extreme; what matters for present purposes is that those were Reagan's core beliefs, which, together with his understanding of the United States and of its great opponent in the Cold War, shaped the key decisions of his presidency and, most notably, the expansion of defense spending with which it must be associated.

The Defense Buildup

The Reagan defense buildup is, arguably, the largest peacetime expansion of military spending in American history, assuming that the defense expansion of the years immediately before Pearl Harbor was part of a wartime buildup. In calendar year 1981, defense outlays were roughly $180 billion in current-year dollars; by 1989, they were nearly $294 billion. With prices adjusted for inflation, the increase in annual budget authority was 12 percent in 1981 and again in 1982, 9 percent in 1983, 5 percent and over 7 percent in 1984 and 1985, respectively, before the beginning of a decline. National defense spending had gone from roughly 5 percent of GDP to 6 percent, in an expanding economy. Put differently, in inflation-adjusted dollars, military budget authority went up by more than 50 percent in the five years between 1980 and 1985.[9]

In retrospect, some have pointed out that the budget plan as laid out in the last budget of the Carter administration (January 1981) called for an expansion of the budget not much short of what Reagan ended up with—6 percent of GNP under the Carter plan in 1986 and an actual 6.4 percent of GNP under Reagan.[10] And undeniably, the large defense buildup that we associate with Ronald Reagan began under his predecessor, as did many of the weapons development programs that were later associated with Reagan, to include advanced fighter aircraft and tanks, precision guided weapons, and stealthy platforms.

To some extent, however, this begs the question: planning defense budgets five years out is one thing, actually executing them is another, and one may question whether a second term of the Carter administration would have been quite so resolute as it was in the immediate aftermath of the Iranian revolution and the Soviet invasion of Afghanistan. Moreover, there were important differences in emphasis. The Reagan buildup, although productive of minor increases in numbers of men and women in uniform, was overwhelmingly oriented toward procurement. From roughly a quarter of the defense budget, it went up to a third, with the result that when American forces went to war in the Persian Gulf in 1991, they did so with an arsenal that was filled with modern equipment, abundant and well-maintained.

Reagan's tenure coincided with, moreover, an overhaul of the military begun under his predecessor. In each of the services, struggling still to cope with the end of the draft, there had been since the late 1970s a drive to purge the ranks of troublemakers or merely incapable soldiers, to professionalize the noncommissioned officer corps, to introduce advanced training on automated ranges like Nellis Air Force Base or the National Training Center, to upgrade equipment, and to develop doctrine for the employment of forces such as the Army's AirLand Battle concept. The Reagan era, with its abundant resources and wholehearted support of the services, was conducive to this massive recovery from the Vietnam era in intellectual and staffing terms, as well as material acquisition.

The Reagan buildup aided all services and programs and continued the revitalization of the conventional forces begun under Carter, but it was particularly focused on the nuclear programs. At the center of this was not merely the modernization of the deterrent, but the Strategic Defense Initiative (SDI), an attempt to create a defense against nuclear weapons that cut to the heart of Reagan's conception of national defense. He believed that the problem of his age was preventing nuclear annihilation while not yielding to a totalitarian ideology: "What, then, is our course? Must civilization perish in a hail of fiery atoms? Must freedom wither in a quiet, deadening accommodation with totalitarian evil?"[11] Many of his critics thought that his response to the second rhetorical question was the most important and deprecated the sincerity of his response to the first. In fact, however, Reagan advocated SDI neither as a bargaining tool nor merely as a ploy to drive the Soviet Union to an accommodation via bankruptcy, but as a measure to shield the country from a threat that preoccupied him.[12]

It is difficult, in retrospect, to credit the passion that Reagan's advocacy of defenses against ballistic missiles evoked. Since the early 1960s, a belief in mutual assured destruction had been central to Democratic policymakers' understanding of nuclear issues. Under this theory, the key to peace, indeed, to survival in the Cold War between the Soviet Union and the United States was the ability of either power to annihilate the other reliably and effectively. Defenses against ballistic missiles were, in this view, dangerous because of destabilizing. Should the Soviets, in particular, conclude that the United States could protect itself against a nuclear attack—indeed, should they believe that such was the American aspiration—a dangerous element of volatility would enter their strategic thinking, and the result could well be nuclear war. When Reagan began not only making the case for defense, but actually launched a Strategic Defense Initiative, the reaction was not only one of deep doubt about the feasibility of the technologies proposed, but a far deeper alarm at the strategic consequences of even appearing to attempt them. To be sure, in many ways Reagan merely tapped a vein of American strategic history going back to the great fortification schemes of the early nineteenth century, but his opponents either did not know or dismissed that.[13] Moreover, where Reagan's critics believed that SDI undermined deterrence, the president took precisely the opposite view: make the United States harder to attack, and one made it far less likely that the Soviets would try it.

What his critics never understood, however, was that Reagan's antipathy to nuclear weapons was deep and abiding. In his 1976 speech to the Republican National Convention, for example, the prospect of annihilation was on his mind: "Who kept our world from nuclear destruction?" was, he said, the question future generations would ask.[14] The president was probably entirely sincere in his desire to see the abolition of nuclear weapons. Certainly, he was willing to entertain a deal with the Soviet Union, particularly under the leadership of Mikhail Gorbachev, to severely reduce their numbers.

Reagan's calculation, however, was based not on mutual confidence, but on a hardheaded estimate of the Soviets:

I have never believed in any negotiations with the Soviets that we could appeal to them as we could to people like ourselves. Negotiations with the Soviets is really a case of presenting a choice in which they face alternatives they must consider on the basis of cost. For example in our arms reductions talks they must recognize that failure to meet us on some mutually agreeable level will result in an arms race in which they know they cannot maintain superiority. They must choose between reduced, equal levels or inferiority.[15]

Reagan, in this area of defense policy at least, integrated high ideals and realpolitik in a way scholars still have trouble accommodating.

The Use of Force

Reagan's defense buildup left behind tangible consequences: an American military that was better equipped than any other in the world. Indeed, a quarter century later, the U.S. armed services are still—and at their peril—living off the accumulated capital of those eight years. The buildup coincided with the replacement of the geriatric leadership of the Soviet Union—Brezhnev, Chernenko, Andropov—by Mikhail Gorbachev and a younger, reform-oriented leadership. Students of Soviet history will argue about the role played by the buildup in convincing the Gorbachev generation that the Cold War was pointless, too costly, and unwinnable. Having come to that conclusion, however, much to their own surprise, Gorbachev and his successor, Boris Yeltsin, presided over the demise of the Warsaw Pact and the Soviet Union itself, ending the Cold War with a wholly unforeseen collapse.

Reagan did indeed use force. In 1982, he deployed a marine amphibious unit (a reinforced infantry battalion) to Lebanon in the wake of Israel's invasion of that country, a force that subsequently became engaged in a low-level conflict with Syria's proxies there, culminating in the bombing of the Marine barracks and a set of retaliatory raids and shelling by U.S. forces. In October 1983, Reagan authorized URGENT FURY, the invasion of Grenada, a small Caribbean island ruled by a government aligned with Cuba, which was, in fact, building a base there. In 1986, following the bombing of a discotheque in Berlin frequented by American service personnel, Reagan authorized Operation EL DORADO CANYON, a sharp set of retaliatory strikes against Libyan leader Muammar Gaddafi, killing a number of individuals including, it was claimed, Gaddafi's daughter. Reagan also authorized aggressive campaigns of

subversive warfare in Central America, directed against the Sandinista movement in Nicaragua, and, far more successfully, against Soviet forces in
Afghanistan who were opposed by a range of Afghan guerrilla groups. Although
constrained by Congress, he also presided over a remarkably successful, if bloody,
effort to support the government of El Salvador against left-wing guerrilla
movements.

Grenada was a far, far smaller conflict than the Gulf War of the 1990s or
the Afghan and Iraq wars of 2001 and 2003; the Libya raid was a one-off affair, unlike the sustained campaigns of aerial attack prosecuted by the Bush
and Obama administrations in Pakistan, Yemen, and elsewhere; only the support to Afghan guerrillas matched the scale of the wars that followed in the
next two decades. In the context of the times, however, and in particular in
the wake of Vietnam, Reagan's willingness to use hard military and paramili-
tary power was notable. It was not entirely successful, let it be noted, and it
was not until the 1991 Gulf War that the American military restored and indeed surpassed the reputation for complete competence that had been lost in
Vietnam. More important, from the point of view of this chapter, Reagan made
no sustained commitments of conventional forces.

Reagan's statesmanship was more visionary than conceptual: from World
War II, he took away a deep admiration of the American military and appreciation of American strength; from Vietnam, a sense of shame at what he understood as a political more than a strategic or organizational failure; from the
Cold War, a belief that the United States was still engaged in a contest that
could, conceivably, come to blows; from his innermost core, a belief that the
United States could never be too strong, on the one hand, but as well a conviction that with adequate strength came the likelihood that military power
would not have to be used. What Reagan did *not*, however, possess was a well-
defined approach to the actual employment of force. He does not seem to have
thought of himself as a wartime leader; he had, among other things, no apti-
tude for that part of the job that required mastery of detail, close questioning
of subordinates, and the swift and brutal relief of some of them (in uniform or
not) and equally swift promotion of others. He was not particularly a student
of military history or inclined to immerse himself in the details of military
operations. He disliked the kind of sharp, open controversy in his presence
that is indispensable to strategic decision making. His subordinates disagreed
among themselves, but rarely argued out their convictions in front of their com-
mander in chief. Perhaps most important, Reagan did not need to be deeply

engaged in thinking about the conduct of war because that was not the predicament in which the United States found itself. His great strategic challenge was managing the Cold War and in particular confronting a Soviet Union that seemed militarily powerful, but he knew was economically weak and politically calcified. To do this, he needed a powerful American military in which public confidence had been restored, but he did not face geopolitical challenges requiring prolonged commitments of military forces. Nor, indeed, is it likely that the American people, still fresh from the trauma of Vietnam, would have tolerated it.

But a fierce internal debate about how to use force emerged, nonetheless, between Reagan's two most formidable cabinet secretaries, Caspar Weinberger at Defense and George Shultz at the Department of State. Weinberger and Shultz had both served on the front lines in the Pacific during World War II, in the Army and the Marine Corps, respectively. Both were readers of history, experienced in business and in government, and formidable intellects.

George Shultz fired the first shot, as it were, in what became the most serious debate in recent times about the conditions and ways in which the United States should use military force. Shultz had become increasingly preoccupied with the spread of international terrorism. On October 25, 1984, barely two weeks after an Irish Republican Army bomb attack had nearly killed the prime minister of Great Britain, Margaret Thatcher, he gave a speech on "Terrorism and the Modern World" (at the Park Avenue Synagogue in New York). At the beginning of the year, the Department of Defense had withdrawn U.S. Marines from Beirut, where almost exactly a year to the day before Shultz's speech, a suicide bomber had blown up the Marine barracks, killing some 241 Americans, most of them Marines. In neither case, interestingly, was the Soviet Union involved: here were lethal conflicts that were at most ancillary to the Cold War.

Shultz believed that it was important for the United States to act and, if necessary, act violently; many of his colleagues did not agree, and when a National Security Decision Directive was issued in April of that year, a section authorizing action to "neutralize" terrorists was changed by those who, according to Shultz, feared that it might be construed to approve assassination.[16] Twenty-five years later, when Americans were inured to routine drone attacks on suspected terrorists, even American citizens who merely inspired them, such compunctions seem remarkable.

Shultz declared that the United States could not "allow ourselves to become the Hamlet of nations, worrying endlessly over whether and how to respond.

A great nation with global responsibilities cannot afford to be hamstrung by confusion and indecisiveness."[17] "Terrorism," he continued, "represents a return to barbarism in the modern age. If the modern world cannot face up to the challenge, then terrorism, and the lawlessness and inhumanity that come with it, will gradually undermine all that the modern world has achieved and make further progress impossible." Shultz believed that the Soviet Union could be deterred and that subversion could be countered. But to cope with terrorism, in addition to effective police and intelligence work, the use of force would be necessary.

Secretary of Defense Weinberger took little time to respond, in a speech delivered on November 28, 1984, at the National Press Club. His immediate concerns, at least according to his memoirs, were rather different from Shultz's: the Pentagon was under pressure to begin escorting oil tankers in the Persian Gulf, where war between Iraq and Iran was endangering commerce. His newly appointed secretary of the navy, James Webb, a veteran of Vietnam, expressed grave doubts about an open-ended commitment there.[18] Weinberger, however, had been brooding on the subject of guidelines for the use of force for months, ever since the Beirut debacle during which he, and not only he, had thought the mission was vague and the prospects for success minimal, and he had been circulating a version of what became his six famous tests for the use of force—tests that he included as an appendix to his memoirs.[19]

Included, most notably, were these six famous tests for the use of force:

The United States should not commit forces to combat overseas unless the particular engagement or occasion is deemed vital to our national interest or that of our allies.

If we decide it is necessary to put combat troops into a given situation, we should do so wholeheartedly and with the clear intention of winning.

If we do decide to commit forces to combat overseas, we should have clearly defined political and military objectives. We should know precisely how our forces can accomplish those clearly defined objectives. And we should have and send the forces needed to do just that.

The relationship between our objectives and the forces we have committed . . . must be continually reassessed and adjusted if necessary.

Before the United States commits combat forces abroad, there must be some reasonable assurance that we will have the support of the American people and their elected representatives in Congress.

The commitment of U.S. forces to combat should be a last resort.[20]

There may be no Reagan doctrine for the use of force, but Weinberger's six rules were widely applauded within the military. His military assistant, General Colin Powell, recounts that he had some initial hesitations about them, but that in practice he found them invaluable. "Clausewitz would have applauded," he declared.[21]

Probably not, actually. In fact, Weinberger's rules were the antithesis of the thinking of the Prussian general, who thought the relationship between war and politics hardly amenable to, as he put it, finding truth by "planting a hedge of principles on either side." In a formal sense, at least, Shultz got in the last word, in a speech delivered a few weeks later.

> Americans have sometimes tended to think that power and diplomacy are distinct alternatives. This reflects a fundamental misunderstanding. The truth is that power and diplomacy must always go together or we will accomplish very little in this world. Power must always be guided by purpose. At the same time, the hard reality is that diplomacy not backed by strength will always be ineffectual at best, dangerous at worst.[22]

That would have been a lot closer to Clausewitz, who would probably have questioned each of Weinberger's propositions and rejected most if not all of them. The notion of "vital interests," for example, was exceedingly slippery—did Grenada count as a "vital interest" of the United States? "Winning," Clausewitz believed, was not the appropriate way to define a nation's purpose in war; achieving a set of political objectives was. Douglas MacArthur (under whom Weinberger had served) famously said that "there is no substitute for victory," but as Clausewitz knew, that was meaningless, because victory can only be defined in political terms.[23] It was one of Clausewitz's students at the war college in Berlin, Helmuth von Moltke, who wisely declared that no plan survives contact with the enemy, a statement of fact that calls into question the notion of knowing "precisely" how military force will achieve the ends of policy.[24]

Adjusting the relationship between objectives and means makes sense up to a point, but then again, as Clausewitz argued, because war is a contest of wills, and because it takes place in an atmosphere of uncertain information and shifting aims, a continual recalculation of strategy is likely to cause chaos. Politics being politics, domestic support can never be guaranteed—and as Clausewitz knew (and political scientists have confirmed) support as often follows success as the other way around. And finally, Clausewitz understood war not as a last resort, but as an intermediate choice, since it is always possible, after all, to yield to an opponent's demands.

Weinberger's principles were too rigid and far too incompatible with the nature of war to survive prolonged contact with reality. Had Abraham Lincoln applied them in 1861 or Franklin Delano Roosevelt 80 years later, both would either have avoided the Civil War and World War II or likely made disastrous choices about how to wage them. But although Shultz's case is ultimately the more persuasive, Weinberger's principles had more of a lasting impact and in some ways were the truer reflection, if not of Reagan's thinking, then of his era as president, an era in which it seemed possible for the United States to succeed in many directions without having to sacrifice.

Reagan, as we have seen, believed that it was possible to be so strong as never to need to use one's strength; he thought of the military in idealized terms, rather than as a set of fallible institutions; he sought a triumphant America that would not require, at the same time, sacrifices. He opposed a return to conscription—a possibility seriously debated as he became president—partly out of a commitment to individual liberty and partly because he (correctly) believed that it would not be necessary. He was not averse to using force, but neither was he enamored of it, and indeed, when he had the choice to hold back or go in (as in Central America), he held back; when he had the choice to double down on a policy in Lebanon that required military power, he folded his hand.

The world that Reagan's successors inhabited was very different. His own vice president, George H. W. Bush, attempted to wage a war in the Persian Gulf following Weinberger's rules. He succeeded in the short run but at the price of leaving the festering sore of a crippled but malignant Iraq. Bill Clinton did not seek a Balkan war and, indeed, was desperate to avoid one: he fought two. George W. Bush ended up waging one war in Afghanistan and another in Iraq that was occasioned in part by the failure of his father to finish off a wounded dictator. Barack Obama, while liquidating two guerrilla wars, expanded programs of assassination and air strikes on even more countries than his predecessor. All four post-Reagan presidents found themselves resorting to limited uses of force that had much more of Shultz than Weinberger in them.

Reagan's legacy in defense resembles, in some ways, his legacy in domestic politics: unwavering faith in America's ideals and strength, a belief in simple (if difficult) solutions to complex problems, and not too much interest in the details of how to bring the former to bear in accomplishing the latter. The good news, for his successors, was that he bequeathed to them the most powerful military on earth; the bad news, unfortunately, was that he, or at least some of his key subordinates, left behind misleading or inadequate ideas of how to employ it. He left behind a record in defense policy that seemed to suggest that there were no difficult strategic choices to be made, no need to call upon Americans to sacrifice treasure (let alone service) to defend themselves, and that strength alone, without judgment, skill, and determination in its use, would suffice.

For his time, Reagan was probably correct. The American military did indeed require across-the-board strengthening in 1980; his defense spending did not wreck the economy; he was fortunate in that war did not come to the United States on his watch and that he did not have to conduct one. But in retrospect, this was an anomalous set of circumstances. The norm, at the end of the twentieth and beginning of the twenty-first century, as it had been earlier in American history, was a much more difficult set of choices and challenges to be met by presidents and Congress. Reagan's heirs had every reason to be grateful for his rebuilding of American military power. Ironically, it is in part because of his achievements that they had to cope with a world less easily adapted to the grand strategic simplicities that had made him uniquely effective.

IV

THE GREAT DEBATE

Reagan and Negotiating the End of the Cold War

8

A World of Fewer Nuclear Weapons

Ronald Reagan's Willingness to Negotiate

PAUL KENGOR

In considering Ronald Reagan in a world transformed, we cannot neglect one of his most dramatic impacts: the greatly reduced number of nuclear weapons in the world—and, by extension, reduced risk of nuclear war—negotiated by Reagan and Mikhail Gorbachev and their respective staffs. This included the complete elimination of all intermediate-range nuclear missiles, achieved by Reagan and Gorbachev with their signing of the Intermediate-Range Nuclear Forces (INF) Treaty in December 1987. That treaty banned an entire class of nuclear missiles, more than 1,000 in total—deadly weapons perched on the doorsteps of Western and Eastern Europe. In addition, Reagan and Gorbachev entered into intense negotiations to cut massive arsenals of long-range nuclear missiles, ultimately leading to the signing of the Strategic Arms Reduction Treaty (START Treaty) by Gorbachev and by Reagan's successor, George H. W. Bush, in July 1991. The START Treaty went into effect in 1994 under President Bill Clinton and Russian President Boris Yeltsin. It was an extraordinary achievement, eliminating roughly 80 percent of the thousands of intercontinental missiles the two superpowers had aimed at one another for decades.

In all, thanks to these negotiations, which featured much drama in cities like Geneva and Reykjavík and Washington and Moscow, there were thousands fewer nuclear weapons in the world. International relations in the decades prior to and during Reagan's presidency were dominated with incessant fears of nuclear conflict between the United States and the Soviet Union. International relations in the decades since the Reagan presidency have not been plagued by those same fears. Sure, the planet faces new problems and nightmares, but the nuclear one that persisted between the United States and the Soviet Union for decades was, mercifully, ended.

Young people today cannot grasp the trepidation once endured by their parents and grandparents. Entire generations of Americans were schooled in duck-and-cover drills, learning in class and at home about the certain nuclear holocaust to come. They went to bed worrying about "the big one." These fears were woven into the fabric of the culture, dramatized in TV shows like *The Twilight Zone* and the widely watched 1980s movie *The Day After,* a genuine horror show. From the 1950s through the 1980s, humanity dreaded some kind of nuclear apocalypse, with millions to perhaps billions dead, from mushroom clouds over Manhattan and Moscow to nuclear winter worldwide.

Instead, nuclear Armageddon was averted, a joyous reality that cannot be stressed or celebrated enough. And if a prophet had said at the start of the 1980s that within a decade the Berlin Wall would be rubble, the Soviet Union would cease to exist, and the Cold War would be over and effectively decided in favor of the United States, the first scary thought on all minds might have been *"Oh, my. How many perished in the nuclear exchange?"*

That no one died at all, that there was no exchange at all, and that the Berlin Wall and the Soviet Union and the Cold War all ended peacefully is a credit to many good people, but especially to the leaders of the two superpowers: Ronald Reagan and Mikhail Gorbachev. This leap to a safer world was the result of unprecedented negotiations between the American president and Soviet general secretary. This better world was the legacy of Reagan's and Gorbachev's commitment to peace and arms control. It was also the legacy of Reagan's personal commitment to negotiating with his main international adversary, a commitment that surprised many. In fact, there was in Reagan a commitment and a consistency that many never expected and might still struggle to accept today.

Reagan, of course, was the ultimate anti-communist, excoriating the Soviet Union as an "Evil Empire," as the "heart of darkness," calling communism a "disease," a "form of insanity."[1] But he also detested nuclear weapons and the prospect of nuclear war. Reagan was willing to talk to that communist empire to reduce those weapons and prospects. Indeed, the phrase "peace through strength"—which was Reagan's underlying philosophy and chief tactic for getting to those negotiations—became synonymous with Ronald Reagan. Like one of Reagan's favorite proverbs directed at the Soviets, "trust but verify" (in Russian, *dovorey no provorey*), "peace through strength" defined Reagan's path toward negotiations with the Soviet Union.

And yet, here may be the most interesting aspect of Reagan's desire to negotiate with the Kremlin: these were negotiations that Reagan had hoped for and sought not only with Gorbachev but (much less appreciated) *prior* to Gorbachev, *prior* to Reagan's second presidential term, and even *prior* to Reagan's presidency. Other chapters in this book, including those by Beth A. Fischer and Julian E. Zelizer, consider various influences (foreign and domestic) on Reagan and his willingness to negotiate, as well as influences that Reagan had on the Soviet leadership. This chapter looks earlier, examining Reagan's willingness to negotiate with the Soviets well *before* the advent of Gorbachev in March 1985. That willingness would have startled observers from all sides of the political spectrum in the 1980s. Some believed that Reagan's willingness to negotiate in his second term was the result of an evolution or dramatic change from the first term, a very different Reagan in, say, 1986, than in 1982. It was not. Tactics might have changed, and, most significant, Soviet leaders changed, but Reagan's willingness neither ebbed nor evolved; it remained steady and unchanged across all Soviet leaders, even as it gained a more receptive man (and reformer) in the Kremlin.

In the years since Reagan's presidency, some scholars—including Beth A. Fischer, Paul Lettow, Melvyn Leffler, and David Hoffman—have illuminated that Reagan willingness,[2] especially with Gorbachev as his negotiating partner, and it is more understood today than at the time or even 5 or 10 years ago; yet, it arguably still has not garnered the wider public knowledge or appreciation it deserves, nor has it been rigorously detailed in a single essay. This chapter looks primarily at Reagan's openness to negotiations and overtures to the Soviet leadership in the Brezhnev era; it finishes with shorter sections (given space constraints) on Reagan likewise reaching out to the two Soviet general secretaries who followed Brezhnev—Yuri Andropov and Konstantin Chernenko. The Andropov and Chernenko sections provide a briefer treatment, but they further affirm the thesis of this chapter.

Importantly, Ronald Reagan did not act in a vacuum or alone, and none of this is to detract from the good work of his determined aides and counterparts. Yet, his willingness to broker substantive agreements with the Soviet leadership in his second term was most assuredly not the result of a sudden, altogether new transformation in his thinking. That willingness had much deeper roots.

"Never Broke Off the Dialogue"

In his July 1980 acceptance speech to the Republican National Convention, Ronald Reagan jolted some of the hard-liners in his party when he implored his fellow conservatives: "We must always stand ready to negotiate."[3]

That constant readiness would surprise Mikhail Gorbachev, and the Soviet leader's many advisers who later attested to the fact.[4] "What I particularly appreciated," said Gorbachev, "is that Ronald Reagan never broke off the dialogue."[5] Cold War historian John Lewis Gaddis discerned just that, stating: "Reagan was careful never to rule out negotiations." Gaddis noted that "a careful reading of the public record" shows that Reagan was aiming to improve U.S.-Soviet relations "from the moment he entered the White House."[6]

Not only was Reagan willing to negotiate with the Soviet Union but also he had great confidence in his ability to do so. Biographer Lou Cannon said of Reagan: "He was a very good negotiator."[7] When asked about Reagan's "hidden talents," Cannon unhesitatingly pointed to Reagan's negotiating skills.[8] Don Oberdorfer, Cannon's colleague at the *Washington Post,* agreed. "He wanted to engage," said Oberdorfer, "and he did engage consistently." Oberdorfer noticed that even before Gorbachev came to power, even before Reagan "found [that] smiling face and eyes that he could meet," Reagan was eager to have the likes of Soviet Foreign Minister Andrey Gromyko (a hard-line communist) come to the White House. "And Gromyko was hardly a guy who Reagan could easily associate with."[9]

Princeton's Fred Greenstein, the renowned presidential scholar, called Reagan the "principal negotiator of his presidency." "Reagan was an active and able negotiator," stated Greenstein, who otherwise was sparse in praising Reagan. What is more, "It turns out that the face-to-face persuasion and negotiating capacities of Ronald Reagan were a significant component of that historical transformation." That "historical transformation," said Greenstein, was the "political endgame of the Cold War."[10]

Reagan's staff certainly saw this trait. "For all his distaste for the Soviet system, he nevertheless believed that it could change if subjected to sufficient pressure and his personal negotiating skill," wrote Jack Matlock, U.S. ambassador to the Soviet Union.[11] Attorney General Ed Meese affirmed: "Reagan was a very effective negotiator. His skill as a negotiator is a talent for which he hasn't received due credit."[12] Adviser and Reagan historian Martin Anderson emphasized that Reagan "loved to negotiate."[13]

According to George Shultz, who, by spring 1982, as Reagan's new secretary of state, had already discussed with Reagan a joint approach of "quiet diplomacy" with the Soviets, the president never wavered or hesitated when given the opportunity to dialogue with the Soviets, despite opposition from some close associates in the administration.[14] Robert McFarlane, deputy national security adviser and then national security adviser (1982–1985), ascribed this willingness to a "self-confidence that he was an historic figure and that he was terribly effective in persuasion. . . . He had enormous self-confidence in the ability of a single heroic figure to change history."[15]

As Reagan himself said, in a September 1984 radio address, "I've said from the outset of my public life that a successful U.S. policy toward the Soviet Union must rest on realism, strength, and a willingness to negotiate."[16]

A year after that statement, once he began meeting with Gorbachev, Reagan's commitment to sitting down with his Soviet counterpart was seen in many quarters as paradoxical, an unexpected switch in his anti-Soviet thinking, a sudden change in mind. That was not the case. It had been Reagan's plan all along. And that plan included talking tough and building up the military as precursors to prodding the Soviets to the table. Reagan's willingness to reach out to the Soviets is one of the most consistent, verifiable aspects of his presidency. As we shall see, Reagan was the initiator of negotiations with Soviet leaders; he was consistently proactive. This was true for each Soviet leader from Leonid Brezhnev to Mikhail Gorbachev. All the Soviet leaders merely needed to react to Reagan's many overtures. To his credit, Gorbachev reacted most, offering his own proposals, particularly at Reykjavík. Nonetheless, it was Reagan, as we shall also see, who first approached Gorbachev.

Reagan's tendency and talent for negotiation dates back to his time in Hollywood, where he headed the actors' union, the Screen Actors Guild. It was there that Reagan (then a registered Democrat) began developing this unappreciated talent. It continued into his gubernatorial years, where Reagan several times squared off with the Democratic leadership in the California legislature. Reagan learned that he was good at negotiating, that he enjoyed it. And as he watched presidents and public officials (Republicans and Democrats) in the 1970s sign what he considered flawed détente-based agreements with the Soviets, from Helsinki to the Strategic Arms Limitation Talks (SALT), Reagan was greatly frustrated and felt he could do better. He yearned for the day when he might sit across from a leader like Brezhnev and tell him, "Nyet."[17]

That does not mean Reagan was opposed to any agreement with the Soviets—quite the contrary. For a long time, and especially throughout the 1970s, Reagan believed that U.S. officials were driven by a mentality that any agreement with the Soviet Union was a good agreement. Reagan called this "the treaty trap."[18] He feared America was willing to give up too much, all in the name of an agreement that merely suggested improved relations or a Cold War thaw. Reagan was always willing to walk away, even at Reykjavík, where Gorbachev seemed to offer what Reagan professed to be his "dream": a "world without nuclear weapons." He ordered George Shultz to grab his briefcase: "The meeting is over. Let's go, George, we're leaving."[19] Gorbachev was stunned.

Reagan was willing to let talks collapse, irrespective of Moscow's protests and the American media denouncing him for "blowing" historic reductions. He was as willing to walk away from negotiations as he was willing to pursue them in the first place. That was a sign of an experienced negotiator, of someone who had done it long before the White House.

The Dual Approach—Words as Weapons

Before considering Ronald Reagan's offers to negotiate prior to his presidency and prior to Mikhail Gorbachev's arrival, it is crucial to understand that his often brutal words toward the Soviet Union were not disconnected from his desire to negotiate. To the contrary, Reagan employed a dual approach of blasting the Soviet communist system and building up the U.S. military while also offering to talk. His frank rhetoric always had this deliberate goal in mind. Or vice versa, the entire time that he was reaching out to the Soviets and expressing a willingness to confer with them, he also issued scathing public denunciations, forcefully articulating a clear moral distinction between the democratic American system and the totalitarian Soviet state.

This was not a contradiction in intentions. The two were inextricably linked. In Reagan's mind, peace could only come through strength—and strength took many forms, from conventional weapons to verbal ones. From the bully pulpit of the presidency, words could be weapons; actually, words could be more effective than literal weapons, since words could be readily fired, whereas Reagan certainly did not want to launch missiles.

Reagan stated: "We learned long ago that the Soviets get down to serious negotiations only after they are convinced that their counterparts are determined to stand firm. We knew the least indication of weakened resolve on our part would lead the Soviets to stop the serious bargaining, stall diplomatic progress, and attempt to exploit this perceived weakness."[20] Phrases like "Evil Empire" were not mere shooting from the hip (or lip); they had larger purposes.[21] As Reagan said of the March 1983 Evil Empire speech, "Although a lot of liberal pundits jumped on my speech at Orlando and said it showed I was a rhetorical hip-shooter who was recklessly and unconsciously provoking the Soviets into war, I made the 'Evil Empire' speech and others like it with malice aforethought."[22]

John Lewis Gaddis grasped this dual approach: "Even while indulging in the strident Cold War rhetoric that characterized his first two and half a years in office, Reagan was careful never to rule out negotiations."[23] Gaddis noted that while other administrations had pursued a tactic of negotiating from strength, Reagan "differed from previous presidents" in that "he took the principle literally: once one had achieved strength, one negotiated."

Those who did not comprehend this dual approach later found themselves puzzling over how Reagan supposedly "changed" once he sat across from Gorbachev. *How could the man who called the Soviet Union the "Evil Empire" end up negotiating with it?* They did not understand what Reagan was trying to do or the intent of his harsh language. "I haven't changed my views since I've been here," Reagan could accurately tell reporters in January 1985, the start of what would become a historic year in the Cold War.[24]

Reagan's chief of staff, Don Regan, is among those who understood the dual approach as it related to the big picture. "Reagan's every action in foreign policy," wrote Regan—listing the military buildup, rejection of Soviet adventurism, pursuit of the Strategic Defense Initiative (SDI), and "public rhetoric of confrontation and the private signals of conciliation toward the Soviets"—had been carried out with "the idea of one day sitting down at the negotiating table with the leader of the USSR and banning weapons of mass destruction."[25]

One who keenly internalized the dual approach was Tony Dolan, the chief speechwriter who crafted many of Reagan's strongest speeches, including the Evil Empire address. These speeches involved multiple drafts and constant give-and-take (weekly and sometimes daily) between Dolan and Reagan. Drafts now on file at the Reagan Library show multiple page-long Reagan deletions and insertions.[26]

In 1993, Dolan published an illuminating piece, "Premeditated Prose: Reagan's Evil Empire."[27] He explained how Reagan employed "a new, intensely controversial approach to the Soviet-American dialogue and mutual relations: candor as part of a strategy to exploit the psychological vulnerabilities of totalitarianism and weaken its intransigence."[28] Reagan frequently fired away, boldly predicting that the "evil" Soviet Union was rapidly heading for the "ashheap of history." At the same time, Reagan also exhibited care in choosing when *not* to deploy antagonizing words. "Reagan kept an eye out for statements that he thought unnecessarily provocative or excessive toward the Soviets," wrote Dolan. He noted that Reagan removed a section from a 1981 text Dolan prepared, judging it "too searing" toward Moscow.[29] On September 1, 1983, on the occasion of the scandalous Soviet shoot-down of the Korean passenger airliner KAL 007, Reagan declined portions of a draft he thought "breathed far too much fire at the Soviets." On another occasion, in 1984, Reagan called Dolan to excise sentences he believed might hinder prospects for a summit. Dolan explained:

> In addition to keeping a careful watch on the tone of his anticommunist formulations, Reagan insisted that his major anti-communist addresses make clear his desire for a new relationship with the Soviets, and in most of those same speeches, he made or repeated an unprecedented number of proposals for arms control and bilateral exchanges. . . . So Reagan not only paid close attention to his anti-Soviet rhetoric, he insisted that it be closely intertwined with diplomatic initiatives.
>
> All this had two results that struck some of his critics as startling ironies of the postwar era. First, the president who issued the strongest denunciations of the Soviets also kept up the steadiest stream of proposals to them for arms reductions, intergovernmental meetings, and people-to-people exchanges. But what his critics saw as merely ironies, Reagan viewed as the logical outcome of a dual strategy that combined candor and diplomacy, conciliation and confrontation. . . . His anticommunist statements were not blundered into but were deliberate and, along with his diplomatic proposals, led—as Reagan had argued explicitly on many occasions that they would—to Cold War breakthroughs.[30]

Reagan himself later confirmed: "Once we'd agreed to hold a summit, I made a conscious decision to tone down my rhetoric to avoid goading Gorbachev with remarks about the 'evil empire.'"[31]

We will see this Reagan dual approach frequently in the chronological treatment that follows.

Willingness to Negotiate: Prepresidency

The Soviets themselves witnessed an early indication of Ronald Reagan's willingness to negotiate in a brief but telling moment in June 1973. At the invitation of President Richard Nixon, Soviet leader Leonid Brezhnev visited the United States. Among his stops, he stayed as a guest in Nixon's private home in California. Nixon arranged a gala reception to which the "flower of California 'high society' had been invited," as Andrey Gromyko remembered it. The California governor, Ronald Reagan, was among the guests. There was a long queue waiting in line to briefly shake hands with the Soviet delegation, which featured Brezhnev, Gromyko, and Anatoly Dobrynin, ambassador to the United States. These were precisely the men that Reagan often said were hell-bent on "world domination." Nonetheless, Reagan cordially shook hands and quickly said to the three men: "Representatives of our two countries should meet each other."[32]

At this point, still long before his presidency, Reagan had already spent 20 years lambasting the Soviet Union as a diabolical slave state. Nonetheless, his choice of words to the Soviet leadership at that brief moment focused not on Soviet criminality and misdeeds, but on dialogue. That short encounter became a symbol of what was to come once Reagan arrived at the White House.

Likewise, another interesting aspect of this encounter was Gromyko's reaction. The communist ideologue was struck that Reagan had "made plain his warm feelings toward us."[33] It was the same warm feeling that Gromyko's comrades would sense throughout the 1980s, as Reagan charmed them in private meetings, albeit eviscerating their system in public statements.

Reagan was elected governor in 1966. Then and prior, he argued that the key to peace was a strong defense, which offered both preparation against an aggressor and the ability to negotiate peace. In the 1960s and 1970s, he made innumerable statements calling for increased defense spending for precisely such purposes.[34] "While we work for peace among men of good will," said Reagan in July 1968, "we must rebuild and maintain our strength; building peace will take time and strength is the currency which can buy that time."[35] In an October 1972 statement, he said: "Let me make it perfectly clear that along with a willingness to negotiate, America can best protect the peace by maintaining a realistic and credible ability to defend itself should the need occur."[36]

Such Reagan quotes from this period are too numerous to list here.[37] One of the better testimonies was a May 1976 interview with *U.S. News & World Report.* Said Reagan:

> I think we have to make darn sure that we improve our military position to the point that we're not second best [to the Soviet Union], so that we can be truly dealing for peace through strength. . . . If the U.S. would do this and the Soviets see this demonstration of will, they might say: "Oh, wait a minute. If we're going to keep up an arms race, this is going to go on forever and we can't catch them or match them." Then I think you could have legitimate reduction of arms.[38]

Reagan maintained that a buildup in military strength would not only decrease the likelihood of war but also increase the likelihood of bringing the Soviets to the table and thereby achieving arms reductions. America had to *build up* before both superpowers could *build down*.[39]

During the 1980 presidential campaign, Reagan said this constantly. One of his many articulations was a 1980 interview with the Associated Press:

> I don't think we should sit at the table the same way we have in the past. We have been unilaterally disarming at the same time we're negotiating supposed arms limitation with the other fellow, where all he has to do is sit there and not give up anything and his superiority increases. He will be far more inclined to negotiate in good faith if he knows that the United States is engaged in building up its military.[40]

During the campaign, Reagan recommended that President Jimmy Carter use the "trump card" of threatening an arms race if the Soviet Union did not agree to acceptable limits on nuclear arms. Carter had "one trump card that has never been used," averred Reagan. "We know and the Soviet Union knows that if there is to be an arms race, they can't even get in the same ballpark as us." If the Soviets "have to compete with us, I'm sure they'll come running to the table and say 'wait a minute,' because they know they can't."[41] He asserted flatly: "The Soviet Union cannot possibly match us in an arms race."[42]

While identical Reagan quotes from the period could be cited over and over,[43] particularly notable was a two-hour June 1980 interview Reagan did with *Washington Post* editors and reporters, including Lou Cannon. In his write-up of the interview, Cannon focused on what he found most remarkable: "Ronald Reagan said yesterday that a rapid U.S. arms build-up would be good for the United States because it would strain the defense-burdened Soviet economy and force the Soviets to the arms control bargaining table."[44] Reagan said: "The very fact that we would start [a rapid arms buildup] would serve a notice on the Soviet Union. I think there's every indication and every reason to believe that the Soviet Union cannot increase its production of arms. . . . They've diverted so much to the military that they can't provide for the consumer needs."[45]

Cannon today recalls this interview, realizing the magnitude of what Reagan said. In an oral history testimony at the University of Virginia, Cannon recounted the moment, with added insight:

> We asked him if he feared an arms race with the Soviet Union. He replied that he welcomed an arms race because he was convinced the Soviets couldn't compete with us. Reagan believed that showing we were serious about a build-up would lead to negotiations with the Soviet Union because their economy could not support an arms race. Reagan was right. Of course, one never knows what the road not traveled might have held. Still, it seems that the fact that the United States was intent on technological competition with the Soviets was certainly a factor influencing a wise leader like Gorbachev in deciding to negotiate a lower level of armaments. . . .
>
> Many people were surprised by the foreign policy developments and the fact that you finally wound up with Reagan and Gorbachev strolling through Red Square proclaiming a new era. I wasn't surprised with that because I knew Reagan envisioned this sort of rapprochement.[46]

So consistent was this theme in 1980 that Cannon noted in his *Post* write-up that it had "become a familiar message from the former California governor as he tours the East, meeting publishers and politicians."[47]

Among those occasions was a speech Reagan delivered in Chicago on August 18, 1980, his second foreign-policy speech in Chicago that year. As he had since his days making speeches to GE plants as a General Electric spokesman in the 1950s and 1960s, Reagan wrote these speeches himself—handwritten drafts of which were found after his presidency by Kiron K. Skinner.[48] Reagan titled the speech simply "Peace." He made it clear that a strategy for peace required both strength and a constant willingness to negotiate:

> Arms control negotiation can often help to improve stability but not when (like with détente) the negotiations are one-sided. And they obviously have been one-sided and will continue to be so if we lack steadiness and determination in keeping up our defenses.

> I think continued negotiation with the Soviet [Union] is essential. We need never be afraid to negotiate as long as we keep our long term objectives (the pursuit of peace for one) clearly in mind and don't seek agreements just for the sake of having an agreement. It is important, also, that the Soviets know we are going about the business of building up our defense capability pending an agreement by both sides to limit various kinds of weapons.[49]

The United States, insisted Reagan, needed to muster the will and determination to build up its forces. Only then might the Kremlin agree to a course of genuine arms limitation.

Pursuing Negotiations: The First Term and the First Steps

As president, Reagan remained committed to this peace-through-strength philosophy and strategy, literally from day one. "We will maintain sufficient strength to prevail if need be," stated Reagan in his January 20, 1981, Inaugural Address, which he wrote himself, "knowing that if we do so we have the best chance of never having to use that strength."[50]

Once in the White House, Reagan wasted no time expressing his willingness to negotiate. In his first press conference on January 29, 1981, he said the United States "should start negotiating on the basis of trying to effect an actual reduction in the numbers of nuclear weapons." Reagan was calling for not merely a limitation in the growth of arms (which Presidents Nixon, Ford, and Carter had pursued) but actual arms reductions. And yet, in this memorable first press conference, Reagan also unhesitatingly blasted the Soviets, declaring that "the only morality" the Soviet leadership recognized "is what will further their cause, meaning they reserve unto themselves the right to commit any crime, to lie, to cheat."[51] Here we see the dual approach from the very beginning of Reagan's term.

Reporters from *Time* magazine followed up with Reagan in an interview at the White House. They noticed the dual approach. "Reagan sent some blunt signals to Moscow," reported *Time*. "He repeated his harsh characterization of Soviet leaders, but also said he would be willing to negotiate a new treaty on limiting strategic arms 'any time that they want to sit down and discuss a legitimate reduction of nuclear weapons.'"[52]

Soon thereafter, in a March interview, CBS News anchor Walter Cronkite asked Reagan whether his views seemed too "hard line toward the Soviet

Union." Cronkite noted that "there are some who . . . feel that you might have overdone the rhetoric a little bit in laying into the Soviet leadership as being liars and thieves, et cetera." Reagan reiterated to Cronkite that he was "willing for our people to go in to negotiate" an "actual reduction in the numbers of nuclear weapons" at "any time" the Soviets were willing.[53]

Reagan's words were not mere rhetoric. Formal gestures were soon exchanged between Reagan and the Soviet leadership, specifically General Secretary Brezhnev, a long-delayed follow-up of sorts to Reagan's words to Brezhnev in California in 1973. We can see these exchanges today in letters declassified in 1999–2000, available at the Reagan Library. They offer a revealing behind-the-scenes look.

As if he were responding to Reagan's statements to the American media, Brezhnev sent a letter to the new president on March 6, 1981. The letter offered dialogue and discussion of actual reductions in strategic weapons. The letter also had real problems, revealing irreconcilable differences in the thinking of the two leaderships. For one, it demanded no U.S. deployment of INFs in Western Europe, citing Pershing II missiles by name, even as Soviet INFs (SS-20s) already existed in Eastern Europe (more on this later in the chapter). Brezhnev also insisted there was a "strategic military equilibrium" between the two powers, which Reagan believed was untrue. Brezhnev defended an unacceptable situation in Afghanistan, a country the Red Army had brutally invaded. Worse, in Reagan's mind, the general secretary's letter pushed for broad U.S. acceptance of the détente status quo, meaning continued Soviet domination of Eastern Europe.[54]

Nonetheless, Reagan was eager to reply to Brezhnev's letter. His team slowly contemplated a response—much slower than Reagan preferred. And then, on March 30, 1981, came a literal life-or-death development when Reagan was shot by a would-be assassin. Did this halt progress? Not for long. The shooting heightened Reagan's urgency. He responded by personally seizing the initiative, which was now much more personal; it was even spiritual, as Reagan was filled with a sense of Divine Providence. "As I sat in the sun-filled White House solarium in robe and pajamas that spring . . . I wondered how to get the process started," said Reagan of the negotiating process. "Perhaps having come so close to death made me feel I should do whatever I could in the years God had given me to reduce the threat of nuclear war; perhaps there was a reason I had been spared."[55]

The shooting thus resolved the lingering issue of how to respond to Brezhnev. The Reagan administration had been kicking around a draft written by Secretary of State Al Haig and the State Department, which was amended, slashed, and argued over by State, the White House, and the National Security Council (NSC).[56] It was the classic bureaucratic rigmarole. The matter was finally settled when Reagan, literally given a new lease on life, insisted on writing the letter himself in his own pen and language. A week after leaving the hospital, he pulled out his trademark yellow-pad paper. Haig and State were reluctant to have Reagan draft the response, thinking the "professionals" should compose such things. Reagan told Haig he intended "to send a personal letter to Brezhnev aimed at reaching him as a human being."

Today, scholars will be confused to find two different Reagan handwritten letters on file at the Reagan Library. Reagan opted for his second draft, which was sent on April 24, 1981.

The first 10 paragraphs of the letter lacked surprise, as Reagan fairly succinctly defended America's record as a peacemaker. Lines he used were very similar to those in his writings in the 1970s and even his General Electric days in the 1950s and 1960s. In the 11th and final paragraph, however, came a significant gesture from Reagan: "It is in this spirit, in the spirit of helping the people of both of our nations, that I have lifted the grain embargo. Perhaps this decision will contribute to creating the circumstances which will lead to the meaningful and constructive dialogue which will assist us in fulfilling our joint obligation to find lasting peace."

This was a real token of peace (or at least Reagan so hoped) reflecting a surefire enthusiasm to begin talking. But the olive branch seemed ineffective. On May 25, the president received what he described as an "icy reply" from Brezhnev, with the general secretary saying he was against making immediate plans for a summit. The letter "repudiated everything I'd said about the Soviet Union," said Reagan, "blamed the United States for starting and perpetuating the Cold War, and then said we had no business telling the Soviets what they could or could not do anywhere in the world. So much for my first attempt at personal diplomacy."[57] The Soviet letter attacked U.S. conduct after World War II and essentially blamed post–World War II tensions on U.S. behavior. Brezhnev's reply made no mention whatsoever of Reagan lifting the grain embargo.[58]

Over the next few months, several other "chilly" letters (Reagan's word) were exchanged.[59] "Chilly" is a polite description for Brezhnev's seven-page letter of October 15, 1981.[60] Nonetheless, Reagan continued to move ahead with more letters, including September 22 and November 18 dispatches.[61] Among them, Reagan so butchered a November 16 draft of the November 18 letter—initially drafted by his national security adviser, Richard V. Allen—that he handwrote an apology to Allen: "Dick—I felt it should be shortened so forgive my slashing. Also I tried to give it something of the tone of my first letter. Ron."[62]

June to November 1981

Reagan's pursuit of peace (via strength) was evident in his public statements. "I have to believe that our greatest goal must be peace," he said in a June 16, 1981, press conference, "and I also happen to believe that that will come through our maintaining enough strength that we can keep the peace."[63] In an October 19, 1981, speech at Yorktown, Reagan added: "Military inferiority does not avoid a conflict, it only invites one and then ensures defeat. . . . We're rebuilding our defenses so that our sons and daughters never need be sent to war."[64]

A major manifestation of Reagan's ongoing commitment in the face of "icy" responses from Brezhnev was his November 18, 1981, address at the National Press Club, which he wrote mainly himself.[65] The speech was broadcast live via Worldnet, a worldwide satellite system developed by the director of the U.S. Information Agency (USIA), Charles Wick, a close Reagan friend. Reagan could rightly say it had been "the most important speech on foreign policy I'd ever made."[66]

Reagan hoped the speech would be sincerely received.[67] He called for the elimination of all INF weapons in Europe (current Soviet missiles and U.S. missiles to be built and deployed), a proposal known as the "zero-zero" option. He proposed abolition of the entire class of INF missiles by both the United States and the Soviet Union. In addition, Reagan invited the Soviet Union to enter new negotiations aimed at reducing mutual stockpiles of long-range strategic nuclear weapons to equal and verifiable levels. He therein proposed that, instead of referring to the next round of negotiations as SALT, for Strategic Arms *Limitation* Talks, they instead adopt a "more positive approach" and call them "START: "Strategic Arms *Reduction* Talks." That change was significant. It signaled that Reagan wanted to actually *reduce* nuclear arsenals, not merely *limit* their growth, as previous administrations had sought. He also suggested the two sides begin negotiations to bring down conventional forces in Europe.

This meant, said Reagan later, understanding the irony in his strategy, that the journey leading me to arms reduction . . . had to begin with an *increase* of arms. . . . It was obvious that if we were ever going to get anywhere with the Russians in persuading them to reduce armaments, we had to bargain with them from *strength*, not weakness. If you were going to approach the Russians with a dove of peace in one hand, you had to have a sword in the other.[68]

Peace via strength.

The speech was very well received, including by the press. Laurence Barrett of *Time* credited Reagan: "He was firm and confident without being tendentious. He spoke to posterity as well as contemporaries." The *New York Times* and *Washington Post* glowed in lead editorials the next day. "At long last," cheered the *Times* (albeit with a backhanded compliment), "President Reagan has made a sound and shrewd foreign policy speech." The *Post* found it "an awfully good speech. . . . He was well prepared, forceful and he made a lot of sense. Serious people in this country, in Europe and in the Soviet Union ought to study his message."[69]

One European who was impressed, having watched the speech along with an estimated 200 million viewers worldwide, was West German Chancellor Helmut Schmidt, who (until then) Reagan had found difficult and disrespectful. He called to tell Reagan that he was meeting with Brezhnev in a few days. Was there anything Reagan would like him to bring up with the general secretary? Yes, Reagan told Schmidt, "Tell him I really mean it about the SS-20s."[70]

Notably, the speech was also a quiet indicator of Reagan's greatly unappreciated role as a balancer among competing factions within his administration. Consider that on the question of INFs, he had received multiple layers of advice from staff. Behind the scenes, there was a back-channel contest among the principals over the specifics of the START proposal. Secretary of Defense Cap Weinberger lobbied in favor of a draft authored by Richard Perle. Haig relied on Judge Bill Clark, his deputy at State, while Clark worked to get favorable consideration of a version crafted by Lawrence Eagleburger. Meanwhile, a third alternative was composed by NSC staffer Dennis Blair. Reagan considered all before deciding that State's approach was best.[71]

December 1981 through May 1982

After the November 18 address, additional letters were initiated between Reagan and the Soviet leadership.[72] In December and January 1981, five letters were exchanged, which included some fireworks regarding Poland, where on December 13, 1981, martial law had been imposed by the communist government under orders from Moscow.[73] In the words of Richard Pipes, the chief NSC expert on Poland, Reagan was "livid," filled with a "mounting fury at the communists" for their actions in Poland.[74] It is quite telling that Reagan did not give up his desire for negotiations even with the outrage of martial law.

Five months later, on May 9, 1982, Reagan kept up the momentum with another major foreign-policy speech, this time at his alma mater, Eureka College. Reagan was critical of the Soviets: "So far, the Soviet Union has used arms control negotiations primarily as an instrument to restrict U.S. defense programs and, in conjunction with their own arms buildup, a means to enhance Soviet power and prestige." He charged: "Unfortunately, for some time suspicions have grown that the Soviet Union has not been living up to its obligations under existing arms control treaties."[75] This, Reagan told his audience, was all the more reason why the United States "must" establish firm criteria for arms control, including seeking agreements that were verifiable, equitable, and militarily significant. Otherwise, "agreements that provide only the appearance of arms control breed dangerous illusions."[76]

Reagan reminded his Eureka friends that in November he had committed the United States to seek "significant" reductions in nuclear and conventional forces. He gave an update on the progress of U.S. efforts: in Geneva, his team had since proposed limits on American and Soviet INFs, including the complete elimination of "the most threatening systems." In Vienna, his team was busy negotiating reductions in conventional forces. In the 40-nation Committee on Disarmament, the United States was seeking a total ban on chemical weapons.

If that was not enough, Reagan detailed his multiphase approach for START. He reported: "I have written to President Brezhnev and directed Secretary Haig to approach the Soviet government concerning the initiation of formal negotiations on the reduction of strategic nuclear arms, START, at the earliest opportunity. We hope negotiations will begin by the end of June."[77]

Reagan finished with a flurry of first-person references intended to demonstrate his willingness and apparently placing the ball in the Soviet court:

We will negotiate seriously, in good faith, and carefully consider all proposals made by the Soviet Union. If they approach these negotiations in the
same spirit, I'm confident that together we can achieve an agreement of enduring value that reduces the number of nuclear weapons, halts the growth
in strategic forces, and opens the way to even more far-reaching steps in the
future. . . .

The fifth and final point I propose for East-West relations is dialogue. I've always believed that people's problems can be solved when
people talk to each other instead of about each other. And I've already
expressed my own desire to meet with President Brezhnev in New York
next month. . . .

I'll tell him that his government and his people have nothing to fear from
the United States. . . .

And I'll ask President Brezhnev why our two nations can't produce mutual restraint. . . .

Why can't we reduce the number of horrendous weapons?[78]

The line "I've always believed that people's problems can be solved when people
talk to each other instead of about each other" was penciled into the speech by
Reagan. It was not part of the speechwriter's initial draft.[79]

This was Reagan's second major speech on arms reductions within a six-
month period, with more statements to come.[80] At the same time, Reagan continued to speak frankly regarding Soviet repression. Recounting this period
in his memoirs, he wrote:

> In the spring of 1982, in a speech at a Eureka College reunion marking the
> fiftieth anniversary of my graduating class, I renewed my invitation to the
> Soviets to initiate the START (Strategic Arms Reduction Talks). . . . At
> the same time, in speeches at the United Nations and other places, I made
> it a point to speak with frankness on what I thought of Soviet expansionism.
> I wanted to remind Leonid Brezhnev that we knew what the Soviets were
> up to and that we weren't going to stand by and do nothing while they sought
> world domination; I also tried to send out a signal that the United States
> intended to support people fighting for their freedom against Communism
> wherever they were. . . . I felt it was time to speak the truth, not platitudes,
> even though a lot of liberals and some members of the State Department's
> Striped Pants Set sometimes didn't like my choice of words.[81]

Amid these spring 1982 remarks, Reagan had sent another letter. On May 7,
two days before the Eureka speech, he signed a letter to be delivered to Brezhnev
in which he recommended a resumption of arms-control talks in Geneva be-

fore the end of June.[82] The timing was no doubt intended to coincide with the sentiments in the Eureka speech.

Brezhnev responded with a May 20 letter. In his memoirs, Reagan said Brezhnev's response "was not cordial." That was an understatement. In June 2000, a copy of Brezhnev's five-page, double-spaced letter, marked up by Reagan's personal annotations, was declassified. In eight different spots in the right-hand margin, Reagan handwrote objections to Brezhnev's statements. Some of these were snide. In one spot, he wrote, "He has to be kidding." In another, where the Soviet leader purported to speak on behalf of the "Soviet people," Reagan penciled the comment: "How will they know? They haven't been told the truth for years." At the end of the letter, at Brezhnev's signature, Reagan wrote: "He's a barrel of laughs."[83] Nonetheless, as Reagan conceded, Brezhnev did agree to new talks in the letter. There was hope.

And that hope was evident in various statements and negotiations in the summer,[84] as the president and his diplomats continued to huddle. To cite just one example, veteran diplomat Eugene Rostow underscored an incident from July 1982. Rostow was in Geneva to assess INF negotiations. He met with Ambassador Paul Nitze, who had been engaged in talks with his counterpart, Ambassador Yuli Kvitsinski. The two ambassadors sketched an approach for presentation to their governments. Rostow provided some revisions. The revising went back and forth. The final plan became known as the "walk-in-the-woods" proposal, and was presented to each government. The Soviet government rejected it with "great vehemence," as Rostow put it, while the United States (President Reagan) "did nothing of the sort."[85]

After a moment of potential promise, it was another setback. Or was it? Reagan insisted that the approach be further discussed and channels remain opened. Rostow recalled Reagan's role in crafting amendments to the proposal: "The most important was suggested by President Reagan himself at the first White House meeting on the proposal in order to correct a political flaw which neither Nitze nor I had spotted." Rostow and Nitze pressed ahead again. "Our NATO [North Atlantic Treaty Organization] allies were briefed on the episode," recalled Rostow, "and warmly approved President Reagan's response."[86]

"If I Could Ever Get in a Room Alone"

Progress remained slow and then suddenly halted when Leonid Brezhnev died in November 1982. After all the initial breaking of the ice, the letters back and forth, the debate and jabs and ebb and flow, Ronald Reagan's steady movement toward that coveted one-on-one with Brezhnev was moribund. Reagan felt that "if I could ever get in a room alone with one of the top Soviet leaders, there was a chance the two of us could make some progress in easing tensions between our two countries. I have always placed a lot of faith in the simple power of human contact in solving problems."

With Brezhnev's death, there was for the first time in almost two decades a new leader in the Kremlin, former KGB head Yuri Andropov. "I didn't expect him to be any less of a doctrinaire Communist than Brezhnev," wrote Reagan later, "but at least there was a clean slate." He would try anyway: "I decided to experiment with some personal diplomacy using back channels to the Kremlin, outside the spotlight of publicity."[87]

Then came a major breakthrough. On February 15, 1983, Reagan finally got himself a one-on-one. He and Soviet ambassador Anatoly Dobrynin met at the White House. Secretary of State George Shultz later explained how the meeting came about. He had told Reagan: "I will be meeting with Dobrynin again late Tuesday afternoon. What would you think about my bringing Dobrynin over to the White House for a private chat?" Reagan responded: "Great. We have to keep this secret. I don't intend to engage in a detailed exchange with Dobrynin, but I do intend to tell him that if Andropov is willing to do business, so am I." Shultz recorded what happened next:

> Rather than the brief meeting I expected, the president talked with us for almost two hours. He clearly had thought about the meeting a great deal. Ronald Reagan is the master of the personal encounter, and he impressively engaged Dobrynin on all the issues and argued our positions effectively on START, on INF, and on Afghanistan and Poland. He spoke with genuine feeling and eloquence on the subject of human rights, divided families, Soviet Jewry, and refuseniks. He also talked with sincere intensity about the Pentecostals, a small group of Christians who had taken refuge in our embassy in Moscow almost five years earlier. The Pentecostals wanted to pursue their religion, and they wanted to emigrate from the Soviet Union. . . . "If you can do something about the Pentecostals or another human rights issue," Reagan told Dobrynin, "we will simply be delighted and will not embarrass you by undue publicity, by claims of credit for ourselves, or by 'crowing.'"
>
> Afterward, Dobrynin and I went back to State and continued until almost 8:00 PM. Before he left, Dobrynin said to me, "We should handle the 'special subject' [the Pentecostals] privately." I agreed.[88]

Dobrynin later remarked on Reagan's enthusiasm and sense of command. "It was evident from Shultz's behavior during our White House conversation and long afterward that Reagan was the real boss, and the secretary of state carried out his instructions," the Soviet ambassador recorded. "Shultz hardly intervened in the conversation and ostensibly agreed with Reagan throughout. I even had the impression, perhaps an erroneous one, that the secretary of state was somewhat afraid of the president."[89]

As Dobrynin recalled, the president urged that the delegations "keep on working" to find agreement on arms, and "succinctly" told the ambassador: "I should like to repeat the conclusion that, like Andropov, I favor good relations between our countries. I want to remove the threat of war in our relations. . . . Please communicate this to the general secretary and the whole Soviet leadership."[90] Reagan wanted Andropov's assistance in removing the threat of war.

Dobrynin followed through on Reagan's various requests. In his immediate report to Moscow, he recommended that "as a first step" the Soviet government should "clear up the problem" of the Pentecostals. He later said that the resolution of this "small gesture" requested by Reagan "was to figure with unusual symbolism in the turn in our relations."[91] Indeed, the Pentecostals were released, and Reagan did not "crow" about it. As Shultz later pointed out, Reagan "didn't say a word."[92]

Reagan's silence is impressive in light of the political pressures he faced at the time. It was 1983, the year before the presidential election. The nuclear-freeze movement was eviscerating Reagan, calling him a nuclear warmonger and worse. Vice President Bush was in Europe arguing in favor of Reagan's Pershing II deployment, where he met mass protests. Reagan was being portrayed around the globe as a crude militarist bent on confrontation and war. The temptation for Reagan to score political points from this meeting must have been immense.

According to Shultz, the situation showed two important things to the Soviet leadership: first, Ronald Reagan keeps his word. This was vital. Reagan learned long ago that a good negotiator bargains in good faith. Second, it showed he really cared about human rights.[93] Thus, almost two years before Mikhail Gorbachev came to power, Soviet officials learned they could work with Reagan as an honest broker.

More still, the meeting was revealing of Reagan in another notable way: Reagan had been nearly alone in favoring the meeting with Dobrynin. Shultz noted that other than himself, Reagan, and Michael Deaver, the president's entire entourage opposed the meeting.[94] "They didn't want him to meet with him [Dobrynin]," remembered Shultz. "But he just brushed them off and said bring him in."[95] Reagan had been pushing and squeezing the Soviets for two years, and now he jumped at an opportunity.

Reagan and Yuri Andropov

One week after the Dobrynin meeting, Reagan twice (February 22 and 23) publicly expressed his desire to meet with Andropov. On February 22, he said that both he and Vice President Bush had expressed "willingness to meet with Mr. Andropov" at "anytime, anyplace."[96]

The conventional view today is that if Andropov had lived throughout Reagan's second term, in lieu of Gorbachev, the Cold War may not have ended, certainly not as peacefully. That is a reasonable assertion that I endorse, and we should not (in retrospect) project undue promise upon a Reagan-Andropov partnership that might have surfaced had the hard-line former KGB head lived. That said, there is unmistakable evidence of significant steps initiated by Reagan with Andropov prior to Gorbachev—unexpected, unreported strides worthy of our attention, given that they reflect Reagan's continued commitment. This, too, is shown in the many confidential Reagan-Andropov letters declassified after the Reagan presidency.

The Reagan-Andropov efforts seemed to bear some fruit in the summer of 1983, only months after Reagan's Evil Empire and SDI speeches in March. Reagan would not see that as a coincidence, interpreting the Soviet response as vindication of his dual approach. The Reagan-Andropov letters increased in length as they went on, particularly Reagan's last letter. There were at least six letters exchanged over 10 weeks in mid-1983, approximating (if not exceeding) the frequency of letters initially exchanged between Reagan and Gorbachev.

Reagan got it going. He wrote the first letter, dated June 17, 1983, congratulating the ex-KGB head on his selection as general secretary, with Reagan no doubt holding his nose. On June 22, Andropov thanked Reagan. A substantive letter from Reagan offering dialogue, written in his own hand, followed on July 11. Andropov's next letter followed on August 4. Another from Reagan came on August 24. Andropov sent another on August 27. While these letters were not earth-shattering, none were irrelevant or unimportant; all revealed an undeniable degree of progress and (at the least) stepped-up interest and communication by both sides.[97]

Imagine, here were the two hardest of hard-liners, devout communist and anti-communist, rapidly making commendable progress (in private) that would have stunned the public. This was the behind-the-scenes actions the world did not see—on top of further striking moves that cannot be addressed in the limited space of this chapter.[98] And they were not the end, as Reagan followed up with still more significant overtures, even in the wake of the Soviet shoot-down of KAL 007 on September 1, 1983. There again, Reagan was enraged at Soviet behavior but not enough to extinguish his desire to talk.

That desire was expressed in several public overtures by Reagan in the months that followed, including a widely reported October 3, 1983, speech at the Heritage Foundation; a November 23, 1983, White House statement on Soviet withdrawal from INF negotiations; and an extremely important January 16, 1984, East Room statement on U.S.-Soviet relations and arms negotiations, which has been underscored at length in important works by Beth A. Fischer.[99]

Nothing could quell Reagan's desire to negotiate. Not even Andropov's death in February 1984.

The Chernenko Period

Even with the demise of Yuri Andropov, Reagan still remained "even more anxious to get a top Soviet leader in a room alone."[100] Because of space constraints, this chapter cannot do justice to the equally prolific Konstantin Chernenko period that followed Andropov. Here is a short summary of the activity.

The moment that Chernenko took over the Soviet leadership, Reagan immediately sent a letter hand-delivered by Vice President Bush on February 11, the occasion of Andropov's funeral. Chernenko replied on February 23.[101] A substantive Reagan letter was sent March 6, with Chernenko replying in a seven-page letter on March 19. (In between, Reagan dispatched U.S. official Brent Scowcroft to talk to the general secretary while in Moscow.) Reagan was impressed by the March 19 letter, writing at the top this instruction to his advisers: "I think this calls for a very well thought out reply and not just a routine acknowledgment that leaves the status quo as is. RR."[102] On April 16, Reagan sent a seven-page, single-spaced letter with a personal handwritten P.S. at the end. He shared his "pledge" to a "lasting reduction of tensions between us."[103] This jump-started the process. Between June 6 and July 31, 1984, Reagan and Chernenko exchanged seven letters in seven weeks, more than Reagan-Andropov and more than Reagan-Gorbachev at *any point*.[104] To repeat: even more than Reagan and Gorbachev.

And then came still more goodwill, more formal offers, and more meetings, ranging from a key Reagan one-on-one with Soviet foreign minister Gromyko on September 28, 1984, in the Oval Office—which Reagan excitedly referred to in his diary as "the big day"[105]—to at least five more letters exchanged between Reagan and Chernenko in the six weeks after the November 1984 election.[106]

"They Keep Dying"

Unfortunately, the dialogue with Chernenko, like Andropov, like Brezhnev, was abruptly ended by the general secretary's death. Once again, mortality stood in the way. Reagan famously quipped that he would be happy to sit down with Soviet leaders if they would "quit dying on me." There was ironic truth to that. From 1917 to 1982, the Soviet Union had mainly four leaders: Lenin, Stalin, Khrushchev, and Brezhnev. Between 1982 and 1985, it had four leaders in three years.

Reagan's deadly misfortune began with Brezhnev. He had tried to get a meeting on the basis of Brezhnev's coming to New York for a United Nations disarmament session. Reagan believed that Brezhnev's health may have factored in the lack of response.[107] But Reagan kept trying. And his persistence finally paid off in the form of the vibrant and vital Mikhail Gorbachev. Gorbachev, as Reagan noted, was a "different type of Soviet leader," not least because he did not die.

On the day of Chernenko's funeral, Reagan again wasted no time. He sent Vice President Bush to Moscow not only to attend another grim communist funeral but also to propose a summit with Gorbachev. Here, too, the previous general secretary literally had not yet been buried, and Reagan was already goading his replacement.

• • •

Once Mikhail Gorbachev took the reins on March 11, 1985, Reagan still encountered frustration. There were stops and starts that tested his patience.[108] In an April 1, 1985, interview with the *Washington Post*, Reagan said that the killing of a U.S. soldier by Soviet troops in East Germany a week earlier had not discouraged him from a summit with Gorbachev: "I want to meet him even more . . . to sit down and look someone in the eye and talk to him about what we can do to make sure nothing of this kind ever happens again."[109] Moreover, Gorbachev took aggressive actions in places like Afghanistan, where he was committed to initially trying to win the Soviet war, a commitment that gravely concerned and even outraged Reagan—an outrage that Reagan expressed directly to Gorbachev.[110] This was hardly the only place or episode where Gorbachev pursued policies that Reagan firmly rejected.

It was a credit to both Reagan's willingness and Gorbachev's receptivity that the two set aside some serious differences and came to the table proposing major cuts in nuclear weapons. Working with their dedicated staffs, the two men changed history together.

It was ironic that on January 9, 1985, his first press conference of the year, three months before Gorbachev came to power, Reagan had estimated: "It's also my hope that as 1985 unfolds, this year will emerge as one of dialogue and negotiations, a year that leads to better relations between the United States and the Soviet Union." Commenting on Secretary of State Shultz's Geneva discussions with Gromyko, Reagan said that U.S. objectives would be not merely the reduction of nuclear arms but the "ultimate goal" of a "complete elimination of nuclear weapons."[111]

Surely, most observers, including the press contingent, chuckled at the president's idealism or dismissed it as mere rhetoric. Even Reagan's most stalwart conservative supporters must have thought him naive. Yet, this was precisely what Reagan and Gorbachev would move toward in that historic year, a road that ran from Geneva in November 1985 to Reykjavík in October 1986 to summits in Washington in December 1987 and Moscow in May–June 1988. The two negotiating partners and their lieutenants embarked on a path of dizzying accomplishments that reduced the chances of nuclear war more quickly and dramatically than any three years in history. They created a safer world, one absent of the multiple thousands of nuclear weapons once aimed at one another and their allies. There had been enough nuclear weapons in both sides' arsenals to kill billions of people, whether directly through a first strike or through the aftereffects. The vast presence of so many truly deadly, destructive weapons—literally the most powerful weapons in the history of humanity—had increased the chances of mishaps or deliberate launch by mad or malicious military commanders or leaders. Dramatically reducing the number of weapons dramatically reduced the likelihood of doomsday.

It was a nuclear world transformed, a world transformed, a world substantially better, a world minus thousands of devastating weapons that once threatened its existence. It is a world that no longer faces the same nuclear nightmare it once dreaded. And it is a world that Ronald Reagan wanted to negotiate all along. That is a global legacy and impact, ultimately negotiated by both Ronald Reagan and Mikhail Gorbachev, that people worldwide would be well served to remember.

9

Building Up and Seeking Peace

President Reagan's Cold War Legacy

BETH A. FISCHER

We now live in a world in which the threat of a superpower nuclear war seems remote, if not downright preposterous. For many, nuclear weapons are little more than a remnant of another era, serving little real purpose in deterring contemporary threats to American security. In the post–Cold War world, both Republicans and Democrats have sought to reduce superpower nuclear arsenals. It is hard to remember an age when such reductions seemed dangerously destabilizing.

What many forget is that President Ronald Reagan ushered in this age of nuclear disarmament. Reagan's predecessors had—from time to time—sought to reduce the rate at which superpower arsenals could grow, but none of them believed nuclear weapons should be reduced, much less abolished. Since the 1950s, the conventional view had been that nuclear weapons were necessary to deter the Soviet Union from attacking the West. It was only the threat of nuclear annihilation that prevented Moscow from invading, it was believed. President Reagan rejected this view, arguing instead that true security could only be achieved once nuclear stockpiles were eliminated. While in office, Reagan revolutionized American nuclear policy: the president repeatedly called for the elimination of nuclear weapons and entered into the Intermediate-Range Nuclear Forces (INF) Treaty, which eliminated an entire class of nuclear weapons.

Given this record, it is ironic that President Reagan is often remembered as a militaristic hawk. It is commonplace to hear that Reagan's military buildup won the Cold War by crushing the Soviet Union. In this view, Soviet leader

Mikhail Gorbachev and his colleagues were fearful of renewed American power and sought to match it. Moscow could not keep pace, however, and therefore had no option but to surrender. The buildup had brought Moscow to its knees. This perspective emphasizes President Reagan's strength and resolve but ignores his commitment to disarmament. In this view, Reagan's primary legacy is the military buildup, which vanquished the Soviet Union.

This perspective begs several questions: What were President Reagan's objectives when introducing the buildup? How did the Soviet Union respond? What role *did* the military buildup play in ending the Cold War and the subsequent transformation of the international political system?

President Reagan and the Military Buildup

When President Reagan took office in 1981, administration officials believed the United States had fallen behind the Soviet Union in the arms race and U.S. forces needed to be both modernized and expanded.[1] Consequently, in March the president embarked on the largest peacetime military buildup in U.S. history. Although President Carter had significantly increased defense spending before leaving office, President Reagan proposed to spend an additional 7 percent per year between 1981 and 1985. Defense expenditures would cost $1.5 trillion and consume more than 30 percent of the federal budget over the next four years. The administration planned to use these resources to strengthen forces, improve combat readiness, and enhance force mobility.[2] In addition, in 1983 President Reagan introduced the Strategic Defense Initiative (SDI), a research program aimed at developing a space-based defense against a potential Soviet nuclear strike. The president hoped that SDI would be a shield to protect Americans from incoming missiles, thus rendering a Soviet attack futile.

Reagan officials explained that the goal of the buildup was twofold. In the short term, a restored military might would deter Soviet expansionism. Officials reasoned that Moscow had invaded Afghanistan in 1979 because America appeared weak and the Kremlin assumed it could invade with impunity. Renewed American strength would prevent future adventurism. But the administration's long-term objective was to pressure Moscow to agree to arms reductions.[3] The president's strategy was to build up military strength to pressure the Soviets to enter into arms reduction talks. He assumed—wrongly, as it turned out—that Moscow would not agree to disarmament unless it was forced to do so. As President Reagan explained in 1982:

> Some may question what modernizing our military has to do with peace. . . .
> A secure force keeps others from threatening us, and that keeps the peace.
> And just as important, it also increases the prospects of reaching significant
> arms reductions with the Soviets, and that's what we really want. The United
> States wants deep cuts in the world's arsenal of weapons, but unless we dem-
> onstrate the will to rebuild our strength and restore the military balance, the
> Soviets, since they're so far ahead, have little incentive to negotiate with us.[4]

The ultimate objective of the military buildup was to usher in an era of dialogue and disarmament. Secretary Shultz explained in 1983, "Strength and realism can deter war, but only direct dialogue and negotiation can open the path
toward lasting peace."[5] Reagan made his objectives clear in January 1984. "Neither we nor the Soviet Union can wish away the differences between our two
societies and our two philosophies," he noted. "But we should always remember
that we do have common interests. And the foremost among them is to avoid
war and reduce the level of arms."[6]

Ronald Reagan abhorred nuclear weapons and repeatedly spoke of his desire to reduce and eventually eliminate them. "I believe there can only be one
policy for preserving our precious civilization in this modern age: a nuclear
war can never be won and must never be fought," he declared in November
1983. "I know I speak for people everywhere when I say our dream is to see
the day when nuclear weapons will be banished from the earth."[7] President
Reagan called for the abolition of nuclear weapons approximately 150 times
during his years in the White House and nearly 90 times before Mikhail Gorbachev took office.[8] At the time, his aspiration was radical, if not quixotic. The
conventional view, as embodied in the doctrine of mutual assured destruction
(MAD), was that nuclear arsenals had kept the peace for 40 years. Because
each side had enough nuclear weapons to withstand a nuclear attack and to
retaliate in kind, each would be deterred from launching a first strike. An attack would prove suicidal. Reagan found MAD to be morally repugnant and
likened it to "two westerners standing in a saloon aiming their guns at each
other's head—permanently." "MAD [was] madness," he insisted. "It was the
craziest thing I ever heard of." It rendered the world "a button push away from
oblivion," he believed.[9] "The concern about nuclear war and the challenge to
diminish that war was always foremost in [Reagan's] mind," the president's adviser and long-term friend Martin Anderson has explained. "It was not something he talked about a lot in public. But he had strong feelings and strong
convictions about what could and should be done."[10]

The Strategic Defense Initiative was rooted in President Reagan's antipathy for nuclear weapons and MAD. "I've become more and more deeply convinced that the human spirit must be capable of rising above dealing with other nations and human beings by threatening their existence," he explained. "To rely on the specter of retaliation, on mutual threat . . . [is] a sad commentary on the human condition."[11] From Reagan's perspective, a defensive system against a nuclear attack could facilitate disarmament: if both the United States and the Soviet Union had effective defenses, then nuclear weapons would become obsolete, thus paving the way for their elimination. Consequently, the president repeatedly offered to share SDI with Moscow, much to his advisers' dismay.[12] Reagan hoped that SDI research would "begin to achieve our ultimate aim of eliminating the threat posed by nuclear strategic missiles. This could pave the way for arms control measures to eliminate the weapons themselves. We seek neither military superiority nor political advantage. Our only purpose—one all people share—is to search for ways to reduce the danger of nuclear war."[13]

Reagan's advisers opposed the abolition of nuclear weapons and tried to convince the president to change his mind. "My dream [was] a world free of nuclear weapons," Reagan explained in his memoirs. "Some of my advisers, including a number at the Pentagon, did not share this dream. They couldn't conceive of it. . . . But for the eight years I was president I never let my dream of a nuclear-free world fade from my mind."[14] The foreign policy experts in the administration insisted that MAD had kept the peace during the Cold War. If the threat of nuclear annihilation were removed, there would be nothing to prevent Soviet expansionism, they believed. Secretary of State George Shultz recalls that the speechwriting process was often "an agony of pulling and hauling" as the president inserted remarks calling for the elimination of nuclear weapons and his advisers removed them. "Every meeting I go to the president talks about abolishing nuclear weapons," Shultz once reprimanded underlings. "I cannot get it through your heads that this man is serious. We either have to convince him he is barking up the wrong tree or reply to his interests with some specific suggestions." Shultz tried to convince the president that nuclear weapons were necessary, but he eventually gave up, acknowledging that he "had no real impact on the president. . . . [Reagan] stuck with his own deeply held view of where we should be heading."[15] British Prime Minister Margaret Thatcher also tried to dissuade the president from calling for the elimination of nuclear weapons, insisting that MAD was indispensable. "We are going to have to live with [this] same doctrine for a considerable period of time," she insisted. Reagan held firm. "I don't think there is any morality in that at all," he replied.[16]

The president's advisers did not share his devotion to SDI either. While Reagan envisioned a defensive system that would shield the American people from a nuclear attack, most of his advisers thought the plan was unrealistic as best and dangerously destabilizing at worst. An effective defense would undermine MAD. The technology did not exist. It was grossly expensive. Once Reagan's advisers understood how deeply wedded the president was to the program, however, they had little choice but to go along. Perhaps it could be used as a bargaining chip, they grudgingly reasoned. Maybe SDI could be traded away for deep cuts in the Soviet nuclear arsenal. "Star Wars might be the leverage needed to get the Russians to decrease their number of land-based ICBM warheads," National Security Adviser Robert McFarlane hoped.[17]

Reagan officials were overwhelmingly opposed to the president's desire to share SDI technology with the Soviet Union.[18] "President Reagan was not only a true believer in SDI, he was definitely a true believer in sharing," National Security Council (NSC) member Jack Matlock explained in 1993. "This was something that most of the bureaucracy, virtually the entire bureaucracy . . . said we can't do." Matlock recalled an instance in July 1986 in which he was drafting a letter to send to the Kremlin and the president wanted to insert a section declaring his intent to share SDI technology with Moscow. The original draft did not contain such a commitment. Matlock "sent the draft in, and [Reagan] changed it," the NSC staffer has recalled.

> [The president] changed the section and made a very strong commitment to sharing . . . the research. I checked this out and all the experts said, "We can't do that." So I changed it back and sent it to him. It went back to him four times. And finally, he called me in, and he said, "Jack, is this my letter?" And I said, "Yes, sir, Mr. President." He said, "This is what I want to say." And I said, "Look, Mr. President, everybody tells me we can't do that." And he said, "Damn it, it is my letter. That's what I am going to do!" And well, that's the letter he sent.[19]

Frank Carlucci, who was both Reagan's national security adviser and secretary of defense, recalls,

> [The president] did, as best I could tell, sincerely believe that he could give [SDI] to the Russians and everything would be fine. And I and others tried

to explain to him that technically that just was not feasible. And the only thing that finally convinced him, I remember [was] one day I said to him, "Mr. President, you have just got to stop saying that because Gorbachev, among others, doesn't believe you." And he said, "Well, I guess you are right. He really doesn't believe me." . . . But it took a number of years to get him to that realization.[20]

The administration did not embark on SDI for the purpose of causing the Soviet Union to collapse. The president's intent was to protect civilians from nuclear annihilation and, ultimately, to render nuclear weapons obsolete. This explains the president's steadfast refusal to abandon or restrict the project as Gorbachev so often insisted, as well as his repeated offers to share the technology with Moscow. Other members of the administration valued SDI as a bargaining chip, however. For them, SDI was not a means to bankrupt Moscow, but rather something to be traded away in exchange for arms reductions.

Soviet Defense Spending and Military Doctrine

As it happened, the Kremlin did not need to be pressured to agree to arms reductions, as the Reagan administration had assumed. By 1980, many Soviet officials had independently concluded that the arms race was no longer in their economic or strategic interests.[21] The four decades of the Cold War had taken a toll on the Soviet economy. Mikhail Gorbachev has estimated that by the late 1970s total defense-related expenses, including indirect costs, consumed approximately 40 percent of the Soviet budget. This was higher than Soviet defense expenditures in 1940 at the outset of World War II. Anatoly Chernyaev, Gorbachev's foreign affairs adviser, has claimed that "70 or 80 per cent" of Soviet spending went to military expenditures in the decades before President Reagan came to office.[22] While this statistic may be questionable, the bottom line is that the Soviets devoted a large percentage of their resources to military expenditures over a long period of time. This trend undermined innovation, as well as the Soviet Union's capacity to produce consumer goods, causing the standard of living to stagnate. Consequently, reformers sought to revitalize the Soviet system. Their aim was to redirect resources away from the military and toward economic revitalization. To do this, the arms race had to end.

There were strategic reasons for ending the arms race as well. Reformers in the Soviet military challenged the logic that drove the arms race: more weapons did not necessarily bring more security, they argued. In fact, at a certain point, large arsenals undermine security by appearing to be offensive in nature and, thus, threatening to the adversary. The adversary will then respond with its own buildup. The reformers' conclusion was paradoxical: having too many weapons undermines security. According to this logic, then, security would be enhanced by reducing armaments, particularly those suited for offense rather than defense. Soviet reformers urged the Politburo to adopt a doctrine of "reasonable sufficiency" in which the Soviet Union would retain only those weapons that were necessary for its defense. As Soviet Colonel Makhmut Gareyev explained, genuine security "is guaranteed by the lowest possible level of strategic balance, not the highest."[23] This doctrine opened the door to slashing Soviet arsenals.

Mikhail Gorbachev came to office in March 1985 convinced that the arms race had to end. Within weeks of taking office he declared a moratorium on nuclear testing, and in February 1986 he made the doctrine of reasonable sufficiency official policy. "When I saw the monster that we and the United States had created as a result of the arms race, with all its mistakes and accidents with nuclear weapons and nuclear power, when I saw the terrible amount of force that had been amassed, I finally understood what the consequences, including global winter, would be," Gorbachev has reflected.[24] "The roots of New Thinking [in Soviet foreign policy] lay in the understanding that there would be no winners in a nuclear war and that in any such event both 'camps' would be blown to kingdom come," he explained.[25]

In the spring of 1986, Gorbachev became even more devoted to reducing nuclear arsenals. On April 26, the nuclear reactor at Chernobyl exploded, spewing huge amounts of radioactive material into the atmosphere across the Soviet Union, Europe, and Scandinavia. The disaster ruined the environment, caused mass relocation of the local population, and sickened thousands. First responders were woefully unprepared, and medical facilities were overwhelmed and ill-equipped. Civilian and military leaders alike were slow to understand the gravity of the situation.

The Chernobyl disaster drove home the potentially devastating effects of a nuclear war and inspired Gorbachev to pursue an end to the arms race with even greater vigor. "The accident at Chernobyl showed again what an abyss will open if nuclear war befalls mankind," Gorbachev told his fellow citizens during a televised address about the accident on May 14, 1986. "For inherent in the stockpiled nuclear arsenals are thousands upon thousands of disasters far more horrible than the Chernobyl one." During the address, Gorbachev beseeched the United States to join him in ending the arms race. "We again urge the United States to consider most responsibly the measure of danger looming over humanity, and to heed the opinion of the world community. . . . The nuclear age forcefully demands a new approach."[26]

The disaster had a profound effect on the general secretary. "One can say that [Chernobyl] marked the border between two Gorbachevs: one before, the other after 26 April," Gorbachev's spokesperson, Andrei Grachev, has observed.

> In a way Chernobyl became for him the equivalent of his personal Cuban missile crisis. Before 26 April his intention to propose a curb on the arms race along with a radical reduction of nuclear weapons was mostly based on economic and security concerns, while after Chernobyl his attitude towards nuclear weapons transformed into a psychological aversion, a moral rejection bringing him in this respect closer to Reagan. The fight for a non-nuclear world . . . became a personal challenge.[27]

Reformer Yevgeny Velikhov recalled that the Chernobyl accident induced Gorbachev to make "a great, instinctive leap to break the old cycle of secrecy, stubbornness, and deadlocked negotiations [with the United States]."[28] "We need negotiations," Gorbachev informed the Politburo on May 8, 1986. "Even with this gang, we need to negotiate. If not, what remains? Look at the Chernobyl catastrophe. Just a puff and we can all feel what nuclear war would be like."[29]

Thus, for economic, strategic, and moral reasons, the Soviets never sought to match Reagan's increased defense expenditures. The U.S. buildup had a negligible effect on Soviet sustainability.

The Strategic Defense Initiative

But what about SDI? Was SDI the straw that broke the Soviet camel's back, forcing them to concede the Cold War?

The Soviet Union had been working on missile defense systems since the late 1950s. In 1978, it had even considered developing a project similar to SDI, which had been proposed by Soviet military scientist Vladimir Chelomei. After careful consideration, however, it was determined that pursuing a comprehensive ballistic missile defense system was not worthwhile, and the project was abandoned.[30]

When President Reagan unveiled SDI in 1983, some Soviets were initially alarmed. "When we [at the Soviet military institutions] received the information that the United States was ready to create a multi-stage anti-missile defense system, we the military initially were put into a state of fear and shock because we understood that this could be realistic due to the economic and financial capabilities of the United States," General Vladimir Slipchenko, a leading Soviet military scientist, recalled in 1998. "The Soviet Union was not ready or prepared to respond adequately."[31]

The Strategic Defense Initiative complicated plans for ending the arms race. Soviet military hard-liners—who opposed the idea of arms reductions as well as the doctrine of reasonable sufficiency—played up the potential threat of SDI. They used SDI as an excuse to lobby for additional funding and repackaged old programs to sell to the Politburo as a way to counter the new American menace. As one observer described it, Soviet military hard-liners behaved like "a hunting dog sensing new quarry."[32] According to Grachev, the response "proposed by Soviet generals and weapons manufacturers envisaged 117 scientific [programs], 86 research projects and 165 experimental programs with approximate spending during the ten-year period amounting to between 40 and 50 billion rubles."[33] Many of these programs had originated years (if not decades) earlier, however.

In late 1983, the Kremlin established a committee to evaluate SDI. The commission was comprised of scientists who had evaluated the Chelomei proposal five years earlier and therefore had unparalleled expertise on missile defense. After careful consideration, the chairman, Evgeny Velikhov, "concluded that building a global anti-missile system that could protect against a first strike by the Soviet Union was impossible—at least it would not be possible during the next 15 to 20 years."[34] The Chelomei proposal enabled Soviet scientists "to respond to Reagan's speech rapidly and energetically," Velikhov has recalled. "The Chelomei affair was killed and this was a very good inoculation for Russia against the Star Wars proposal by Reagan, because five years before, we had already had these internal discussions, with a very detailed analysis on the technical engineering level."[35] Velikhov and other experts advised the Politburo to forgo building a Soviet version of SDI and to focus instead on arms reductions. It made far more sense to reduce arsenals, they reasoned, than to build a system to neutralize them.

The more Soviet scientists delved into SDI, the more their initial concerns were allayed. General Slipchenko recalled:

In figuring out our response we modeled many times the kind of SDI that the US could realistically have created. We became convinced that even the most reliable system of anti-missile defense, let's say 99 percent effective, still has holes, and out of 6400 warheads which could be launched in the direction of the United States, 60 warheads would have found their targets. . . . The retaliatory strike of even one nuclear warhead would cause unacceptable damage to a country. Therefore, we decided that this American policy must be of a political nature. To be more specific, the US was trying to economically ruin the Soviet Union by involving it in an arms race.[36]

However, SDI did not require a costly response. Soviet scientists determined that it would be considerably less expensive to try to counter SDI than to match it. Slipchenko recalled in 1998:

We found over 200 alternative solutions [to SDI], . . . We chose 20 to 30 of them to look at more closely. We evaluated our anti-SDI measures against a realistic SDI of the United States and found out that it would cost us about 10 per cent of what the Americans would have to spend on SDI. Then we were happy. Actually, we would have been quite glad if the Americans continued building SDI . . . because we realized that SDI could be fought very successfully—not by means of creating a similar system, but by way of creating means to overcome the system.[37]

Pursuing countermeasures would not only be far less costly than building a Soviet version of SDI, it could be put off until the Americans had deployed their system—something that would likely never happen, they reasoned.

Gorbachev favored an even more cost-effective response to SDI: a full-court diplomatic press.[38] If Gorbachev could persuade Reagan to abandon or restrict the program, Soviet military hard-liners would have little reason to request or receive additional funding. Domestic resistance to Gorbachev's plan to end the arms race would be undermined. The Soviet leader already sought to reduce nuclear arsenals, so trading such reductions in exchange for concessions on SDI was perfectly acceptable. Consequently, throughout his first two years as leader, Gorbachev tenaciously battled Reagan's program. SDI dominated every summit meeting and every discussion about arms control. There would be no agreements on reducing nuclear arms, Gorbachev insisted, until Reagan agreed to restrict SDI.

Gorbachev's plan backfired, however. His diplomatic offensive had the unintended effect of making the Americans value SDI more highly. The more

Gorbachev pressed Reagan to restrict SDI, the more American officials be-lieved SDI gave them leverage over Moscow, and the more committed they became to the project. Thus, SDI became a roadblock on the path toward disarmament.

By 1987, Gorbachev determined that his fixation on SDI had undermined progress toward his primary objective: ending the arms race. Thus, he shifted course. On February 28, the Soviet leader announced that Moscow would be willing to discuss the reduction of nuclear missiles separately from the Stra-tegic Defense Initiative. This decision constituted a major breakthrough. Al-leviated of the need to find common ground on SDI, the Cold War began to unravel quickly. "From late 1987, . . . we began to register significant results in all parts of the US-Soviet agenda," Jack Matlock has recalled. "The speed of change was dizzying for those of us who had worked for decades on what had long seemed the intractable problems of dealing with the USSR."[39] In De-cember 1987, Gorbachev not only visited the United States for the first time but also joined the president in signing the INF Treaty, a landmark agreement that eliminated an entire class of nuclear weapons. Captivated by the revolu-tionary changes in the Soviet Union, "Gorby mania" swept through the United States. By the time Reagan strolled through Red Square in May 1988, he de-clared that the Cold War had been "another time, another era." Many agreed. A majority of Americans polled in the spring of 1988 believed that the Soviet Union posed only a minor threat, if any at all. By the spring of 1989, leading American newspapers were running editorials with titles such as "Beyond the Cold War" and "The Cold War Is Over." In May, President Bush declared it was time for the United States to "move beyond containment."[40]

The Cold War was largely over by the spring of 1989, but the Soviet Union continued to exist for two and a half more years. During this time, American and Soviet policymakers collaborated closely, seeking to continue to reduce nu-clear arsenals and to navigate toward a more peaceful era.

• • •

Nowadays many portray President Reagan as a hawkish leader whose legacy is nothing more than a military buildup that forced the collapse of the Soviet Union. But this stereotype is flawed. Ronald Reagan was a visionary leader who helped to end the nuclear arms race and thus transform the international system. Reagan embarked on a military buildup to deter Soviet expansionism but, more important, he sought to induce Moscow to agree to nuclear arms reductions. The president's ultimate objective was to eliminate nuclear weapons. This vision was radical for the time. During an era in which the so-called experts were bogged down in the minutiae of throw weights, MIRVs, and counting warheads, the president envisioned a world beyond MAD, a world in which the threat of nuclear annihilation had been eliminated.

President Reagan was a leader in the true sense of the word—someone who was willing to defy close advisers, longtime friends, and key allies to pursue his vision of a more moral, more humane approach to global security. Perhaps even more difficult, he was able to rise above ideological differences and reach out to his adversary to accomplish his goals. "Our people look to us for leadership, and nobody can provide it if we don't," the president had written to Gorbachev in November 1985. "But we won't be very effective leaders unless we can rise above the specific but secondary concerns that preoccupy our respective bureaucracies and give our governments a strong push in the right direction."[41] And while President Reagan's calls for nuclear disarmament were considered quixotic at the time, this vision has since come to be embraced by Republicans and Democrats alike.

As it turned out, the Soviet Union never sought to match President Reagan's increased defense expenditures. The buildup did not bankrupt the Soviet Union, nor did it compel Moscow to surrender the Cold War. Likewise, SDI did not force the Politburo to concede. If anything, the buildup complicated Gorbachev's plan for ending the arms race. Soviet military hard-liners used the buildup to play up the American threat and to advance their own interests: Washington is preparing for war, they argued; so must we.

Would the Cold War have ended absent the U.S. military buildup? Probably so. It was not the buildup that brought the two sides together but rather Reagan's and Gorbachev's mutual desire to eliminate the threat of nuclear annihilation. The leaders' mutual antipathy for nuclear weapons was the foundation upon which the Cold War ended. It was this issue that first brought the two leaders together and that formed the stepping-stone to transforming global security. Aleksandr Bessmertnykh reflected in 1993:

[Gorbachev and Reagan] were very idealistic. . . . This is what they immediately sensed in each other and this is why they made great partners. . . . And if it were not for Reagan, I don't think we would have been able to reach the agreements in arms control that we later reached: because of Reagan, because of his idealism, because he really thought that we should do away with nuclear weapons. Gorbachev believed in that. Reagan believed in that. The experts didn't believe, but they did.[42]

It is this visionary leadership, this revolutionary antinuclearism that led to the peaceful conclusion of the Cold War. This is President Reagan's most enduring legacy.

10

Ronald Reagan, Liberalism, and the Politics of Nuclear War and National Security, 1981–1985

JULIAN E. ZELIZER

One of the central puzzles in the historiography about Ronald Reagan is how a conservative president, who spent much of his career before the 1980s railing against international arms agreements and insisting on an aggressive stance toward communism, ended his tenure by negotiating a historic arms agreement with the Soviet Union.

There have been four major answers to this puzzle. The first posits that Reagan shrewdly had a strategy all along that anticipated this outcome and he made it work. Early in the 1980s, according to this account, Reagan initiated a huge buildup in the defense budget that forced the Soviets into an arms race that they could not afford. Reagan, in some of this controversial work, is depicted as a long-time nuclear abolitionist who skillfully used his hawkish posture as a tool to achieve his real objective.[1] The second explanation claims that a series of international events in 1983 literally scared Reagan into understanding that his hawkish stance could easily result in nuclear war.[2] These events, in turn, caused him to back down. The third explanation centers on the claim that Reagan turned out to be a skilled and pragmatic diplomat as well as politician who seized opportunities as they arose.[3] Finally, those who discount the centrality of Reagan place the greatest weight on Soviet Premier Mikhail Gorbachev and internal changes that had changed the Soviet Union since the 1970s.[4]

But historians have not paid sufficient attention to the domestic political environment within which Reagan operated. Liberalism and its continued impact on American politics in the 1980s played an important role in constraining Reagan and pushing him toward a more circumscribed national security agenda that would have major international effects. For many years, the standard narrative about this period revolved around the "rise of the right," the story about the emergence of a grassroots conservative movement that swept through American politics and fundamentally transformed public debate. In this familiar account, the late 1960s and early 1970s witnessed the death of the New Deal coalition and thereafter produced a realignment of politics that lasted for decades.

But a new wave of scholarship has started to raise important questions about the first generation of scholarship on conservatism, questions that offer important insights into Reagan's presidency.[5] Historians are now beginning to explore the challenges that confronted conservatives when they finally came to power. Being a conservative was different on the campaign trail than it was in Washington, where compromises had to be made and where it became evident that the opposition continued to have a significant hold on power. One of the most difficult challenges that conservatives in power encountered was that liberalism did not disappear after the 1960s. In fact, liberal institutions, policies, and ideas remained inscribed in the polity. Liberal programs also had a strong hold on the public, given how long and deeply entrenched these forms of public spending had become by the 1980s within the electorate. Like most kinds of federal spending, whether military contracts or pork barrel funds for congressional districts, liberal programs became much harder to retrench over time, regardless of the political environment, as Americans became accustomed to the services.[6]

Nowhere are these emerging historiographical changes as relevant as with national security. In the traditional narrative, Democrats had divided in the 1960s over the war in Vietnam. The left wing of the party rejected the arguments of liberal internationalism that had guided the party since World War II. At the same time, the hawkish Republican rhetoric that called on America to be tough against communism played extremely well with voters who were seeking to restore the nation's standing overseas. Reagan's presidency thus resulted in a huge intensification of defense spending and military strength.

Yet a closer look at the Reagan presidency reveals a very different picture. What has received less attention from scholars are the political limits that Reagan confronted when dealing with national security as a result of the continued impact of liberal ideas, activists, and politicians. Most of the aforementioned literature on the changes in Reagan has focused on the second term. They juxtapose those years with the hawkish era of 1981–1985. But a closer look reveals that in the first term Reagan encountered a myriad of political challenges from the left that limited and constrained his course of action, pushing him in certain directions and away from others.

Revitalizing Military Strength

When Reagan entered the White House, he was determined to overcome concerns about the national security state that were born out of Vietnam. He was also a staunch opponent of negotiations and arms agreements with the Soviet Union that had been championed by Republican presidents Richard Nixon and Gerald Ford—as well as Democrat Jimmy Carter—through the policy of détente. When he challenged Gerald Ford for the Republican nomination in 1976, nearly winning, Reagan said that détente was a "one way street. We are making the concessions, we are giving them [the Soviet Union] the things they want; we ask nothing in return."

The president, who had opposed every major arms agreement until that time, made it clear that he was not interested in talking with the Soviet Union until they agreed to very stringent terms. The Soviets, he felt, were not yet prepared to do so, and the administration did not make arms negotiation a top priority. Instead, Reagan staffed many key positions in his administration with Republicans and neoconservative Democrats who had spent most of the 1970s railing against détente. Reagan, for example, nominated a former assistant to Democratic senator Henry "Scoop" Jackson, Richard Perle, to be assistant secretary of defense for international security policy, Paul Wolfowitz to serve in the State Department, and Paul Nitze as the main person to negotiate with the Soviet Union over arms control. Jackson, according to one of the leading members of the neoconservative Coalition for a Democratic Majority, "feels that Reagan's election mandate was due to the same things he has been talking about for years."[7] National Security Adviser Richard Allen was very close to conservative movement activists and likewise a skeptic of arms treaties. His successor, William P. Clark, held a hard line against the Soviets.

Touting a vision of peace through strength, Reagan argued that military strength was the only way to win substantive concessions from the Soviets before the negotiations really began. This entailed a major military buildup and aggressive response to communist forces around the globe. In November 1981, Reagan introduced the zero-zero option, a controversial offer to end the planned deployment of the Pershing II and ground-launched cruise missiles in Western

Europe on the condition that the Soviets disband every intermediate-range weapon that threatened the continent. This offer would force the Soviets to abandon their SS-20 missiles, as well as approximately 600 other intermediate missiles already in place, in exchange for the United States not deploying weapons that were not yet in Europe.

Reagan, who had been influenced by conservative theories in the 1950s about rolling back communism (as opposed to containment, which accepted the permanence of communism in certain parts of the world and just wanted to limit its expansion), believed that the U.S. government had to fight for the human rights of those living under communist rule. His assistant secretary of state for human rights and humanitarian affairs, Elliott Abrams, was a staunch neo-conservative Democrat who proclaimed that the "center of any human rights policy was going to be anticommunism, because the greatest threat to human rights was the Soviet Union."[8]

The centerpiece of Reagan's first term was the massive increase in the defense budget that took place under Secretary of Defense Caspar Weinberger. Weinberger stated: "The goal is to insure that America is strong enough in all respects so that we would be able to deter any kind of attack upon us from any quarter by making it very clear to any potential enemy that the cost of such an attack would be unacceptably high to them and they would be deterred . . . from undertaking it."[9]

In 1981, Reagan proposed the largest military budget since World War II, and over the next four years, defense spending reached 30 percent of the federal budget. "I believe my duty as President requires that I recommend increases in defense spending over the coming years. Since 1970, the Soviet Union has invested $300 billion more in its military forces than we have."[10] The administration reversed the decline in military spending that Congress had undertaken since 1968. Spending for defense had fallen from 9.4 percent of GDP in 1968 to 4.7 percent of GDP in 1979.[11]

The tenor of Reagan's first few years in office was unmistakable. The president set out to fulfill the arguments that he had been making for decades about how to deal with the Soviet Union. Through his appointments and his policies, as well as tough rhetoric about the need to destroy communism, Reagan sought to revitalize American military strength and establish a tough posture toward the Soviets.

Domestic Opposition

Yet during his first term, Reagan also ran into many obstacles as he undertook these initiatives. One of the biggest sources of political opposition came from the nuclear freeze movement, an international network of pacifists, socialists, religious leaders, environmental groups, scientists, geographers, psychologists, unions, creative and performing artists, senior foreign policymakers, and others. Within the United States, the movement included more than 26 organizations that joined the Citizens against Nuclear War.[12] The movement rejected the logic behind Reagan's defense buildup. "The nuclear arms race has gone on long enough and its time to stop it," argued Randall Forsberg, a top figure in the movement. "The next generation of nuclear weapons will make nuclear war much more likely and decrease our security rather than increase it."[13]

Within the United States and overseas, the freeze movement demonstrated the kind of protests that it could generate in response to Reagan's zero-zero decision to deploy 572 intermediate-range nuclear force (INF) missiles in Western Europe, based on a NATO agreement that had been finalized in 1979. The decision had originally been made in response to the Soviet deployment of SS-20s in the late 1970s. While many European leaders supported Reagan's decision, tens of thousands of moderate and left-wing European activists mounted demonstrations warning that this could escalate into nuclear war. They found strong support in the United States.

Movement politics was not the only challenge that Reagan confronted. The fact was that many Americans, as evident in public opinion, did not have much stomach for military operations after Vietnam.[14] Reagan was very eager to provide military and economic assistance to anti-communist forces in Central America, particularly rebels in Nicaragua, as well as to the government of El Salvador. However, the White House was aware from the start that there was not much public or congressional support for military intervention in the region. On March 29, Reagan's adviser Richard Wirthlin wrote James Baker, "The emergence of 'world peace' and defense-related issues on the number one problem list is very sensitive to current news events. . . . Regarding El Salvador, the biggest fear expressed by the American people is that involvement with the Central American country would lead to another Vietnam. Over two-thirds of the public feel that giving aid in particular would precipitate involvement similar to that experienced by the U.S. in Southeast Asia."[15]

Congressional Democrats, who still controlled the House, understood these fears and were unwilling to provide the administration with a blank check. Democratic speaker Tip O'Neill stood in Reagan's way. O'Neill, a Massachusetts Democrat who had turned against Lyndon Johnson and the war in Vietnam in 1967, did not believe that the United States should fund efforts in Central America. O'Neill had backed covert support to the anti-Soviet rebels in Afghanistan, but he rejected the idea that Central America was a region where the United States should intervene militarily. O'Neill knew that most House Democrats did not support Reagan. "Do we slip into another Vietnam," asked Massachusetts Democrat Edward Markey when the House was considering whether to support assistance, "or do we begin to stop another Vietnam from occurring?"[16] O'Neill was also influenced by his conversations with left-wing Jesuits and missionaries who were stationed in Central America, including his aunt.

Reagan's advisers realized that he was vulnerable politically on these issues. In May, the White House launched a public relations program to build support for his nuclear policies. One internal memorandum reported that the "American public is concerned about the possibility of the U.S. and the Soviet Union stumbling into a nuclear war. Only about 30% are confident that a nuclear war between the superpowers will not occur within the next decade." Although the public supported Reagan's tough stand against the Soviets, the memo stated, "The public is increasingly concerned that the President does not genuinely desire to negotiate with the Soviet Union on nuclear arms."[17] This was not the age of Rambo, notwithstanding popular myth. "The issue in the general arena of foreign relations that could swamp us," warned Wirthlin, "if we do not handle it with great care, is the proposed freeze on the production and deployment of nuclear weapons. Even when apprised of the difficulties of verification of this plan, 75% of all Americans favor the freeze."[18]

Even if the president wanted to ignore public opinion and take on movement opposition, his hands were limited or tied. One problem was the limited size of the military in 1981. In 1973, under Republican Richard Nixon, the U.S. government had dismantled the permanent draft (which had been on the books for almost the entire period since 1940). The absence of a draft was one of the most powerful pieces of evidence that liberal opposition to Vietnam had impacted American politics. While conservatives had opposed the draft, Nixon moved to end the system because he thought it would undercut liberal opposition to the war.

The draft had been replaced with a professional volunteer army. Reagan, like many conservatives, had supported this change on the grounds that it was more efficient and did not empower the government to require service from citizens. Yet the professional military remained in terrible shape in the early 1980s. In 1979, the Pentagon did not meet its recruitment targets, and that was after substantially lowering the standards used to gauge whether someone was fit to serve. Few experts had much confidence in what the professional army could accomplish, should any kind of major conflict take place.

There was evidence from Reagan's appointments after his first year that he was coming to understand the growing importance of different kinds of voices in his administration. When Secretary of State Alexander Haig resigned in July 1982, Reagan replaced him with George Shultz. A respected intellectual who was educated at Princeton and MIT, a former professor at the University of Chicago, and a veteran of the Nixon administration, Shultz was more sympathetic to the notion that there needed to be negotiation with the Soviets.

The midterm elections of 1982 constituted a blow to the White House. Although the midterms were mainly shaped by the severe recession, many House Democrats also ran on platforms opposing Reagan's Central America policies and in support of the nuclear freeze. Democrats enjoyed a 26-seat gain in the House, reaching a total of 269. Nuclear freeze initiatives passed by almost 60 percent in eight states and 26 cities. In California, voters approved Proposition 12 by 52 percent to 48 percent, requiring their senator to deliver a letter to the president demanding his support on nuclear freeze legislation. The number of House Democrats who said that they would support the freeze rose from 49 percent to 55 percent.[19]

Members of the administration decided to handle Central America through a covert CIA operation to overthrow the Sandinista regime in Nicaragua. This was part of the Reagan Doctrine, which sought to undermine Soviet strength by supporting wars of liberation against allied regimes. The decision to handle Central America through covert action likewise meshed with the political options that were available to Reagan by 1982, when any recommendations for a muscular political operation would have encountered stiff political resistance.

Around the time of the midterm elections, *Newsweek* published a story on the CIA operation. Speaker O'Neill was livid about the program. Congress responded. O'Neill worked with fellow Massachusetts congressman Edward Boland to attach an amendment to an appropriations bill in December 1982 that prohibited assistance to the contras if the money was to be used to overthrow the Nicaraguan government. Boland said, "That language, and listen to it, that language expresses the sense of the conferees that no funds authorized by the act should be used 'to overthrow the Government of Nicaragua or to provoke a military exchange between Nicaragua and Honduras.'" Boland believed that the amendments would check the administration, telling one reporter, "It's pretty plain and simple. If there was any effort to use funds for that purpose, the Administration would have to justify it and I don't know how they would."[20] The Boland Amendment angered the president, but he had no choice other than to sign it. The alternative was Iowa representative Tom Harkin's bill that would ban support for any assistance to groups working against the Nicaraguan government (even if they were not attempting to overthrow it).

Nuclear Freeze and Missile Defense

By the start of 1983, the freeze movement had strong support all over the world and within the United States. The message of the freeze movement reached into American popular culture. Reagan, who said that the arguments of the freeze movement were simplistic even though he agreed with their objectives, realized that they had enough support to cause political problems.

As Reagan continued to push for higher defense budgets and used increasingly strident rhetoric against the Soviets (such as calling them the "Evil Empire"), polls showed that the public was moved by warnings about war and criticism of Reagan's policies. According to a Harris poll, 66 to 31 percent felt that the president was doing an unsatisfactory job in his negotiations with the Soviets. While 85 to 9 percent believed that the Soviets were hostile toward the United States and willing to use nuclear force, by a margin of 76 to 21 they favored some kind of agreement with the Soviets on a nuclear freeze.[21] Reagan allies such as the conservative physicist Edward Teller took the movement seriously and believed that it was having an impact.[22]

The centerpiece of Reagan's response to the freeze movement was the Strategic Defense Initiative (SDI), which was introduced in a speech on March 23, 1983. Reagan thereby committed the United States to major research on a missile defense system that would allow the nation to continue taking an aggressive military stand toward the Soviets and its allies without much risk from Americans.

While there were strategic reasons behind this initiative, politics was also on the mind of the White House. According to one of its architects, SDI was "a uniquely effective reply to those advocating the dangerous inferiority implied by a 'nuclear freeze.'"[23] Just as with the decision to focus on covert operations in Central America, politics influenced the types of strategic decisions made by the administration.

SDI aimed to abandon the policy of mutual assured destruction. For Reagan, the idea had long roots, dating back to a 1967 meeting he had with Edward Teller at Lawrence Livermore National Laboratory while governor.[24] In Congress, Wyoming Republican senator Malcolm Wallop and New York representative Jack Kemp were the primary supporters for the plan.

A coalition in the White House and external supporters lobbied aggressively for the plan. *New York Times* columnist and former Richard Nixon speechwriter William Safire wrote that despite the ridicule of the establishment, Reagan was "lurching forward to a new era in arms control."[25] According to one pollster who worked for the coalition, SDI "appears to have the potential to form a broad based voter consensus. Since it is non-nuclear, it appeals to those voters opposed to nuclear weapons, while attracting strong support from those voters who favor a strong national defense. Simply, the . . . strategy eases voter anxiety over nuclear weaponry by maintaining a strong national defense without nuclear weapons."[26]

But they did not get a free ride. Respected experts challenged the plan. They said that an antimissile shield would never work and only end up triggering an arms race in outer space. Administration officials admitted that the response to the plan was "skepticism."[27] Opponents labeled the program "Star Wars" in reference to a popular science fiction film of the era, with Senator Edward Kennedy (D-MA) using that label the morning after the speech.

The Soviets warned that SDI would create an arms race in space and would violate the 1972 agreement to limit antiballistic missile (ABM) technologies. If the technology ever worked, there would be no incentive for the United States to refrain from launching a first strike. Given that the United States was not reducing its offensive power, expanding the defense system constituted an aggressive action. Reagan turned these arguments against the Soviets: "I wonder why some of our own carping critics who claim SDI is an impractical wasted effort don't ask themselves, if it's no good how come the Russians are so upset about it?"[28]

The nuclear freeze movement responded by saying that SDI was impossible and dangerous. They turned to scientific data as proof. Activists insisted that the only viable path to peace was through both countries agreeing that they would not produce as many weapons. "The endless cycle of nuclear escalation is more and more likely to end in nuclear conflagration," said Senator Edward Kennedy and Oregon senator Mark Hatfield. Another freeze supporter, Representative Markey, said, "The worldwide arms race is getting out of control."[29] SDI supporters dismissed the claims of activists, warning that a freeze would never work and spreading information that movement officials were linked to Soviet propaganda efforts.

On May 4, 1983, the House passed a freeze resolution that would stop the production of new nuclear weapons and maintain current levels for existing nuclear armaments, by a margin of 278 to 149, with 60 Republicans supporting the measure. There was not yet enough support in the Senate, however, which defeated the freeze on October 31 by a vote of 58 to 40, with 12 hawkish Democrats joining 46 Republicans.

At the same time that he encountered intense opposition to his national security policies, the president became more sensitive to his opponents in the fall of 1983, when he came to genuinely believe that the world had entered into a dangerous period, with the potential for nuclear war.[30] The events that took place in those months would challenge Reagan's core arguments about military force and also cause him to rethink his approach to negotiations.

The rapid turnover of leaders in the Soviet Union caused great concern for U.S. policymakers. When Brezhnev died on November 10, 1982, his successor, Yuri Andropov, got off a poor start with Reagan. During Andropov's short term, tensions escalated between the Soviet Union and the United States. Andropov assumed that the United States was considering a first-strike strategy under a trigger-happy president.

The period between September and November was terrifying to many Americans and to Reagan himself. On September 1, the Soviets shot down a Korean airliner when the plane entered Soviet airspace, killing 269 passengers and crew. The 61 Americans on board included Georgia Democratic representative Larry McDonald. Tensions were high, as some Republicans like Newt Gingrich told the president that this was the "deliberate murder" of Americans, and others called for a military response.[31] But the call for sanctions against the Soviets came from both sides of the political aisle. According to O'Neill, "The world is aghast. This isn't the U.S. versus Russia. This is Russia versus the world."[32]

The president resisted, however, saying that the issue would work against the Soviets. Public opinion did not support confrontational policies after the incident. Reagan instead said that they needed to let the situation cool down and to publicly condemn the action. He delivered a speech doing so, which was well received by many, including Democrats.

The next month, another event involving hundreds of casualties, this time in Lebanon, tested the limits of how much bloodshed America's political system would tolerate. The Lebanese crisis had begun a year earlier. Secretary of State Haig had given the green light to Israel to invade Lebanon to destroy the military bases of the Palestinian Liberation Organization and diminish the power of Syria. After the invasion, Lebanon continued to slide further into civil war. Reagan responded by sending troops. His commitment was modest, with only 1,800 Marines dispatched to the country. By contrast, in 1958, President Eisenhower had sent 18,000 there to stabilize civil conflict.[33] Reagan made his decision over the opposition of the Joint Chiefs of Staff (JCS), which feared the operation would turn into a disaster. The JCS were soon proved right.

An attack on the military barracks resulted in significant bloodshed. Although initially the president warned that the terrorists would see the withdrawal of troops as a sign of weakness, under intense congressional pressure, he decided against ordering any military operation and in February 1984 brought the troops home. Neoconservatives were frustrated.

Two days after the bombing, U.S. troops invaded the small Caribbean island of Grenada following a coup that could have endangered American students living on the island. It was a political success, though Reagan's critics accused him of having manufactured a crisis to distract the nation from the Lebanon disaster. Even Secretary Shultz admitted, "The situation was bizarre. Here we had a Pentagon that seemed to take any means to avoid the *actual use* of American military power but every opportunity to *display* it."[34]

Big Changes in 1984

It was in this atmosphere of tense international relations that the administration began planning for the 1984 presidential elections. The polls showed that the public was unhappy with many of Reagan's policies and worried about the possibility of war. One internal study warned that in terms of the top "bad things" that Americans thought could happen during a Reagan term, 51 percent of those polled were worried about the possibility of nuclear war. According to a Reagan campaign document, the polls strongly recommended that "we should emphasize (if there have been no major foreign policy setbacks by late

Fall of 1984) that our dealings with the Soviets have succeeded because they were based on realism (we have dealt with the Soviets as they are—not as we wish they would be), strength and reciprocity. Further, we should emphasize that we are committed to peace—to arms reduction, and to developing 'people' programs to help nations of Central America and South America."[35]

This message became even more important as U.S.-Soviet relations disintegrated in November. Early in the month, the U.S. military and Western allies conducted an extensive computer war simulation called Exercise Able Archer. The Soviets were aware that the exercise was taking place but could not discern whether it was a simulation or real attack. As a result, the Soviets placed their troops on high alert and prepared for nuclear attack. Although the Soviets soon realized that Able Archer was a simulation, the two sides came close to war. According to Anatoly Dobrynin, the early years of Reagan's presidency were extraordinarily difficult and dangerous.

The power of antiwar arguments was captured in the popularity of a television movie, *The Day After*, that focused on the aftermath of a nuclear war in small town in Kansas. A hundred million Americans saw the show when it broadcast on November 20, 1983. The broadcast took on the aura of a national event. People discussed it at college campuses, schools, and churches. Lee Loveland, who hosted 20 members of the St. Stephen and Incarnation Church in Washington for a potluck dinner to watch the show, said "I feel very strongly that we should see this together as a group." California senator Alan Cranston, a supporter of the freeze and presidential candidate, hosted a party in Spokane, Washington, that was just one of 136 events that he sponsored in 26 states. The nuclear freeze movement established a massive advertising campaign to promote the film.[36] "It's very effective and left me greatly depressed," Reagan noted after viewing it in a preview. Reagan became so worried about what kind of impact the film would have that he had the administration embark on a public relations campaign in response. The president said, "We know it's 'anti-nuke' propaganda but we're going to take it over & say it shows why we must keep on doing what we're doing."[37] The Republican National Committee and the White House Director of Communications, David Gergen, headed the efforts.

House Democrats continued their focus on Central America. Congress passed another series of Boland amendments, this time prohibiting allocating money to the contras. The House approved the amendments by a vote of only 228 to 195. Democratic candidate Walter Mondale, former vice president under Jimmy Carter and Minnesota senator, called Reagan "trigger happy."[38] Angry with Democrats, Reagan, who responded to reporters that he was not "trigger happy," wrote in his diary that "whenever it is us versus the Soviets or Cubans they [Democrats] always come down on the wrong side."[39]

With the House Democrats pushing for further restrictions on activities in Central America, some members of the administration turned to other tactics to achieve their goals. They continued to focus on covert operations from within the executive branch. On June 25, 1984, President Reagan met with Vice President George H. W. Bush, Secretaries Weinberger and Shultz, CIA Director William Casey, United Nations ambassador Jeanne Kirkpatrick, National Security Adviser Robert McFarlane, and several other officials to discuss what to do about the Nicaraguan contras. They wanted to figure out how to provide assistance despite the congressional bans. McFarlane said that "the bad news includes the fact that there seems to be no prospect that the Democratic leadership will provide for any vote on the Nicaraguan program." Casey and Kirkpatrick believed that the United States needed to turn to third parties to help with this operation.[40]

Some members of the administration were uncomfortable with these discussions. Secretary Shultz said that Chief of Staff James Baker had said that, based on his legal training, "if we go out and try to get money from third countries, it is an impeachable offense." Baker believed that the United States could "raise and spend" funds for the program only through congressional appropriation.

But others were not deterred by the warnings. They held ambitious views about presidential power and were determined to use it to overcome the kind of political resistance they had encountered toward their national security agenda. Vice President Bush asked, "How can anyone object to the U.S. encouraging third parties to provide help to the anti-Sandinistas under the finding? The only problem that might come up is if the United States were to promise to give these third parties something in return so that people could interpret this as some kind of exchange." McFarlane ended the meeting by telling his colleagues not to repeat any of the conversations that had taken place about third-party support until they were more certain about what they could do. Reagan himself warned that if this story was revealed, "we'll all be hanging by our thumbs in front of the White House."[41]

The meeting was significant in signaling a new direction for Central American policy, a response to the limitations that Republicans felt on their power in the 1980s. The first term of the Reagan administration had been filled with frustration and disappointment, as conservatives learned that a revolution had not taken hold. For Reagan, living up to his own national security rhetoric proved to be enormously difficult, as Congress opposed direct military intervention. Besides the military budget and his tough rhetoric about communism, much of the administration's policies were conducted through covert, executive-centered operations. This was part of a broader strategy within the administration as Reagan cemented the marriage between conservatism and executive power.[42]

As the 1984 election approached, Reagan changed the tone of his discussions with the Soviets. He took a series of steps to improve relations with the Soviet Union and to break with the hard-liners. The political pressures and the strategic pressures were converging. Many members of the administration were starting to believe that there was a possible turning point in the Soviet Union because of the fragile condition of the economy.[43] Mondale had promised voters in early September that if they elected him as president he would request that the Soviets meet with him to negotiate a freeze in the arms race. "Every day we fail to open negotiations with the Soviets is another day we slip toward Armageddon," he told the annual convention of the American Legion.[44]

●   ●   ●

At the United Nations on September 24, Reagan made his first public conciliatory speech to the Soviets. Pointing to the Soviet and U.S. representatives sitting before him, Reagan said: "In this historic assembly hall it's clear that there's not a great distance between us." The speech was as much a political act as it was an act of diplomacy, one that sent signals to the Soviets about the possibility that Reagan was changing his outlook. Soviet Foreign Minister Andrey Gromyko listened in silence, having met the previous day with Walter Mondale. Campaign officials believed that the speech was the start of a more moderate tone for his campaign, one that aimed to take away likely candidate Mondale's possible advantage on the "war and peace issue." Campaign officials were reading polls showing that voters were concerned the administration would take them to war. The more Reagan spoke about negotiation, the stronger his polls became.[45] Reagan planned to talk more about possible negotiations when he met with Gromyko at the end of the week. The speech and messages were effective. According to one of Mondale's advisers, "The Reagan people have so far succeeded in just taking the wind out of our sails on nuclear issues."[46]

Democrats understood that this was a political danger for Reagan, and they tried to make the most of his hawkish reputation. That August, Reagan made a joke during a sound check, not realizing that the microphones were on. "My fellow Americans," he said, "I am pleased to tell you today that I've signed legislation that will outlaw Russia forever. We begin bombing in five minutes." Democrats pounced on the statement, condemning the president for joking about nuclear war.

Mondale was a New Deal liberal on social policy and a strong supporter of the nuclear freeze movement. Running with New York representative Geraldine Ferraro, Mondale warned that Reagan's policies were causing danger internationally.

Reagan stressed both his hawkishness and his efforts to calm tensions. Speaking about the Soviets, he said, "I told Mr. Gromyko we don't like their system. They don't like ours. . . . But between us, we can either destroy the world or we can save it." Although Reagan assured voters that he would do a better job achieving peace with the Soviets, it was peace through strength, as he continued to remind them that Democrats were weak on defense. One Republican adviser said: "The increasing 1984 emphasis on jingoism, anti-Communism and defense spotlights three issues that have historically driven a major wedge into the Democratic coalition. This is in sharp contrast to economic issues like fairness and joblessness that reinforce the Democratic coalition."[47] The president's campaign team felt that national security was one of Mondale's greatest areas of vulnerability. "Mondale as a Senator, later as understudy to Jimmy Carter," Reagan said, "and still today has seemed possessed with one simple but very wrong idea: American strength is a threat to world peace." According to Reagan's staff, Mondale's biggest area of weakness was his "weak record on defense and foreign affairs."[48]

One of the most powerful advertisements aired by Republicans showed a bear walking in the woods. As viewers watched the bear, the narrator warned: "There is a bear in the woods. For some people, the bear is easy to see. Others don't see it at all. Some people say the bear is tame. Others say it's vicious and dangerous. Since no one can really be sure who's right, isn't it smart to be as strong as the bear? If there is a bear?"

Reagan received strong support from a younger group of congressional Republicans in the House who were hammering away at Democrats for stifling initiatives in Central America. Newt Gingrich and Pennsylvania's Robert Walker honed in on this theme. They called Democrats "blind to communism," charging that they were defeatist on foreign policy and did not believe in American military strength. Members of their caucus, the Conservative Opportunity Society (COS), made use of one-minute speeches at the start of each day (where any member could stand up before the cameras) and "Special Order" speeches in the evening hours to attack Democrats. On May 8, 1984, members of the COS appeared on the floor, covered by C-SPAN cameras, to speak about the Democratic record on fighting communism. Republicans asked the Democrats they accused of withholding funds from operations in Central America to defend their positions. The cameras showed only the speaker, hiding the fact that the chamber was empty. It looked on television as if the Democrats had no reply, even though they were not present. When Gingrich made a speech about Congressman Boland, who happened to be O'Neill's roommate in Washington, the speaker exploded. He ordered the cameras to pan across the chamber as Robert Walker spoke. This violated the agreement that had been reached in 1978 when the House decided to let television cameras into the chamber. Walker was unaware that viewers could see the chamber was empty—that is, until Mississippi representative Trent Lott stormed onto the floor to tell Walker what was happening. The following day O'Neill called Gingrich's operation the "lowest thing" that he had witnessed on Capitol Hill. Republicans claimed that O'Neill had violated the rules of decorum, and as a result, the speaker's words were stricken from the record. The entire episode backfired on Democrats as Republicans accused the leadership of blatantly disregarding the rules of the chamber.[49]

Democrats responded to these national security attacks by warning of how close the nation had come to war in 1983. Mondale said that with SDI the president would escalate and expand the arms race into space. He said that the president could not be effective in negotiations, given his strident rhetoric. The Republicans did not deter House Democrats. They passed another round of Boland Amendments, the most restrictive thus far, saying that "no funds available" to the Department of Defense, the CIA, or any intelligence agencies could be used to support the contras either directly or indirectly.

Mondale's message resonated with many voters, and congressional Democrats were on target with public opinion. But Mondale could not match Reagan's charisma. Mondale struggled against Reagan in his public appearances. He also was having trouble retaining voters in once-Democratic areas in the South. Moreover, though Democrats in many ways had the public on their side, they failed to articulate a convincing message of their own about how to handle international threats. Many Democrats were frustrated that Mondale could not respond well to Reagan's national security attacks and that he had allowed him to present Democrats almost as isolationist.

Reagan defeated Mondale by a landslide, winning 49 of 50 states. His success in 1984 did not include Congress, where House Democrats retained control of the House, even though the GOP picked up 16 seats. The biggest challenge was that more moderate Democrats lost their seats, which made the House more liberal. Republicans retained control of the Senate.

Beyond the 1984 Election

Following the election, Democrats continued to impose immense pressure on the administration. Administration officials complained of the lethargic operations in Central America. Some members of the administration were even more explicit in discussing the limits they faced. During a speech at the National Press Club on November 28, 1984, Secretary of Defense Cap Weinberger promised reporters that the United States would not be brought into a war in Central America. He outlined a doctrine that was rooted in the limitations of the period. He said that the United States would only use force when the nation was willing to unleash its full force and there was a national consensus over goals. The key guidelines included several pillars: the first was that the United States would rely on military force only in defense of the national interest. The second was that the government would demonstrate its total commitment to victory. The third was that the president and Congress needed to state clear military objectives, including a coherent plan about how to achieve them. The fourth was that policymakers would reevaluate those objectives regularly and make sure they would work. Fifth, the United States would only take on a mission if there was strong public and congressional support. Sixth, the use of military force would be a weapon of last resort. Weinberger admitted that this grew out of the Vietnam experience.

During his first term, Reagan had brought the conservative movement back into the halls of power, and for most of the time, he had remained true to the kind of hawkish rhetoric that he had employed in previous years. He made it clear that he continued to support peace through strength and that he would bring the Soviets to the negotiating table through military strength rather than through an invitation to negotiate.

But conservatives learned that being a hawk was much easier on the campaign trail than in power. Too much of liberal ideas, both from the era of internationalism as well as from the 1960s, remained an integral part of the fabric. The public did not support a massive sweep to the right on national security questions. Rather than acting like a hawk, Reagan had to compromise to advance his agenda and often switched course quite dramatically. There were many reasons behind these changes, including his own growing fears of war, but the power of oppositional institutions, ideas, and policies was quite integral.

•　•　•

By 1984, Reagan sounded quite different in his campaign than he had when he started. At the start of 1984, he had offered a more conciliatory tone to the Soviets in a speech to the Soviet Union, and throughout the year he continued to talk about negotiation and reaching out to the Soviets. Even many members of his administration were acknowledging the limits of Central American power and fighting through covert action.

To be sure, this did not mean that the Cold War came to a halt. Even while restricting aid, Congress passed some form of assistance to the contras in 1985 and 1986, as well as agreeing to support anti-communist forces in Cambodia, Angola, and Afghanistan. But the support that Congress agreed to was limited and certainly a far cry from the kind of aggressive approach toward the Soviets that Ronald Reagan, when he was out of power, and other conservatives had championed through the 1970s. With the Soviets themselves, he moved toward direction negotiation.

The second term of Reagan's presidency would revolve around national security concerns. Reagan struggled to deal with the fallout from the Iran-contra scandal, where controversial covert operations came to light. After he survived the scandal and investigation, Reagan shocked many conservatives when he entered into arms negotiations with Soviet Premier Mikhail Gorbachev, a younger reformer who believed that the Soviets had to change their economic and foreign policies. The negotiations culminated in the INF Treaty in 1987.[50]

Although the developments in the second term were crucial, the roots for the politics and policies of these years took shape soon after Reagan became president. There were many factors that ultimately limited Reagan's options on national security. But the continued power of liberal ideas, as expressed through social movements, public opinion, public policies, and congressional

Democrats, was extremely important in the 1980s. They undercut the notion of a conservative revolution and counteracted some of the shifts that Republicans had hoped to undertake.

The thawing of the Cold War during the final part of Ronald Reagan's presidency was a watershed moment for international affairs, as the possibility of nuclear war diminished and the defining international tension since the 1940s came closer to an end. Reagan's change in policy was a historic moment, one that had huge global consequences given that he was one of the handful of major players in this struggle, since it dramatically lowered the possibility for a nuclear war.

This was a world transformed. It was a world where the likelihood of nuclear war was reduced significantly and where the Cold War was closing. The defining international conflict that threatened the world before Reagan entered office was reaching an unexpected conclusion. The world after Reagan left office, and since then, is quite different, particularly because of that greatly diminished nuclear threat among the superpowers.

•   •   •

There were many reasons that this moment of possibility was realized. While historians have demonstrated the role of Gorbachev and Reagan in this transformation, domestic politics was an important part of the mix. Domestic politics helped push Reagan in a direction that resulted in his being prepared to enter these discussions. Even though this was the era of conservatism, the persistence of liberalism played a huge role in shaping Reagan's presidency and counteracting the pressures for a more hawkish stand toward the Soviets. Partisanship did not stop at the water's edge, and in this case that helped usher the way toward an end to one of the major conflicts of the twentieth century.

The politics of national security had shifted during the Cold War, resulting in a pushback against conservatism. When Reagan was elected, the president's muscular rhetoric about the Cold War had signaled the potential for a sharp rightward shift in the political culture following the collapse of the Cold War consensus with Vietnam. While there were many pockets of politics that clearly supported Reagan in his early years as president, it became increasingly clear in the 1980s that the political forces pushing against militarism were also quite strong. Their success in the 1980s would encourage and bolster efforts in coming decades to constrain large-scale military ventures and fuel opposition when presidents embarked on wars overseas.

The continued pressures against massive military intervention were even at play after the horrendous attacks of 9/11 and the resurgent support for militarism that was clearly evident throughout the United States. As the nation vastly expanded its military operations with wars in Afghanistan and Iraq, the country took these steps without reinstituting the draft and with government officials facing ongoing, enormous pressure to contain the role of ground troops in these regions. There was no full-scale wartime mobilization. Government leaders opted for wars that centered on special operations forces and targeted air strikes, and the political pressures to withdraw the forces that did enter the field of combat were huge and made it difficult to find support for the kind of sustained intervention that postwar reconstruction required. The United States has also avoided many other conflicts, such as Syria, with U.S. politicians fearing that there would be little public support for military presence.

In that sense, the constraints on military intervention abroad by U.S. presidents and Congress in the post-1989 era are not drastically different from the 1980s. The American public continues to share a distaste and skepticism toward large-scale military action overseas, and there is limited political support for the kind of total mobilization that occurred in World War II. The arguments that many liberals made in the aftermath of Vietnam about the dangers of unbridled militarism continue to resonate in the nation's political culture and are unlikely to disappear anytime soon.

V

REAGAN AND MULTILATERALISM

Two Voices

11

Ronald Reagan's Approach to the United Nations

KIM R. HOLMES

It is not uncommon to hear critics of President Ronald Reagan say that he had little regard for international institutions, preferring instead to operate outside of them. Such criticism is hardly new. In 1986, Robert C. Johansen, professor of political science and peace studies at Columbia University, wrote that "the hostility of the Reagan administration toward the United Nations poses the greatest challenge yet to multilateralism."[1]

Reagan, of course, fueled such conclusions with a plethora of statements critical of the United Nations (UN). A classic example is his response to reporters after a UN General Assembly vote condemning his sending U.S. troops into Grenada: "One hundred nations in the U.N. have not agreed with us on just about everything that's come before them, where we're involved, and it didn't upset my breakfast at all."[2]

Nevertheless, Reagan's approach to the UN and international organizations was not entirely negative. It was, in fact, quite often pragmatic. If this was a surprise to liberals, it was also a surprise to conservatives. As to the latter, Reagan did not walk away from the UN, as some of his conservative allies wanted, nor condemn it as frequently or stridently as they might have wanted. Instead, he engaged it on a piecemeal basis. He worked with it when it suited U.S. interests and was compatible with American values, and he condemned it when it fell short. He supported UN initiatives and multilateralism when consistent with his objectives, but did not when he felt they were ineffective or counterproductive. To be sure, this was not unique among presidents, but, for President Reagan, his attitude toward the UN was not as black-and-white as both opponents and supporters suspected. Reagan challenged the UN to live up to its principles but was not averse to bucking it, and the international community, as he did by refusing to sign the UN Convention on the Law of the Sea that he believed violated U.S. rights and sovereignty.

Reagan stood between two worlds. The first was the traditional legal and international order of nation-states and customary law—a world where sovereign nations jealously protected their rights. It was also one in which the United States unapologetically asserted its moral superiority over international organizations that Reagan believed had been corrupted by the disproportionate influences of totalitarian states like the Soviet Union.

The second was one governed by the internationalist worldview introduced by President Woodrow Wilson and fellow progressives. Once a Truman Cold War liberal himself, Reagan was not automatically opposed to the concepts of international humanitarian law that worldview represented. There were ways in which the Reagan administration remained committed to an international rule of law and cooperation around human rights, trade, and various technical standards. He signed the United Nations Convention against Torture, for example, even though he had reservations. In doing so, Reagan believed as surely as Truman before him that he was asking the international community to embrace and live up to what he understood as America's traditional values of freedom, justice, and decency.

Because his main concern was confronting communism and the Soviets in the Cold War, President Reagan viewed the UN and international organizations as platforms for advancing the cause of freedom. In that respect, the UN was but a backdrop to a larger drama. But it was a stage nonetheless. It was one on which Reagan's stalwart defense of liberty helped succeed in transforming the very nature of world geopolitics, not to mention the way the United States has approached the UN ever since.

The Roots of Reagan's Skepticism

Ronald Reagan's skepticism toward the UN had deep roots. Coming out of the American conservative movement, he carried with him many of the assumptions long held by fellow conservatives. He was suspicious of the anti-American motives of many of the UN's member states. He was repulsed by the "big government" assumptions behind the ideology of international governance prevalent at the UN. He believed the UN had become a forum for many of the world's worst dictators to protect themselves from international criticism and accountability.

Standing up to the anti-American proclivities of the UN was nothing new. The U.S. permanent representative to the UN under John F. Kennedy, Adlai Stevenson, spoke against its admitting Communist China as a member, given its "ridiculous" demands that the Republic of China (on Taiwan) be expelled. He also dramatically exposed Soviet lies regarding their ballistic missiles in Cuba. Gerald Ford's ambassador to the UN, Daniel Patrick Moynihan, did much the same when he forcefully spoke out against the resolution declaring Zionism as racism. Therefore, when Reagan's ambassador to the UN, Jeane J. Kirkpatrick, arrived on the scene, she saw herself as operating within and continuing that tradition. Reagan adviser and attorney general Ed Meese recalls attending a Cabinet meeting when Kirkpatrick characterized her role at the UN as taking off the "kick me" sign. Reagan agreed and would often remind her of this remark.[3] As he recorded in his diaries, Kirkpatrick told him "the U.N. is a worse can of worms than even she had anticipated. We've agreed the U.S. has got to get tough and maybe walk out a few times."[4]

Above all, the UN was for Reagan a political stage upon which he and Kirkpatrick could challenge the Soviet Union. One of the most poignant scenes out of this playbook was Kirkpatrick's confronting the Soviet Union over the 1983 downing of Korean Air Lines Flight 007. In a UN Security Council meeting on September 6, 1983, Kirkpatrick played a recording of radio intercepts of the Soviet pilots who shot down the jetliner.[5] As *Foreign Policy* editor David Bosco described it, "The American delegation took care to situate one [TV] monitor near the Soviet ambassador, and the American team also provided transcripts to the translators."[6] After denouncing the Soviets for "murdering 269 people," Kirkpatrick concluded: "The fact is that violence and lies are regular instruments of Soviet policy."[7]

Thus, Kirkpatrick had placed the specific murderous act of downing a civilian airliner within the larger narrative of denouncing the Soviet system itself. As such, long before Reagan's famous "Mr. Gorbachev, tear down this wall" speech, Kirkpatrick had made the UN a major front in the president's overall strategy of challenging the Soviet Union, not merely accommodating it as previous presidents had done with the policy of détente.

Here is how Reagan put it in a speech to the UN General Assembly's Special Session on Disarmament on June 17, 1982:

The decade of so-called detente witnessed the most massive Soviet buildup
of military power in history. . . . Soviet aggression and support for violence
around the world have eroded the confidence needed for arms negotiations.
While we exercised unilateral restraint, they forged ahead and today possess nuclear and conventional forces far in excess of an adequate deterrent
capability. Soviet oppression is not limited to the countries they invade. At
the very time the Soviet Union is trying to manipulate the peace movement
in the West, it is stifling a budding peace movement at home.[8]

Using the UN as a bully pulpit to denounce Soviet communism was not limited to one or two venues or speeches. Reagan launched a broad assault across
the UN system. In the General Assembly during that session on disarmament,
for example, he also spoke about the Soviet Union's "record of tyranny" since
World War II.[9] He used the International Labor Organization, a UN affiliate
that the United States had rejoined just before he took office, as a forum to
criticize communist states for their treatment of workers, especially Poland regarding Solidarity workers, and to announce America's support for trade union
movements throughout Eastern Europe, Asia, and Africa.[10] A particularly stun-
ning example of using the UN to confront the Soviet Union came in 1986.
After concluding that the Soviet Union was using its UN mission in New York
as a base for espionage in the United States, he cited the host country agreement and demanded that Moscow reduce its personnel there by 38 percent
within two years.[11]

Reagan's Pragmatism

Although Reagan clearly was suspicious of the ability of the UN to advance
human rights and freedom, his confrontation of the Soviets shows that he was
not shy about utilizing the various institutions of the UN to press his case. He
employed three basic methods: (1) aggressively press U.S. interests in the Security Council and other UN bodies such as the Commission on Human Rights;
(2) challenge the UN to live up to its stated lofty standards, particularly concerning human rights, of which he accused the UN of falling short; and (3)
insist that the UN be reformed.

President Reagan did not want to make the Security Council center stage
for all U.S. diplomacy. Its members, during the height of the Cold War, were
too politically divided and the threat of a Soviet veto too real to assure him
that the United States could shepherd major security initiatives through the

council. All too often, either Israel or the United States was the target of co-ordinated attacks at the council. Ambassador Kirkpatrick explained it this way to a reporter: what goes on in the Security Council "more closely resembles a mugging than either a political debate or an effort at problem-solving."[12]

The politicization of issues before a polarized Security Council impeded its ability to resolve conflicts. Reagan no doubt considered this dynamic in de-ciding not to take to the Security Council his decision to send troops into Gre-nada in 1983. He likewise avoided the Security Council when he sent air strikes into Libya after its operatives bombed a West German discotheque, killing American troops who frequented it. Long before charges of U.S. "unilateralism" were hurled at President George W. Bush, Reagan was doing what he felt was necessary to defend American interests without resorting to the Security Council.

Nevertheless, President Reagan did approach the Security Council to ad-vance some U.S. policy priorities. In 1983 and 1986, he vetoed two Security Council resolutions condemning Israeli settlements in Gaza, which he said were ill-advised and unnecessarily provocative but not illegal.[13] He supported a British draft resolution demanding that Argentina withdraw its forces from the Falk-land Islands, thus offering an assist to his ally, Prime Minister Margaret Thatcher. In 1988, he supported setting up three new UN peacekeeping op-erations (the UN Good Offices Mission in Afghanistan and Pakistan, the UN Iran-Iraq Military Observer Group mission, and the first UN Angola Verifi-cation Mission), as well as extending UN missions in the Golan Heights, Cyprus, and Lebanon.[14] American presidents who followed him have turned to the Security Council more frequently, but this is less a shift in policy than in the political environment since the end of the Cold War and the threat of a Soviet veto. The effect can be seen in the fact that, of the 69 peacekeeping and observer missions authorized by the Security Council since 1948, 53 came after Reagan had left office.[15]

Reagan often used America's veto in the Security Council. He turned to it some 40 times, principally on resolutions related to the Middle East.[16] His veto prevented the council from criticizing U.S. military actions in Grenada (1983) and Libya (1986), as well as the British actions in the Falklands. He also ve-toed a resolution on South Africa, a country he said had stood beside us in every war.[17] His administration also abstained on at least 22 Security Council votes, most dealing with Israel and the Middle East. Nevertheless, the United States under Ronald Reagan did join consensus votes 122 times. Thus, despite the deep divisions on the Security Council, the Reagan team was not always at loggerheads with other countries and often found ways to work cooperatively on matters of common concern.

Along with this pragmatic approach to the Security Council, Reagan avoided calls for a complete withdrawal of the United States from the UN. Instead, he called on the UN to live up to its own principles. During his address at the 38th Session of the General Assembly in 1983, Reagan tried to call member states back to the higher principles of the UN Charter:

> The members of the United Nations must be aligned on the side of justice rather than injustice, peace rather than aggression, human dignity rather than subjugation. Any other alignment is beneath the purpose of this great body and destructive of the harmony that it seeks. What harms the charter harms peace. The founders of the U.N. expected that member nations would behave and vote as individuals, after they had weighed the merits of an issue—rather like a great, global town meeting. The emergence of blocs and the polarization of the U.N. undermine all that this organization initially valued.[18]

This strategy was not merely a rejection of the isolationist urge to withdraw completely. It was also the beginning of a conservative strategy that would be picked up later by President George W. Bush (when, for example, he took the issue of Iraq to the UN Security Council). It was practical without sacrificing principle. Reagan, like Bush, believed the UN had some redeeming features that could be used to advance what he perceived as American interests and the causes of freedom and justice if the United States played a leadership role.

Perhaps the best example of this strategy was Reagan's approach to human rights. The Reagan administration sought from the outset to confront the UN system over its record on human rights, particularly the Commission on Human Rights, the principal body charged with defending human rights. More often than not, the UN seemed to shelter abusers of human rights like the Soviet Union and its communist allies than it did their victims.[19] The introduction to the State Department's *Country Reports on Human Rights Practices* for 1981 stated: "During the past year the U.S. has taken the lead in opposing in international fora the double standard applied to human rights violations, and has worked toward encouraging a more regional approach to solving international human rights concerns."[20]

Ambassador Kirkpatrick was particularly outraged. In a statement to the Third Committee of the UN General Assembly in 1981, she said the UN's record "belies the claim to moral seriousness," and as proof, she continued:

The human rights agencies of the United Nations were silent while three million Cambodians died in Pol Pot's murderous Utopia. The human rights agencies of the United Nations were silent while a quarter of a million Ugandans died at the hands of Idi Amin. The human rights organizations of the United Nations have been silent about the thousands of Soviet citizens denied equal rights, equal protection of the law, denied the right to think, write, publish work freely, or to emigrate to some place of their own choosing.[21]

At meetings of the Commission on Human Rights in Geneva, the U.S. delegation would continually draw attention to the double standard. At the 37th session in Geneva in 1981, the delegation stressed "the need to deal with human rights concerns in an even handed way" and said the United States was "particularly concerned that Latin American countries supportive of the West were being singled out for condemnation, while equal or greater human rights violations in Eastern Europe, the Soviet Union and Cuba went virtually unnoticed."[22] Moreover, the United States "insisted that international bodies entrusted with protecting human rights judge human rights performance by a single standard."[23]

The double-standard problem was endemic, rooted in how the UN and the Commission on Human Rights were set up. The voting members of these bodies included authoritarian regimes whose primary objective was to divert criticism from their own domestic abuses. They were able to get elected to bodies like the commission because they had the support of their regional voting blocs. Not only were the Soviet Union and China continually reelected for membership but their client states were as well, often exchanging seats. Belarus, for example, was elected on the commission for the term 1980–1982, Ukraine took the seat for 1983–1985, Belarus reclaimed it for 1986–1988, and then Ukraine for 1989–1991. China came onto the commission in 1982, taking Mongolia's place, and served continuously until 1993. Cuba served from 1976 to 1984 and was voted back on in 1989, serving until 1997.[24]

Reagan, International Conventions, and International Law

Reagan was skeptical of the ability of international conventions to advance the cause of freedom. One in particular he found problematic was the 1982 UN Convention on the Law of the Sea (UNCLOS), also referred to as the Law of the Sea Treaty. In general, Reagan was suspicious of international bodies exercising influence and control over U.S. sovereignty. As a strict constitutionalist, he was concerned that supranational bodies set up either through the UN or by an international convention could make decisions that infringed upon the constitutional rights of Americans to self-government and their system of federalism.

His main objections to UNCLOS were not over its navigational provisions; in fact, he felt they codified much of common practice. Rather, he objected to provisions that he and his advisers believed could establish a "new international economic order" based on the redistribution of wealth.[25] He was deeply concerned about provisions governing the Outer Continental Shelf and deep seabed mining. He especially opposed subjecting U.S. commercial activities to the unaccountable bureaucratic machinery the convention had set up to manage seabed mining. In his "Statement on United States Participation in the Third United Nations Conference on the Law of the Sea," dated January 29, 1982, he wrote that the United States would return to the negotiations with the purpose of achieving "an acceptable treaty."[26]

He listed in that statement the specific changes he sought so as to avoid the "monopolization of [seabed mining] resources by the operating arm of the International [Seabed] Authority,"[27] the international bureaucracy created by UNCLOS to oversee, regulate, collect, and transfer revenues from all seabed mining activity. Reagan wanted to ensure that the United States would continue to have access to its seabed mining resources to advance its economic development. The arbitrary authority of the International Seabed Authority was, to his mind, a potential threat to the sovereign economic interests of the United States. Moreover, concerned that the treaty might be changed in the future in ways that adversely affected U.S. economic interests, Reagan insisted that no new amendments come into force without the approval of all participating states and, in the United States, the advice and consent of the Senate. Reagan also was interested, as he specified in his statement, that the convention "not contain provisions for the mandatory transfer of private technology and participation by and funding for national liberation movements."[28]

His negotiators were not successful in achieving all of the changes, which prevented Reagan from signing UNCLOS. In an entry in his diary on June 29, 1982, he wrote: "Decided in NSC meeting—will not sign 'Law of the Sea' treaty even without seabed mining provisions."[29] According to his long-time legal adviser, Ed Meese, Reagan had not received the assurances he'd asked for and thus was not convinced the treaty would best serve U.S. interests. Meese recalled Reagan telling him that the best defense of American interests in the world's oceans was not an international convention, but the U.S. Navy.[30]

After months of further deliberation, Reagan concluded that, despite not joining UNCLOS, the United States would nevertheless respect its traditional navigation provisions, which he considered little more than a reiteration and codification of international customary law. In his presidential statement on March 10, 1983, he said:

> The United States is prepared to accept and act in accordance with the balance of interests relating to traditional uses of the oceans—such as navigation and overflight. In this respect, the United States will recognize the rights of other states in the waters off their coasts, as reflected in the Convention, so long as the rights and freedoms of the United States and others under international law are recognized by such coastal states.[31]

The United States to this day has not ratified UNCLOS. Some proponents argue that Reagan would have approved the treaty with the changes made to it in 1994.[32] The changes were made to assure the United States that, if it ratified the convention, it would have a guaranteed seat on the International Seabed Authority council, that voting groups (not individual nations) could block substantive decisions that they objected to by consensus, and that the largest donors would be placed on the finance committee that initiates by consensus the policies that the council would vote on.

Nevertheless, many members of Congress have expressed continuing concerns that the United States will be at a disadvantage; so far the Senate has not found enough broad support for the treaty to give its advice and consent. Moreover, despite what treaty proponents say, it is not at all clear that Reagan would have signed the treaty as amended in 1994. Two of Reagan's closest advisers, Ed Meese and William P. Clark—people who surely knew his mind better than those who must rely on surmise or secondhand speculation—still believe that he would not.[33]

Despite his rejection of UNCLOS, Reagan embraced other international conventions, albeit with conditions. Concerning treaties dealing with conflicts, for example, Reagan supported the Geneva Conventions as "improving the international rules of humanitarian law in armed conflict."[34] Nevertheless, in his letter of transmittal to the Senate in January 1987, he requested the Senate consider only Protocol II to the conventions for its advice and consent, taking into consideration his reservations, understandings, and declarations.[35] Protocol II, he explained, expanded the "fundamental humanitarian provision of the Conventions for non-international armed conflicts, such as humane treatment and basic due process for detainees, protection of the wounded, sick and medical units, and of noncombatants from attack and deliberate starvation." Moreover, he said, "If these fundamental rules were observed, many of the worst human tragedies of current internal armed conflicts could be avoided."

However, in that same letter to the Senate, Reagan specifically rejected Protocol I.[36] It had some good provisions, he acknowledged, but it also treated "wars of national liberation" as international conflicts. "Whether such wars are international or non-international," he wrote, "should turn exclusively on objective reality, not on one's view of the moral qualities of each conflict. To rest on such subjective distinctions based on a war's alleged purposes would politicize humanitarian law and eliminate the distinction between international and non-international conflicts." That would thereby grant combatant status to terrorists and other "irregular" forces that might hide among civilians. "These problems," he continued, "are so fundamental in character that they cannot be remedied through reservations." He concluded:

> I therefore have decided not to submit the Protocol to the Senate in any form . . . [and] the Joint Chiefs of Staff have also concluded that a number of the provisions of the Protocol are militarily unacceptable. It is unfortunate that Protocol I must be rejected. . . . We would have preferred to ratify such a convention, which as I said contains certain sound elements. But we cannot allow other nations of the world, however numerous, to impose upon us and our allies and friends an unacceptable and thoroughly distasteful price for joining a convention drawn to advance the laws of war. In fact, we must not, and need not, give recognition and protection to terrorist groups as a price for progress in humanitarian law."[37]

An international convention that met a more positive response from Reagan was the United Nations Convention against Torture, which he signed in 1988. According to Meese, who conferred personally with Reagan on the matter, Reagan saw this convention as extending America's natural abhorrence of the practice of torture into the realm of international law.[38] But he was careful to include appropriate reservations, such as whether the governing committee established by the treaty to oversee its implementation would be recognized as competent by the United States. In his May 20, 1988, letter of transmittal to the Senate for advice and consent, Reagan wrote:

> Should the Senate give its advice and consent to ratification of the Convention, I intend at the time of deposit of United States ratification to make a

declaration pursuant to Article 28 that the United States does not recognize the competence of the Committee against Torture under Article 20 to make confidential investigations of charges that torture is being systematically practiced in the United States . . . [and that the] decision as to whether to accept such competence of the Committee should be withheld until we have had an opportunity to assess the Committee's work.

Some of Reagan's 19 reservations were later watered down or struck either by the George H. W. Bush administration or the Democrat-controlled Senate during deliberations in 1991. The instrument of ratification finally submitted to the UN by Bill Clinton in 1994 contains only three reservations, four understandings, and two declarations. Nevertheless, many of Reagan's concerns have been borne out by subsequent controversies at the UN over, for example, what constitutes torture and what jurisdiction the convention's implementing committee would have. Reagan had anticipated that work of the committee could be politicized, such as it was in 2012 when UN Special Rapporteur on Torture Juan Mendez formally accused the United States of the cruel and inhuman treatment, and possible torture, of Bradley Manning, a U.S. soldier accused of leaking scores of classified government documents in the scandal now known as Wikileaks.[39]

President Reagan committed the United States to other treaties as well. In 1988, he signed into law a bill criminalizing genocide, permitting the United States to ratify the 1948 International Convention on the Prevention and Punishment of the Crime of Genocide. That same year, to further the "war on drugs," he signed the United Nations Convention against Illicit Traffic in Narcotic Drugs and Psychotropic Substances, which he called the "broadest and most far-reaching set of laws and agreements ever adopted in this field." And he signed into law the Montreal Protocol on Substances That Deplete the Ozone Layer, saying its "unique provision" creating a mechanism for adjusting the protocol over time was wise.

Reagan's approach to international conventions and treaties was thus largely pragmatic. If he deemed that international treaties served U.S. interests and protected American sovereignty, he generally was inclined to support them. In this respect, he was merely reflecting the age-old approach to customary international law that for centuries had upheld the sovereignty of nation-states. He was willing to go along with new trends in international humanitarian law, as he did by signing the Convention against Torture, so long as safeguards and reservations were included to prevent its abusive use against the United States.

Reagan's Arms Control Agenda and the UN

One of Reagan's lasting legacies is his new approach to arms control. Before his time, arms control agreements like the Strategic Arms Limitation Treaty (SALT) of 1972 had merely ratified the nuclear arsenals on both sides of the Cold War divide. With his Strategic Arms Reduction Treaty (START) proposal, Reagan introduced into the arms control equation a way for the nuclear powers to actually reduce their nuclear arsenals. START was signed in 1991; by 2001, it had resulted in an 80 percent reduction in the numbers of known strategic nuclear weapons. He negotiated the Intermediate-Range Nuclear Forces (INF) Treaty with the aim to not merely limit the growth of those weapons in nuclear arsenals, but to actually eliminate them.

For Reagan, arms control agreements should distinguish between nonaggressive powers like the United States and aggressive ones like the Soviet Union. Arms control treaties with the Soviet Union must be based on the simple objective of effectively and verifiably reducing the threat of nuclear war. He walked the United States away from the Strategic Arms Limitation Treaty II (SALT II) signed by President Carter after determining that the Soviets were unwilling to abide by it.

Reagan used speeches and statements before the UN Conference on Disarmament (CD) to reiterate his principles and policies toward disarmament. One of his recurring themes was the necessity for strict verification of arms control agreements; he often accused the Soviet Union of violating the agreements. However, by and large the Conference on Disarmament was a sideshow for arms control during his presidency. With the exception of calling for a comprehensive ban on chemical weapons, which Vice President George H. W. Bush presented to the CD in 1984, most of Reagan's actions in this setting were defensive. In 1988, he opposed Soviet proposals for bans on nuclear testing and curbs on space and naval weapons, for example, and he repeatedly opposed Arab efforts to condemn Israel's reported nuclear weapons program.[40]

Reagan and UN Reform

One of Reagan's lasting legacies is the focus of U.S. policy on trying to reform the UN. Since Reagan, every U.S. president, including President Barack Obama, has paid at least lip service to the need to do this. Reagan gave them a blueprint for how to get things done, making it absolutely clear that the United

States was unafraid to withdraw from UN bodies that were deemed to be corrupt and anti-American and to withhold its dues (if need be) to spur reform.

The letter that Secretary of State George Shultz delivered to the United Nations Educational, Scientific, and Cultural Organization (UNESCO) notifying them of Reagan's decision to withdraw in 1984 provides an example: "UNESCO," it stated, "had extraneously politicized virtually every subject it deals with, has exhibited hostility toward the basic institutions of a free society, especially a free market and a free press, and has demonstrated unrestrained budgetary expansion."[41] The persistent efforts of socialist and totalitarian member states to use UNESCO to promote a "new world information order" and to codify restrictions on freedom of speech and of the press drove Reagan to accept the advice of his State Department to withdraw.[42]

In doing this, Reagan clearly recognized the value other nations placed on such institutions. But he also had an unwavering expectation that they should focus on their missions and not fall victim, as UNESCO had, to political agendas that undermine their very purposes. President Reagan could not justify using U.S. tax dollars to finance hostile agendas in these organizations.

The issue of withholding some of the dues the United States paid to the UN took on new significance during his presidency. When he entered office, America was expected to pay 25 percent of the UN's entire regular budget and over 30 percent of its peacekeeping budget. In 1980, in fact, the United States paid 40.2 percent of all contributions for peacekeeping, while France paid 7 percent and the Soviet Union only 3.5 percent.[43] However, early in the Reagan administration, the United States began a process of deferring part of its annual dues until the fourth quarter of each fiscal year as a way to incorporate actual UN budget requests and align its contributions to the U.S. government's fiscal year appropriations process (instead of paying in advance). According to the U.S. General Accounting Office, the purpose was to realize "a temporary U.S. budget reduction, improve the accuracy of U.S. budget requests, and impress upon the [UN] organizations the need for restraining budget growth."[44]

Then, in 1985, Reagan signed the Kassebaum-Solomon amendment into law, which called for withholding 20 percent of U.S. dues to the UN and specialized agencies unless weighted voting on budgetary matters was adopted.[45] Reagan, at least from his official statements, did not appear entirely convinced that this approach would work. In the statement released by the White House when he signed the bill into law, he went so far as to assert that some of these withholdings could "deleteriously affect" organizations that were important to the United States.[46] The provision was rescinded in the 1990s; nevertheless, it had set a strong precedent for Congress and future U.S. administrations to withhold U.S. funding to the U.N. to force reform, such as the legislation introduced by Senators Jesse Helms and Joe Biden and enacted into law 1999.

Ultimately, though weighted voting at the UN was not adopted, the prospect of facing significant withholdings by the United States convinced the UN in 1986 to agree to consensus-based budgeting, an informal process that in effect gives each country a veto over the proposed budgets; it was used for the first time in 1987.[47] That informal agreement helped to greatly constrain UN budget growth. And because of it, toward the end of his second term, Reagan approved paying back some of the U.S. withholdings.[48] The informal consensus-based budgeting process prevailed, in fact, for 20 years until 2006, when the UN General Assembly adopted a budget resolution over U.S. objections.[49]

Lessons for Presidents and the World Today

A healthy skepticism about engaging in international organizations is a virtue for every president. The UN system, to which America now sends a total of more than $7 billion a year,[50] is at its foundation political. Its many agencies include some that are appropriately limited in purpose and do good work—such as protecting and resettling refugees or setting technical standards for international air travel or postal deliveries between countries. In other areas, its agencies and efforts have been inadequate; consider, for example, the UN's record in stopping genocide or promoting economic development.

Leaders today can learn much from Ronald Reagan. Unfortunately, his successors did not always learn from his example. Sensing new possibilities in the wake of the end of the Cold War, George Herbert Walker Bush revived the fortunes of the Security Council in the first Gulf War. In that case, the strategy worked well, but since then reaching out to the Security Council to manage America's wars or protect its vital interests has not been consistently successful. The high expectations of the Gulf War era lived on in the Clinton administration, but even Bill Clinton had to bypass the Security Council to undertake the military operation over Kosovo. Like his father, George W. Bush went to the Security Council to gain approval for an American war—in this case, the Iraq War. But the results of that strategy were largely a mixed bag. Since then, the UN's star has faded in the making of American foreign policy. Even a figure sympathetic to the UN—President Barack Obama—is selective in engaging the Security Council; yes, he went to it in the Libya operation, but he bypassed it on Syria because of the threat of Russia's veto. He also did not sign an agreement granting one of the UN's oldest specialized agencies, the International Telecommunications Union, more authority over the Internet due to concerns that it could harm that medium's growth, freedom, and vitality.[51] As in the days of Reagan, expectations of the UN are often tempered with pragmatism.

Rather than assuming international organizations have everyone's best interests at heart and turning over to them vital decisions affecting the security and prosperity of Americans, U.S. presidents should work to build stronger diplomatic relationships, coalitions, and alliances with countries that share America's values or goals to address specific problems.[52] Like Reagan, they should use the UN and other international organizations to challenge countries that actively undermine liberty and security. And where the UN falls short, they should not hesitate to call it out for its failures. There is nothing morally superior about the decisions of an international body that has, in at least half of its membership, nations that are not full democracies and that do not share a fundamental respect for freedom, human rights, and the rule of law.

Reagan said it best when he addressed the UN General Assembly in September 1986:

> This [UN] organization itself faces a critical hour—that is usually stated as a fiscal crisis. But we can turn this crisis into an opportunity. The important reforms proposed by a group of experts can be a first step toward restoring the organization's status and effectiveness. The issue, ultimately, is not one of cash but of credibility. If all the members of this universal organization decide to seize the moment and turn the rhetoric of reform into reality, the future of the U.N. will be secure. And you have my word for it: My country, which has always given the U.N. generous support, will continue to play a leading role in the effort to achieve its noble purposes.

12

Ronald Reagan, the Pragmatic Internationalist

BARRY E. CARTER

President Ronald Reagan had strong conservative principles and often declared them in soaring, though direct, terms. And yet, during his presidency, he could be—and very effectively was—a pragmatic internationalist when circumstances made such pragmatism the best way to achieve beneficial results for the United States.

This chapter comes from a unique background and perspective. Unlike some of the other contributors in this book, who might have worked for President Reagan or knew him, I was not in the Reagan administration or a Republican. Indeed, as a moderate Democrat in foreign policy, I worked as a full-time foreign policy aide in the 1984 presidential campaign of former Vice President Walter Mondale. President Reagan won that election decisively, losing only Mondale's home state of Minnesota and the District of Columbia.

Watching President Reagan and his team in 1984 roll over the Mondale campaign gave me a firsthand view of how good President Reagan was in creating and delivering a coherent, upbeat message—and reacting effectively to changing situations. I felt like a lineman on an opposing football team who came to appreciate and respect the other side's superb quarterback and his team after getting thoroughly beaten by them.

I recall a moment midway through the 1984 campaign, while listening in on a strategy meeting among former Vice President Mondale and his senior campaign advisers onboard a long plane flight from Texas to Washington, D.C. They were discussing what approach should be taken in the remaining weeks, and Mondale highlighted the problem. Apparently, his campaign advisers had initially recommended attacking President Reagan—with the result that Mondale's poll negatives rose. Then, they had recommended focusing on issues—and the public was saying that Mondale was boring. Here, midway through the campaign, the Mondale camp did not know a way to beat Reagan. In retrospect, I doubt if there was one.

That campaign experience and my other observations during his eight years as president made me recognize and respect President Reagan's formidable abilities. As examples, here I will describe how President Reagan demonstrated these abilities or strengths in three areas: international economic policy, arms control, and the law of the sea.

International Economic Policy

Returning to 1984, the national economy was just beginning to emerge from difficult economic times. When he was inaugurated in 1981, Reagan had inherited high inflation and high interest rates from the Carter administration, and the overall economy declined even further during Reagan's first year, becoming a recession. Fortunately for Reagan's 1984 reelection prospects, the economy began to recover in 1982.

Because its campaign was not run by the party in control of the White House and executive branch, the Mondale campaign relied on many volunteer experts to help on substantive issues. The experts came from the sometimes overlapping circles of former executive-branch officials and other people in academia, think tanks, business, labor unions, law firms, and Congress. On international economics, there was a remarkable consensus that domestic U.S. manufacturing was being hampered by a strong U.S. dollar. The strong dollar meant that U.S. exports were priced higher relative to the products of other countries and that a dollar lower in value would improve the relative pricing of U.S. goods. The advisers urged Mondale, who understood the substance, to call for a lower dollar as a way to promote exports and create jobs.

The speechwriters put such a call into one of Mondale's speeches. Immediately, the same day, the Reagan campaign hit back. Mondale was already somewhat suspect in many voters' minds as not being tough enough because of, among other reasons, the general perception that Democrats were soft on defense and Mondale's specific stand in the past on some issues, like Vietnam and the defense budget. The Reagan campaign played on that and invoked patriotism. The Reagan team's response essentially was: "There's goes Walter

Mondale again. He's for a weak dollar and a weak United States. President Reagan is for a strong dollar and a strong United States."[1]

Outmaneuvered politically, and very quickly so, I do not believe that Mondale or his campaign made an issue of the dollar again.

This response by the Reagan campaign reflected what appears to have been President Reagan's own strongly and consistently held views in 1984 and earlier. For example, he had said he was "firmly opposed to any attempt to depress the dollar's exchange value by intervention in international currency markets. Pure exchange market intervention cannot offset the fundamental factors that determine the dollar's value. . . . The dollar must therefore be allowed to seek its natural value without exchange market intervention."[2]

In fact, the dollar was overvalued relative to other major currencies. After the 1984 campaign was over, President Reagan promptly appointed his White House chief of staff and effective campaign manager, James A. Baker III, to be secretary of the Treasury. As the talented Baker settled into his position, one of his early acts was to reconsider U.S. international economic policy, including the value of the dollar. Baker and his deputy, Richard Darman, embarked on active discussions with U.S. allies, especially the other G-5 countries—Japan, West Germany, England, and France.

The first signs of the change from a hands-off policy in the currency markets were progressively larger interventions starting in January 1985 after an agreement at a G-5 meeting on January 17, 1985. More serious efforts to manage U.S. international economic policy and to coordinate with the other countries began in April 1985 with Japan. After further international discussions and meetings, the G-5 deputies met in London on September 15 to negotiate the key points of an agreement and issue a nine-page communiqué.

On Sunday, September 22, 1985, when the world's currency and stock markets were closed, Baker secretly convened the finance ministers and central bank governors of the G-5 countries at the Plaza Hotel in New York City. Working from the drafts of an agreement and a communiqué prepared by their deputies, the G-5 representatives resolved the remaining issues. The representatives reached a detailed agreement that the countries would intervene significantly in the currency markets by a public announcement of their intentions and concrete actions, primarily selling dollars from a collective "war chest" of up to $18 billion (an unprecedented sum in those days). In a so-called non-paper (because of its sensitivity) that the deputies prepared, the intervention shares of each country were specified, and one objective was that "a 10–12 percent downward adjustment of the dollar from present levels would be manageable over the near term."

On the delicate political issue of whether to describe the effort as one to depreciate the dollar or appreciate other currencies, the U.S. view prevailed. The agreement called for the appreciation of the yen and the deutsche mark, rather than the depreciation of the dollar. The public communiqué read: "Some further orderly appreciation of the main non-dollar currencies against the dollar is inevitable."

On the Monday following the New York meeting and the unexpected announcement, the effect of the announcement and "massive joint intervention" meant that "the dollar fell 4.29 percent against foreign currencies [and even more against the yen], the largest single-day drop in the history of the London and New York currency markets."[3] By the end of October, the dollar had dropped "13 percent . . . from the level at which it had traded during the week before the G-5 meeting in relation to the yen," 10.5 percent compared to the deutsche mark, and 8 percent relative to the British pound. "The goal of 10 to 12 percent realignment had already been accomplished."[4]

In short, the Reagan administration's actual nonintervention strategy and its campaign tactics and rhetoric had given way in 1985 to a pragmatic, reasonable dollar policy.

Similarly important, the successful financial cooperation on currencies of the G-5 countries helped pave the way for more close international economic cooperation among major powers. As other countries have grown economically, the G-5 morphed into the G-7 in 1991, and then the G-8, and now the G-20 is playing a major international economic role.

Arms Control and the INF Treaty

On national security matters, President Reagan was strongly anti-communist—and hardly a friend of the Soviet Union. In 1983, he called the Soviet Union an "evil empire," and in 1987, standing before the Berlin Wall, he called on Soviet General Secretary Mikhail Gorbachev to "open this gate" and "tear down this wall."

Yet, President Reagan was also genuinely aware of the real dangers of a nuclear conflict with the Soviet Union. In a dramatic and eloquent speech on March 23, 1983, that called for the Strategic Defense Initiative (SDI) with defensive interceptors, President Reagan declared: "I call upon the scientific community in our country, those who gave us nuclear weapons, to turn their great talents now to the cause of mankind and world peace, to give us the means of rendering those nuclear weapons impotent and obsolete."

To achieve his goal, the president was willing to address a wide variety of arms-control approaches with the Soviet Union. Maybe the most dramatic illustration was the U.S.-Soviet summit meeting in Reykjavík, Iceland, between Reagan and Gorbachev on October 11–12, 1986. The event was meant to be a "meeting," but the world came to regard it as a "summit." Reflecting President Reagan's desire for summits that were not already preprogrammed from the bottom up, Secretary of State George P. Shultz and others tried to make the event less programmed by avoiding a prenegotiated communiqué and allowing more time "for the leaders to meet alone and engage in real conversation."[5] At the same time, a whole team of experts and representatives from all the relevant U.S. departments and agencies was on hand for analysis and consultation.

The leaders' discussions at Reykjavík were truly wide-ranging on nuclear weapons and led to remarkably unexpected positions on both sides. Their first meeting, on Saturday, October 11, was initially between the two leaders, with only their interpreters and notetakers present. As soon as both leaders sat down, Gorbachev "pulled a set of notes from his briefcase and proceeded to present what he called his 'bold, unorthodox' proposals to limit strategic weapons, intermediate-range missiles, and missiles in space." Gorbachev, however, wanted to confine SDI research to the laboratory.[6]

After more meetings that day and on Sunday, as the two leaders struggled with an impasse over Reagan's commitment to moving forward with SDI, the rapidly evolving positions of both countries led Gorbachev to renew a proposal he had made months ago to do away with all nuclear weapons in 10 years. Notably, Reagan responded, "It would be fine with me if we eliminated all nuclear weapons."[7] The idea was being seriously considered by the two leaders.

Continued disagreement, however, over what would be allowed for the development and testing of Reagan's Strategic Defense Initiative and other issues finally led to no arms-control agreement at the summit. Indeed, Reagan ended the meeting abruptly, and there was not even the usual communiqué.

The conventional wisdom in the United States after Reykjavík was that it had been a failure on arms control specifically and a wider failure more generally. However, as Secretary Shultz has argued, "The accomplishments were immense. The Soviet agreement that human rights belonged on the regular agenda of U.S.-Soviet relations was astonishing."[8] Moreover, Reagan's embrace of eliminating nuclear weapons fertilized a long-growing idea that has since seen other prominent leaders encourage at least steps toward a world free of nuclear weapons.[9]

The Reykjavík summit also provided new momentum that helped yield actual and important results in the near term. Gorbachev suggested in February 1987 that the impasse over SDI could be decoupled from the negotiations for an Intermediate-Range Nuclear Forces (INF) Treaty. This concession helped lead to the treaty, which was signed in December 1987. The treaty called for the United States and the Soviet Union to eliminate all of their nuclear and conventional ground-launched ballistic and cruise missiles with ranges of 500 to 5,500 kilometers. As noted by the Arms Control Association, "The treaty was the first time the two superpowers had agreed to reduce their nuclear arsenals, eliminate an entire category of nuclear weapons, and utilize extensive on-site inspections for verification."[10]

President Jimmy Carter and other NATO leaders had started the INF process in 1979 as a result of Soviet deployment of SS-20 missiles in the Soviet Bloc in the mid-1970s. The SS-20 was an intermediate-range, multiple-warhead missile that increased Soviet capabilities in the European area. Although the United States and the rest of NATO agreed on a strategy of negotiations and deployment of new U.S. missiles, President Reagan became the driving force for negotiations and deployment. Gorbachev, who became secretary general in 1985, was the other key actor in the negotiations.

Reagan's actions began shortly into his first term. First, he continued the push for the deployment of intermediate-range U.S. missiles (cruise missiles and the Pershing II missiles) in Europe to offset the Soviets' SS-20 missiles and to provide some bargaining leverage vis-à-vis Moscow. Second, Reagan proposed in a speech at the National Press Club in November 1981 a clear and dramatic negotiating position, the so-called zero option. He offered to refrain from deploying the U.S. intermediate-range nuclear missiles (INF) if the Soviet Union agreed to eliminate all their SS-20 missiles currently deployed in Europe or Asia. Although U.S. arms control negotiators had departed from this zero option on occasion before 1986, the basic concept of zero was to reemerge at Reykjavík in 1986.

In moving forward with the deployment of the U.S. missiles that was scheduled to begin in 1983, President Reagan overcame political opposition at home and, with the help of West German Chancellor Helmut Kohl and other European leaders, considerable opposition to deployment in West Germany and other European countries. It was a long, difficult, and heated process. Eventually, however, Reagan and Gorbachev's discussions at Reykjavík included major movement on INF negotiations.

The 1987 INF Treaty itself met continued strong opposition from a number of American conservatives. However, President Reagan worked hard to obtain the advice and consent of the U.S. Senate, and the treaty entered into force in June 1988. It abolished an entire class of nuclear weapons. The INF Treaty also demonstrates that there can be benefits and advantages in well-designed and carefully verified arms-control agreements, even with countries that have sharply different ideologies and interests.

Law of the Sea Negotiations and Convention

Although President Reagan announced in July 1982 that the United States would not sign the Law of the Sea Convention (the Convention or LOS Convention)[11] as adopted by the conference that negotiated it, he recognized that the Convention contained "many positive and significant accomplishments." Importantly, Reagan also detailed his specific problems with certain provisions of the deep-sea mining regime in the Convention. His announcement disappointed many people interested in the law of the sea in the United States and in the rest of the world. However, it came as no great surprise because of Reagan's steps leading up to the announcement. Significantly, his listing of specific problems gave hope and a path that might lead to the United States eventually joining the treaty.

Here, I will analyze this issue by first looking at some necessary background history, followed by sections on the Convention, Reagan's position, and, last, the post-Convention situation, which remains a significant issue in the world today.

A little history on this issue can be useful.[12] After centuries in which almost all the rules or laws regarding the seas were found in customary international law that developed and evolved, the pressures for codification of the law increased after World War II. Exploitation of oil and other offshore mineral wealth was a reality, and the depletion of fishery stocks was rapidly increasing.

In 1956, a United Nations Conference on the Law of the Sea (UNCLOS I) was called. It produced four treaties in 1958: the Conventions on the Territorial Sea and Contiguous Zones, on the Continental Shelf, on the High Seas, and on Fishing and Conservation of Living Resources of the High Seas. The United States ratified all four of these conventions, and all four entered into force in the early to mid-1960s.

Although UNCLOS I was considered a great success, a number of issues were left unresolved, and new issues emerged. The unresolved issues included the breadth of the territorial sea and the limits on the continental shelf. There was also concern about a major new issue—mining of the deep seabed beyond any limits on the continental shelf.

In 1960, UNCLOS II was convened, but it was not successful. It failed by a single vote, for instance, to adopt a compromise formula that provided for a territorial sea of six nautical miles, plus a six-mile fishery zone.[13] No formal conventions emerged from the conference.

Supported by the U.S. government (with President Richard Nixon, a Republican, and Secretary of State Henry Kissinger), UNCLOS III began in 1974. Rather than adopt provisions through a straight majority vote, the conference used a system of consensus. Although this undoubtedly lengthened the proceedings, the system sought to ensure that no single group of nations could force their will on a minority; it thereby attempted to secure the ongoing participation of all nations.

From its inception, the Convention was conceived as a comprehensive agreement. The document, opened for signature in 1982, is well over 100 pages long and contains 32 articles and nine annexes. It covers widely divergent subjects, ranging from the nationality of vessels to deep seabed mining. Among other accomplishments, the Convention definitively outlines various zones in the sea where the coastal state and other states have varying rights, such as control of resources or passage of vessels. The regime is divided into areas of descending authority for the coastal states: internal waters, territorial sea, contiguous zone, exclusive economic zone, continental shelf, and high seas.

The Convention and its annexes also established a complicated system for the exploitation of the mineral resources in the deep seabed, the so-called Area. It was the most controversial aspect of the Convention. Many of the Convention's other provisions simply adopted customary international law or have become accepted as international law, but the deep seabed mining regime caused considerable dissension.

As for Ronald Reagan, most of the key provisions in the 1982 Convention had already taken shape by 1980. In his 1980 campaign, Reagan ran on a Republican platform that opposed certain provisions in the draft Convention. Soon after his inauguration in January 1981, President Reagan withdrew the U.S. delegation from consultations.

He sent U.S. negotiators back in January 1982. However, as he carefully explained later in his "Statement on United States Actions Concerning the Conference on the Law of the Sea," dated July 9, 1982, he had decided not to sign the Convention:

> The United States has long recognized how critical the world's oceans are to mankind and how important international agreements are to the use of those oceans. For over a decade, the United States has been working with more than 150 countries at the Third [UN] Conference on Law of the Sea to develop a comprehensive treaty.
>
> On January 29 of this year, I reaffirmed the United States' commitment to the multilateral process for reaching such a treaty and announced that we would return to the negotiations to seek to correct unacceptable elements in the deep seabed mining part of the draft convention. I also announced that my administration would support ratification of a convention meeting six basic objectives.
>
> On April 30 the conference adopted a convention that does not satisfy the objectives sought by the United States. It was adopted by a vote of 130 in favor, with 4 against (including the United States) and 17 abstentions. Those voting 'no' or abstaining appear small in number but represent countries which produce more than 60 percent of the world's gross national product. . . .
>
> We have now completed a review of that convention and recognize that it contains many positive and very significant accomplishments. Those extensive parts dealing with navigation and overflight and most other provisions of the convention are consistent with United States interests and, in our view, serve well the interests of all nations. . . .
>
> Our review recognizes, however, that the deep seabed mining part of the convention does not meet United States objectives. For this reason, I am announcing today that the United States will not sign the convention as adopted by the conference, and our participation in the remaining conference process will be at the technical level and will involve only those provisions that serve United States interests.

Although Reagan here made clear that the United States would not sign the Convention—as currently constituted—his statement was constructive for the longer term in listing the specific objections of the United States. As noted earlier, it provided a path or road map that might lead to the United States eventually joining the Convention. Reagan indicated:

These decisions reflect the deep conviction that the United States cannot support a deep seabed mining regime with such major problems. In our view, those problems include:

—Provisions that would actually deter future development of deep seabed mineral resources, which such development should serve the interest of all countries.

—A decision-making process that would not give the United States or others a role that fairly reflects and protects their interests.

—Provisions that would allow amendments to enter into force for the United States without its approval. This is clearly incompatible with the United States approach to such treaties.

—Stipulations relating to mandatory transfer of private technology and the possibility of national liberation movements sharing in benefits.

—The absence of assured access for future qualified deep seabed miners to promote the development of these resources.

We recognize that world demand and markets currently do not justify commercial development of deep seabed mineral resources, and it is not clear when such development will be justified. When such factors become favorable, however, the deep seabed represents a potentially important source of strategic and other minerals. The aim of the United States in this regard has been to establish with other nations an order that would allow explorations and development under reasonable terms and conditions.

Although the United States did not sign the Convention in December 1982 when other countries began signing, and it has yet to sign the Convention, enough other countries signed and then ratified the treaty so that it came into force in November 1994. As of April 2013, the Convention had 165 states as parties, out of the generally recognized 194 states in the world.

The United States then proceeded on two principal tracks after 1982. First, in spite of his public opposition to the Convention, President Reagan was the pragmatic internationalist. He accepted and implemented important provisions that he correctly saw were in the U.S. national interest.

Starting in March 1983, by a presidential proclamation and executive orders, Reagan announced that the United States would act in accord with the treaty's provisions on navigation and overflight. He also proclaimed an Exclusive Economic Zone (EEZ), in which the United States would exercise sovereign rights over living and mineral sources within 200 nautical miles of its coast. This was a huge extension of U.S. claims over the resources adjoining its shores, especially compared to its previous three-mile territorial sea and claims to the natural resources of the continental shelf and to coastal fishery zones. Five years later, in 1988, President Reagan formally proclaimed that the United States was extending its three-mile territorial sea to 12 nautical miles.

As a law professor, I have to gulp a bit about President Reagan saying in his 1983 proclamation that these new provisions were "consistent with the convention and international law." The LOS Convention would not enter into force until November 1984, and the United States was not going to be a party then. Moreover, the 200-mile EEZ was not a long and consistent practice of states; it would not be considered customary international law. Similarly, Reagan's 1988 proclamation extending the territorial sea to 12 miles said that these were "the limits permitted by international law." Again, the United States was not part of the Convention, and, until it came into force in November 1994, most states had set a range of three to 12 miles as their territorial seas. This was a claim to a very rapid development of customary international law.[14]

What President Reagan effectively did was to move quickly to capitalize on some of the Convention's provisions that were beneficial to the United States, knowing that other countries could hardly complain because the new Convention was pushing international law toward those boundaries.

President Reagan's admirers might recall these steps—seizing upon beneficial provisions—when considering the significant developments in the deep seabed mining area provisions since the initial provisions of the Convention. I will discuss those next.

On the second principal track, the United States moved to negotiate alternative arrangements to the Convention's deep seabed regime through bilateral and multilateral agreements. For example, Belgium, France, West Germany, Italy, the Netherlands, the United Kingdom, and the United States concluded in 1984 the Provisional Understanding Regarding Deep Seabed Mining. Needless to say, many signatories to the LOS Convention condemned this alternative approach.

A number of factors combined, however, to make supporters and opponents of the Convention's deep seabed mining provisions more open to accommodation. In October 1990, consultations among a representative group of countries began under UN auspices to determine whether there was enough common ground between the developing and developed countries to seek more generally acceptable arrangements for deep seabed mining. Representatives of the U.S. State Department during President George H. W. Bush's administration and then President Bill Clinton's administration participated in these new consultations. The consultations led to the Agreement Relating to the Implementation of Part XI of the 1984 agreement on the United Nations Convention on the Law of the Sea.

The new agreement came into force in July 1996. As of April 2013, there are 144 parties of this agreement. The growing acceptance of the LOS Convention and the 1984 agreement, among other factors, led the major countries that had been siding with the United States to begin to become parties to the LOS Convention and the 1984 agreement, isolating the United States.

The United States even signed the 1984 agreement on July 29, 1994. President Clinton then announced in 1998 that he was submitting the LOS Convention and the 1994 agreement to the U.S. Senate for its advice and consent. The Senate had not done this by the end of the Clinton administration.

After George W. Bush became president in 2001, his administration began a review process that led it to support U.S. accession to the LOS Convention and the 1984 agreement. As explained in November 2008 by the U.S. Department of State's legal adviser, John B. Bellinger III, the U.S. government had concluded:

> First, the Convention strongly advances U.S. national security interests because it guarantees our military and commercial vessels—both ships and aircraft—navigational rights and freedoms through the world's oceans. . . . We concluded that these protections are particularly important at a time when the U.S. military is conducting military operations in Iraq and Afghanistan and new initiatives like the Proliferation Security Initiative. . . .
>
> Second, the Convention advances U.S. economic interests. It would codify U.S. sovereign rights over all the resources in the ocean, and on and under the ocean floor, in a 200-nautical Exclusive Economic Zone off our coastline [and further with respect to the continental shelf]. . . .
>
> The third principal benefit of the Convention is that it sets forth a comprehensive legal framework and establishes basic obligations for protecting the marine environment from all sources of pollution.
>
> Apart from the benefits of these substantive provisions, joining the Convention would give the United States a "seat at the table" in the interpretation and development of the law of the sea. . . . Our status as a non-Party puts us in a far weaker position to advance U.S. interests.

In addition, the U.S. Congress passed the Oceans Act of 2000, which went into effect on January 20, 2001. The act established a 16-member Commission on

Ocean Policy to undertake an 18-month study and to make recommendations to the president and Congress. President George W. Bush appointed the commission's 16 members, based on a process that included nominations by both Congress and the president. Admiral James D. Watkins, USN (Ret.), the former chief of naval operations (the Navy's highest uniformed position), was named chairman. Before the commission expired in 2004, the commissioners released a final report containing the commission's findings and recommendations for ocean policy, including the following:

> It is imperative that the nation ratify the United Nations Convention on the Law of the Sea, the preeminent legal framework for addressing international ocean issues. Until that step is taken, the United States will not be able to participate directly in the bodies established under the Convention that make decisions on issues of importance to all coastal and seafaring nations.[15]

With this support from the Clinton administration and the second Bush administration, as well as from the Commission on Ocean Policy, the Senate Foreign Relations Committee, chaired by moderate Republican senator Richard Lugar (after Senator Jesse Helms had retired), voted 17–4 to recommend that the full Senate consent to ratification. The Senate, however, has still not given its consent to the treaty.

Consent by the full Senate is apparently still delayed because of other Senate priorities and because of some residual opposition to the Convention from conservatives who are still concerned that the problems identified by President Reagan in the deep seabed mining provisions have not been resolved, or possibly by other concerns by these conservatives.[16] These opponents and the proponents of ratification can get into a hairsplitting debate over whether each of the five problems identified in Reagan's statement of July 9, 1982, quoted earlier, was resolved by the later 1984 agreement. This debate would require a detailed treatment beyond the level of this chapter.[17]

What can be said is that President Reagan's position on the Convention still allowed him to effectively adopt a number of beneficial provisions through presidential proclamations and executive orders. And his specific objections to ratification led to thoroughgoing efforts by all the countries to negotiate and ratify the 1984 agreement that made substantial improvements in the deep seabed mining provisions.

The views of the Clinton administration, the second Bush administration, and the carefully chosen Commission on Ocean Policy definitively concluded that the benefits of becoming a party to the Convention and the 1984 agreement now outweigh any disadvantages.

•   •   •

On important issues in international economic policy, arms control, and the seas, President Reagan deserves recognition and credit for being a principled pragmatist. That pragmatism stands apart from the conventional view of Reagan at the time.

As noted, President Reagan's foreign policy was often remembered for soaring, intense anti-communist rhetoric and deep ideological conviction. Nonetheless, the president frequently engaged in pragmatic internationalism when such a less-ideological approach promised the best results for America's interests. The three diverse examples considered in this chapter illustrate that unappreciated but important approach. And in all three areas, from international economic policy to arms control to the Law of the Sea Treaty, President Reagan left a legacy that remains with us and the world today.

Notes

Introduction

1. Since 1999, Gallup has regularly asked Americans to name the "greatest president." Reagan finished first in 2001, 2005, 2011, and 2012 and routinely finishes in the top three. To cite one example, a Gallup Poll released for Presidents Day 2011 declared Reagan the "greatest president" of all time, garnering 19 percent of the vote among 44 presidents, beating Abraham Lincoln fairly soundly, who finished second at 14 percent.

2. A June 2005 online poll (not a scientific survey) by the Discovery Channel and AOL (which included 2.4 million responses) declared Reagan the "greatest American of all time," beating Lincoln and George Washington.

3. Starting in 1999, C-SPAN began surveying presidential scholars every 10 years. The 2009 survey by C-SPAN, released for Presidents Day 2009, which included 65 well-known presidential scholars, ranked Reagan tenth most successful, knocking Lyndon Johnson out of the top ten, and behind Woodrow Wilson at ninth.

1. Ronald Reagan and the New Age of Globalization

1. Quote from "George Bush's New World," *New York Times*, January 15, 1989, E26; Robert G. Kaiser, "The U.S.S.R. in Decline," *Foreign Affairs* 67, no. 2 (Winter 1988–1989): 97–113.

2. Alfred E. Eckes Jr. and Thomas W. Zeiler, *Globalization and the American Century* (New York: Cambridge University Press, 2003), 1.

3. Alfred E. Eckes Jr., *The Contemporary Global Economy* (Oxford: Wiley-Blackwell, 2011), 158; "Restructuring of America: Interview with John Naisbitt," *U.S. News & World Report*, December 27, 1982; Theodore Levitt,

"The Globalization of Markets," *Harvard Business Review* 61, no. 3 (May–June 1983): 92–102.

4. Pranay Gupte, "Ronald Reagan, Father of Globalization," *Singapore Straits Times,* June 7, 2004; Robert Skidelsky, "What Russians Can Learn from Ronald Reagan," http://www.skidelskyr.com/print/what-russians-can-learn -from-ronald-reagan.

   For Thatcher's speeches, see http://www.margaretthatcher.org/. Reagan used the term "globalization" in written responses to questions from the Japanese newspaper *Asahi Shimbun,* April 28, 1987, http://www.reagan.utexas.edu/.

5. Ronald Reagan, "Radio Address to the Nation on Free and Fair Trade," August 2, 1986, http://www.reagan.utexas.edu. On Thatcher's support for free and fair trade, see Margaret Thatcher, "Speech at Georgetown University," February 27, 1981, http://www.margaretthatcher.org/document /104580; "Radio Interview for IRN," December 4, 1982, http://www.mar garetthatcher.org/document/105064.

6. Ronald Reagan, "Remarks at the Business Roundtable Annual Dinner," June 22, 1988, http://www.reagan.utexas.edu/; Margaret Thatcher, "Speech to the First International Conservative Congress," Washington, DC, September 28, 1997, http://www.margaretthatcher.org.

7. Eckes and Zeiler, *Globalization and the American Century,* 203.

8. James M. Boughton, *Silent Revolution: The International Monetary Fund, 1979–1989* (Washington, DC: IMF, 2001), 1–2; John G. Ruggie, "International Regimes, Transactions, and Change: Embedded Liberalism in the Postwar Economic Order," *International Organization* 36, no. 2 (Spring 1982): 379–415; http://micpohling.wordpress.com/2009/06/30/top-indi vidual-tax-rates-1980/.

9. Jeffry A. Frieden, *Global Capitalism: Its Fall and Rise in the Twentieth Century* (New York: Norton, 2006).

10. Milton Friedman, *Capitalism and Freedom* (Chicago: University of Chicago Press, 1962).

11. Martin Anderson, "The Reagan Revolution," *Christian Science Monitor,* April 20, 1988, 13; Margaret Thatcher, *The Downing Street Years* (New York: HarperCollins, 1993), 11–12.

12. Ronald Reagan, *An American Life: The Autobiography* (New York: Simon and Schuster, 1990), 105, 117–143; Thomas W. Evans, *The Education of Ronald Reagan* (New York: Columbia University Press, 2006), 6, 57–80.

13. Ronald Reagan, "Remarks on East-West Relations at the Brandenburg Gate in West Berlin," June 12, 1987, http://www.reagan.utexas.edu/.

14. Alfred E. Eckes Jr., *U.S. Trade Issues: A Reference Handbook* (Santa Barbara, CA: ABC-CLIO, 2009).

15. World Bank, *World Development Indicators* (CD-ROM, 2009); World Trade Organization, *World Trade Report 2007* (Geneva: WTO, 2008), 244. World

exports and GDP are stated in 2000 constant U.S. dollars at current prices and exchange rates.

16. United Nations Conference on Trade and Development (UNCTAD) database, January 15, 2010, http://www.unctad.org/; U.S. Bureau of the Census, *Statistical Abstract 1990*, 400, 812.

17. Nelson Lichtenstein, *The Retail Revolution* (New York: Henry Holt, 2009), 151–159.

18. William Niskanen, "Reaganomics," in *The Concise Encyclopedia of Economics*, ed. David R. Henderson, http://www.econlib.org/library/CEE.html.

19. Ronald Reagan, "Remarks to Harley-Davidson Company Employees in York, Pennsylvania," May 6, 1987, http://www.reagan.utexas.edu.

20. U.S. Bureau of the Census, "Historical Series: U.S. International Trade in Goods and Services," http://www.census.gov/foreign-trade/; Susan B. Carter et al., *Historical Statistics of the United States*, millennial ed. (New York: Cambridge University Press, 2006), 5-506, 5-544, 5-560.

21. Ronald Reagan, "Statement on International Investment Policy," September 9, 1983, http://www.presidency.ucsb.edu/.

22. U.S. Bureau of Economic Analysis, Department of Commerce, International Data, Direct Investment and MNCs, http://www.bea.gov/. Comparable inward and outward data not available for 1981.

23. Simon Johnson and James Kwak, *13 Bankers* (New York: Pantheon, 2010), 70–74; Ken Guenther, "He Tore Down the Walls of Regulation," *American Banker*, June 25, 2004, 10; Peter J. Wallison, "A President's Ideas Helped to Reshape Financial Services," *American Banker*, June 25, 2004, 10.

24. Eckes, *Contemporary Global Economy*, 98; John Williamson, "Did the Washington Consensus Fail?," November 6, 2002, http://www.iie.com /publications/papers/paper.cfm?ResearchID=488.

25. "Asia's Lending Hand," *Financial Times*, June 13, 1986, 24; "America's Tough Tactics Add to Turmoil at ADB," *Financial Times*, May 30, 1985, 4; David R. Francis, "U.S. Stepping Up Push for Free Enterprise via Third-World Aid," *Christian Science Monitor*, May 30, 1985, 19; Jonathan Friedland, "Showdown for Prime Asian Bank's Shogun," *Sydney Morning Herald*, February 17, 1987, 25.

26. Devesh Kapur, John P. Lewis, and Richard Webb, *The World Bank: Its First Half Century* (Washington, DC: Brookings, 1997), 22, 1193.

27. Rawi Abdelal, *Capital Rules* (Cambridge, MA: Harvard University Press, 2007), 31–32.

28. Ronald Reagan, "Radio Address to the Nation on Economic Growth and the Situation in Nicaragua," June 18, 1988, http://www.presidency.ucsb.edu/; http://www.worldbank.org/html/prddr/outreach/or3.htm.

29. Ronald Reagan, "Remarks at the Annual Meeting of the Atlantic Council," June 13, 1988, http://www.reagan.utexas.edu/; Milton Friedman and Rose

D. Friedman, *Two Lucky People: Memoirs* (Chicago: University of Chicago Press, 1998), 516–558.

30. Ronald Reagan, "Farewell Address to the Nation," January 11, 1989, http://www.reagan.utexas.edu/.

31. U.S. Office of Management and Budget, "Historical Tables, Summary of Receipts, Outlays, and Surpluses or Deficits in Current Dollars, Constant (FY 2005) Dollars, and as Percentages of GDP: 1940–2018" (table 1.3), http://www.omb.gov/budget/. Because the federal fiscal year extends from October 1 to September 30, and a new president takes office on January 20, nearly four months after the beginning of the fiscal year, it is arguable that we should look at the last two fiscal years. If so, Reagan deficits averaged –2.95 percent in 1988–1989, compared with Jimmy Carter –2.65 percent in 1980–1981; George H. W. Bush, –4.3 percent in 1992–1993; Bill Clinton, –1.85 percent in 2000–2001; and George W. Bush, –6.6 percent in 2008–2009.

32. World Bank, World Development Indicators, http://www.worldbank.org/; Hobart Rowen, "U.S., Japan Set Major Yen Accord, Pact Would Ease Competition," *Washington Post*, May 30, 1984, A1.

33. Oren Dorell, "Eastern Europe Toasts Reagan's 100th Birthday, Influence," *USA Today*, June 27, 2011, 5A.

2. The "Great Expansion"

1. For an example of this literature, see Jeff Madrick, *Age of Greed: The Triumph of Finance and the Decline of America* (New York: Borzoi Books, 2011); Thomas L. Friedman and Michael Mandelbaum, *That Used to Be Us: What Went Wrong with America—and How It Can Come Back* (Boston: Little, Brown, 2011).

2. For the original declinist debate in the late 1980s, see Paul Kennedy, *The Rise and Fall of Great Powers* (New York: Random House, 1987), and the rebuttals, Henry R. Nau, *The Myth of America's Decline: Leading the World Economy into the 1990s* (New York: Oxford University Press, 1990), and Joseph S. Nye Jr., *Bound to Lead: Changing Nature of American Power* (New York: Basic Books, 1990).

3. Robert J. Samuelson, *The Great Inflation and Its Aftermath: The Past and Future of American Influence* (New York: Random House, 2008).

4. See Allan Meltzer, "What Happened to the 'Depression'?," *Wall Street Journal*, August 31, 2009, http://online.wsj.com/article/SB10001424052970204251404574342931435353734.html.

5. See, among others, Nau, *The Myth of America's Decline*, passim and appendix; Allan Meltzer, *A History of the Federal Reserve*, vols. 1–3 (Chicago: University of Chicago Press, 2003); Alfred E. Eckes Jr. and Thomas W. Zeiler, *Globalization and the American Century* (Cambridge: Cambridge University

Press, 2003); and Angus Maddison, *The World Economy in the 20th Century* (Paris: Development Centre of the Organization for Economic Co-operation and Development, 1989).

6. Gary S. Becker and Kevin M. Murphy, "Don't Let the Cure Destroy Capitalism," *Hoover Digest,* no. 3 (July 1, 2009), http://www.hoover.org /research/don't-let-cure-destroy-capitalism.

7. International Monetary Fund, *World Economic Outlook* (Washington, DC: IMF, April 2014), table A-1, 180, http://www.imf.org/external/pubs/ft/weo /2014/01/pdf/text.pdf.

8. For data in this paragraph, see Brad Schiller, "The Inequality Myth," *Wall Street Journal,* March 10, 2008, A15; and Stephen Rose, "5 Myths about the Poor Middle Class," *Washington Post,* December 23, 2007, B03.

9. "Globalization," *Financial Times,* September 14, 2011, 1.

10. See, for example, the popular books by Thomas L. Friedman, *The Lexus and the Olive Tree* (New York: Farrar, Strauss and Giroux, 1999) and *The World Is Flat* (New York: Farrar, Strauss and Giroux, 2005).

11. See tables and appendices in Nau, *The Myth of America's Decline.*

12. Michael J. Boskin, *Reagan and the Economy: The Successes, Failures and Unfinished Agenda* (San Francisco: Institute for Contemporary Studies, 1987), 5.

13. On this point, see Edwin Meese III, *With Reagan: The Inside Story* (Washington, DC: Regnery Gateway, 1992); and Martin Anderson, *Revolution* (San Diego: Harcourt Brace Jovanovich, 1988), chapter 11.

14. Donald Regan, *For the Record: From Wall Street to Washington* (New York: Harcourt Brace, 1988).

15. David Stockman, *The Triumph of Politics: Why the Reagan Revolution Failed* (New York: Harper and Row, 1986).

16. In his autobiography, Reagan lists his diary entries in 1982 reflecting the tug of war going on among his aides. See Ronald Reagan, *An American Life: The Autobiography* (New York: Simon and Schuster, 1990), 315–324.

17. Reagan thought deeply and broadly about security issues as well. See, for example, the breathtaking account of Reagan's views on nuclear weapons, compiled exclusively from declassified NSC records. Martin Anderson and Annelise Anderson, *Reagan's Secret War: The Untold Story of His Fight to Save the World from Nuclear Disaster* (New York: Crown, 2009).

18. Markets and trade are never wholly free or controlled. They move at the margins toward greater freedom or control. Since the Great Depression, the world economy swung broadly away from market policies in the 1930s, back toward freer markets in the early postwar period, back again toward intervention in the 1970s, and finally toward markets again in the last 30 years. When these moves are global, they are powerful and correlate with, if not cause, the swings we observe in economic performance.

19. Steven F. Hayward, *The Age of Reagan: The Conservative Counterrevolution* (New York: Crown Forum, 2009), 199.

20. See the data already evident at the time I wrote *The Myth of America's Decline*, 225–230. For subsequent evidence, see Samuelson, *The Great Inflation and Its Aftermath*, appendix 1.

21. Samuelson, *The Great Inflation and Its Aftermath*, 116. Policy advisers discouraged the use of this term. See Anderson, *Revolution*, 115–116.

22. Samuelson gives equal credit. *The Great Inflation and Its Aftermath*, 106.

23. Quoted in Peter Robinson, *How Ronald Reagan Changed My Life* (New York: ReganBooks, 2003), 51. Robinson was a speechwriter for Reagan from 1982 to 1988.

24. Reagan to Paul Trousdale in Martin Anderson, Annelise Anderson, and Kiron Skinner, eds., *Reagan: A Life in Letters* (New York: Free Press, 2003), 295.

25. Steven R. Weisman, "Reagan and Allied Leaders Agree to Discuss Curbs on Soviet Trade," *New York Times*, July 21, 1981, A1.

26. Hayward, *The Age of Reagan*, 173.

27. Reagan, *An American Life*, 335.

28. That was the point of my critique of Reagan policies written in 1989. See *The Myth of America's Decline*, 254–258.

29. For one comparison, see Allan Meltzer, "What Happened to the 'Depression?,'" *Wall Street Journal*, August 31, 2009, http://online.wsj.com/articles /SB10001424052970204251404574342931435353734.

30. Samuelson, *The Great Inflation and Its Aftermath*, 135.

31. Carmen M. Reinhart and Kenneth Rogoff, *This Time Is Different: Eight Centuries of Financial Folly* (Princeton, NJ: Princeton University Press, 2009).

32. On economic policymaking under the Obama administration, see Peter Baker, "The White House Looks for Work," *New York Times Magazine*, January 23, 2011, MM36.

33. Gary S. Becker, "The Great Recession and Government Failure," *Wall Street Journal*, September 2, 2011, A13.

34. Ben Casselman and Justin Lahart, "Companies Shun Investment, Hoard Cash," *Wall Street Journal*, September 17, 2011, A2.

35. See Gideon Rachman, "The Long Slide into Protectionism," *Financial Times*, September 13, 2011, 11.

36. Ryan Lizza, "Inside the Crisis: Larry Summers and the White House Economic Team," *The New Yorker*, October 12, 2009, 80.

37. See Alan Greenspan, *The Age of Turbulence: Adventures in a New World* (New York: Penguin Press, 2007), chapters 9 and 10.

38. Nick Timiraos, "Cost of Bailing Out Fannie and Freddie Expected to Fall Sharply," *Wall Street Journal*, October 26, 2012, http://online.wsj.com/news /articles/SB10001424052970204598504578080770443540656.

3. "The Balancer"

1. Purposefulness does not necessarily mean that presidents always work from an explicit, fixed, long-term plan or that presidents characterize their guiding philosophy or approach to statecraft in precisely the terms scholars would use in their retrospective analyses. What concern us here are the patterns of consistent strategic behavior across a series of events, places, and policies.

2. On balancing, see Kenneth N. Waltz, *Theory of International Politics* (New York: Random House, 1979); Stephen M. Walt, *The Origins of Alliances* (Ithaca, NY: Cornell University Press, 1987); Robert Jervis and Jack Snyder, eds., *Dominoes and Bandwagons: Strategic Beliefs and Great Power Competition in the Eurasia Rimland* (New York: Oxford University Press, 1991).

3. External balancing itself can be disaggregated into "harder" and "softer" balancing. Soft balancing refers to the use of diplomatic tools (e.g., economic sanctions) and especially international institutions to balance against a foreign challenger. On soft balancing, see Robert A. Pape, "Soft Balancing against the United States," *International Security* 30 (2005): 7–45.

4. For a good concise account of Wilson's balancing strategy during this period, see George H. Quester, "The Wilson Presidency, the U.S. Navy, and Homeland Defense," *White House Studies* 4 (2004): 137–148.

5. See John Mearsheimer, *The Tragedy of Great Power Politics* (New York: Norton, 2001), 323.

6. Nicholas John Spykman, *America's Strategy in World Politics: The United States and the Balance of Power* (New York: Harcourt Brace, 1942).

7. James Kurth, "America's Grand Strategy: A Pattern of History," *The National Interest* 43 (1999): 6.

8. Marc Trachtenberg, "Making Grand Strategy: The Early Cold War Experience in Retrospect," *SAIS Review* 19 (1999): 34–35. See also Melvyn P. Leffler, "The American Conception of National Security and the Beginnings of the Cold War, 1945–48," *American Historical Review* 89 (April 1984): 346–381.

9. John Lewis Gaddis, *Strategies of Containment: A Critical Appraisal of American National Security Policy during the Cold War,* 2nd ed. (New York: Oxford University Press, 2005).

10. As a percentage of GDP, Kennedy's military buildup actually exceeded Reagan's. See Gaddis, *Strategies of Containment*, 203, 393–394.

11. See James Mann, *About Face: A History of America's Curious Relationship with China, from Nixon to Clinton* (New York: Vintage, 2000), 56.

12. Whether Reagan's actions were driven by concerns about his personal legacy is unclear. Reagan, apparently, was aware that his efforts to work with Gorbachev would anger hard-liners in the Republican Party. See Richard Reeves, *President Reagan: The Triumph of Imagination* (New York: Simon and Schuster, 2006), 294.

13. Peter Trubowitz, *Politics and Strategy: Partisan Ambition and American Statecraft* (Princeton, NJ: Princeton University Press, 2011).

14. During the Cold War, successive presidents, Republican and Democratic alike, so feared a domestic political backlash for "losing a country to communism" that they attached value to places of little intrinsic geostrategic interest. Foreign policies that were justified in terms of international commitments often also had a great deal to do with protecting an administration's domestic political credibility and closing off a possible avenue of attack by opponents. Credibility abroad and credibility at home were conflated. See Gordon M. Goldstein, *Lessons in Disaster: McGeorge Bundy and the Path to War in Vietnam* (New York: Henry Holt, 2008); Leslie Gelb, "Vietnam: The System Worked," *Foreign Policy* 3 (1971): 140–167; John Garofano, "Tragedy or Choice in Vietnam? Learning to Think outside the Archival Box: A Review Essay," *International Security* 26 (2002): 143–168; and John Mueller, "Simplicity and Spook: Terrorism and the Dynamics of Threat Exaggeration," *International Studies Perspectives* 6 (2005): 208–234.

15. This section draws on Peter Trubowitz, *Defining the National Interest: Conflict and Change in American Foreign Policy* (Chicago: University of Chicago Press, 1998), 169–234.

16. Walter LaFeber, *America, Russia and the Cold War, 1945–1992*, 7th ed. (New York: McGraw-Hill, 1993), 303.

17. See John R. Petrocik, "Issue Ownership in Presidential Elections, with a 1980 Case Study," *American Journal of Political Science* 40 (August 1996): 825–850.

18. David Hoffman, *The Dead Hand: The Untold Story of the Cold War Arms Race and Its Dangerous Legacy* (New York: Doubleday, 2009), 31.

19. The Republicans also made substantial gains in the House and at the state level.

20. Henry A. Kissinger, *Diplomacy* (New York: Simon and Schuster, 1994), 773. In addition to Kissinger's overview of Reagan's foreign policy, see George C. Herring's useful summary of the Reagan years in *From Colony to Superpower: U.S. Foreign Relations since 1776* (New York: Oxford University Press, 2008), 861–916.

21. Daniel Wirls, *Buildup: The Politics of Defense in the Reagan Era* (Ithaca, NY: Cornell University Press, 1992), 36.

22. In 1980, the Pentagon spent roughly 64 percent of its budget on operations. The remaining 36 percent went to new investment. These funds were lavished on high-tech growth industries. By 1986, investments accounted for more than 50 percent of the military budget, nearly 160 percent more in dollar terms than when Reagan took office. (By comparison, operating funds increased by only 60 percent.) See Wirls, *Buildup*, 46–52.

23. *America's New Beginning: A Program for Economic Recovery* (Washington, DC: General Printing Office, 1981), 1.

24. See James Shoch, *Trading Blows: Party Competition and U.S. Trade Policy in a Globalizing Era* (Chapel Hill: University of North Carolina Press, 2001).

25. See, for example, Stephen Brooks and William Wohlforth, "Power, Globalization, and the End of the Cold War," *International Security* 25 (Winter 2000–2001): 5–53; Richard Ned Lebow and Thomas Risse-Kappen, eds., *International Relations Theory and the End of the Cold War* (New York: Columbia University Press, 1995); Daniel Deudney and G. John Ikenberry, "Who Won the Cold War?," *Foreign Policy* (Summer 1992), 123–138; and Jeffrey W. Knopf, "Did Reagan Win the Cold War?," *Strategic Insights* 3 (August 2004), https://www.hsdl.org/?view&did=444565.

26. See, for example, Robert Kuttner, *The End of Laissez-Faire: National Purpose and the Global Economy after the Cold War* (Philadelphia: University of Pennsylvania Press, 1992); Robert Gilpin, *Global Political Economy: Understanding the International Economic Order* (Princeton, NJ: Princeton University Press, 2001); and Henry R. Nau, *International Reaganomics: A Domestic Approach to World Economy* (Washington, DC: Center for Strategic and International Studies).

27. This section draws on the analysis in Trubowitz, *Defining the National Interest*, 169–234.

28. The industrial Northeast refers here to states in the regions of New England, Middle Atlantic, and the Great Lakes—the traditional manufacturing belt. The Sunbelt refers to states in the South, Southwest, and Pacific Coast regions.

29. On the changing geographical distribution of economic activity during this period, see Joseph H. Turek, "The Northeast in a National Context: Background Trends in Population, Income, and Employment," in Harry W. Richardson and Joseph H. Turek, eds., *Economic Prospects for the Northeast* (Philadelphia: Temple University Press, 1985), 28–84. See also John Agnew, *The United States in the World Economy: A Regional Geography* (Cambridge: Cambridge University Press, 1987), 161–185; and Candace Howes and Ann R. Markusen, "Trade, Industry, and Economic Development," in Nelzi Noponen, Julie Graham, and Ann R. Markusen, eds., *Trading Industries, Trading Regions: International Trade, American Industry, and Regional Economic Development* (New York: Guilford Press, 1993), 1–44.

30. Robert Jay Dilger, *The Sunbelt/Snowbelt Controversy: The War over Federal Funds* (New York: New York University Press, 1982).

31. Ann R. Markusen, Peter Hall, Scott Campbell, and Sabrina Deitrick, *The Rise of the Gunbelt: The Military Remapping of Industrial America* (New York: Oxford University Press, 1991).

32. For accounts about the changing regional composition of the Democratic and Republican parties, see Richard Franklin Bensel, *Sectionalism and American Political Development: 1880–1980* (Madison: University of Wisconsin Press, 1984); Nicole Mellow, *The State of Disunion: Regional Sources of Modern*

American Partisanship (Baltimore: Johns Hopkins Press, 2008); and Earle Black and Merle Black, *Politics and Society in the South* (Cambridge, MA: Harvard University Press, 1987.

33. On foreign economic policy, Democrats edged away from their long-standing commitment to free trade, capital mobility, and equal access. Demands for "fairer trade," job retraining, and industrial policy became as obligatory in Democratic politics as demands for freer trade, "fast-track procedures," and "FTAs" (free-trade agreements) were in Republican circles. See Trubowitz, *Defining the National Interest*, 196–219.

34. On the domestic political impact of Reagan's security and economic policies, see Trubowitz, *Defining the National Interest*, and Bensel, *Sectionalism and American Political Development*.

35. See Trubowitz, *Defining the National Interest*, 219–232.

36. See Benjamin O. Fordham, "The Limits of Neoclassical Realism: Additive and Interactive Approaches to Explaining Foreign Policy Preferences," in Steven E. Lobell, Norrin M. Ripsman, and Jeffrey W. Taliaferro, eds., *Neoclassical Realism, the State, and Foreign Policy* (Cambridge: Cambridge University Press, 2009), 251–279.

37. The administration's policy reversals also reflected stubborn international realities. For a good discussion of Reagan's reversals and the limits imposed by the international system, see Kenneth A. Oye, "Constrained Confidence and the Evolution of Reagan Foreign Policy," in Kenneth A. Oye, Robert J. Lieber, and Donald Rothchild, eds., *Eagle Resurgent: The Reagan Era in American Foreign Policy* (Boston: Little, Brown, 1987), 3–39. See also Beth A. Fischer, *The Reagan Reversal: Foreign Policy and the End of the Cold War* (Columbia: University of Missouri Press, 1997).

38. *Congressional Quarterly Weekly Report*, January 21, 1989, 143.

4. From Containment to Liberation

Special thanks to Robert H. Swindell for his research assistance.

1. Marc Selverstone, *Constructing the Monolith: The United States, Great Britain, and International Communism, 1945–1950* (Cambridge, MA: Harvard University Press, 2009), 25.

2. "The Yalta Conference," Lillian Goldman Law Library, Yale University, http://avalon.law.yale.edu/wwii/yalta.asp.

3. Franklin D. Roosevelt, "Address to Congress on the Yalta Conference," March 1, 1945, *Public Papers of Franklin D. Roosevelt*, http://www.presidency.ucsb.edu/ws/index.php?pid=16591#axzz1mIcOmLdu.

4. Winston S. Churchill, *The Second World War*, vol. 6: *Triumph and Tragedy* (Boston: Houghton Mifflin, 1953), 418–439; "Letter from President Roosevelt to Stalin on an Acceptable Compromise Regarding the Composi-

tion of the Postwar Polish Government," February 6, 1945, http://digitalarchive
.wilsoncenter.org/document/111002.

5. Two of Reagan's closest advisers, Ed Meese and William Clark, said Reagan
had a "preoccupation" with the injustice of Yalta, especially in Poland. See
Paul Kengor, *The Crusader: Ronald Reagan and the Fall of Communism* (New
York: HarperCollins, 2009), 100.

6. Ronald Reagan, "The Brotherhood of Man," Address at Westminster
College, November 19, 1990, http://www.pbs.org/wgbh/americanexperience
/features/primary-resources/reagan-brotherhood/.

7. Melvyn P. Leffler, *A Preponderance of Power: National Security, the Truman
Administration and the Cold War* (Stanford, CA: Stanford University Press,
1992), 145.

8. The names of presidential directives vary across administrations. For
instance, decision directives during the Cold War were called National
Security Councils (Truman, Eisenhower), National Security Action
Memorandums (Kennedy, Johnson), National Security Decision Memoran-
dums (Nixon, Ford), Presidential Directives (Carter), National Security
Decision Directives (Reagan), and National Security Directives (Bush).

9. "U.S. Objectives with Respect to the USSR to Counter Soviet Threats to
U.S. Security," in *Foreign Relations of the United States*, vol. 1 (Washington,
DC: Government Printing Office, 1948), 663–669.

10. John Lewis Gaddis, *Strategies of Containment: A Critical Appraisal of Postwar
American National Security Policy* (New York: Oxford University Press,
1982), 45.

11. Geoffrey Roberts, "Moscow and the Marshall Plan: Politics, Ideology and
the Onset of the Cold War, 1947," *Europe-Asia Studies* 46, no. 8 (1994): 379.

12. Selverstone, *Constructing the Monolith*, 98–100.

13. PPS-59, "U.S. Policy toward the Soviet Satellite States in Eastern Europe,"
August 25, 1949, http://digital.library.wisc.edu/1711.dl/FRUS.FRUS1949
v05.

14. Gaddis, *Strategies of Containment*, 68.

15. NSC-162/2, "A Report to the National Security Council by the Executive
Secretary on Basic National Security Policy," October 30, 1953, http://www
.fas.org/irp/offdocs/nsc-hst/nsc-162-2.pdf.

16. John Lewis Gaddis, *The United States and the End of the Cold War: Implications, Reconsiderations, Provocations* (New York: Oxford University Press,
1992), 71.

17. Gregory Mitrovich, *Undermining the Kremlin: America's Strategy to Subvert the
Soviet Bloc, 1947–1956* (Ithaca, NY: Cornell University Press, 2000),
167–168; see also Thomas Alan Schwartz, *Lyndon Johnson and Europe: In the
Shadows of Vietnam* (Cambridge, MA: Harvard University Press, 2003),
134–135.

18. Gaddis, *Strategies of Containment*, 208.

19. *Foreign Relations of the United States, 1961–1963*, vol. 16: *Eastern Europe, Cyprus, Greece, Turkey*, Office of the Historian, United States Department of State, http://history.state.gov/historicaldocuments/frus1961-63v16/comp1.

20. Memorandum of Conversation, December 12, 1961, http://history.state.gov /historicaldocuments/frus1961-63v16/d6.

21. Special Report by the Central Intelligence Agency, March 27, 1964, http:// history.state.gov/historicaldocuments/frus1964-68v17/d2.

22. National Security Action Memorandum No. 352, July 8, 1966, http://history .state.gov/historicaldocuments/frus1964-68v17/d15.

23. *Foreign Relations of the United States, 1964–1968*, vol. 17: *Eastern Europe*, Office of the Historian, United States Department of State, http://dosfan.lib .uic.edu/ERC/frus/summaries/960812_FRUS_XVII_1964-68.html.

24. Notes of Emergency Meeting of the National Security Council, August 20, 1968, http://history.state.gov/historicaldocuments/frus1964-68v17/d81.

25. National Security Decision Memorandum 212, http://history.state.gov /historicaldocuments/frus1969-76v29/d27.

26. National Security Study Memorandum 129, June 15, 1971, http://history .state.gov/historicaldocuments/frus1969-76v29/d227.

27. Memorandum from the Executive Secretary of the Department of State (Springsteen) to the President's Deputy Assistant for National Security Affairs (Scowcroft), Washington, January 23, 1975, http://history.state.gov /historicaldocuments/frus1969-76ve15p1/d12.

28. *Foreign Relations of the United States, 1969–1976*, vol. E-15, *Part 1, Documents on Eastern Europe, 1973–1976*, Preface, http://history.state.gov/historical documents/frus1969-76ve15p1/preface.

29. Kim Willenson, "Ford's Big Gamble on Détente," *Newsweek*, August 4, 1974.

30. Notes of a Meeting of European Chiefs of Mission Conference, London, December 14, 1975, http://history.state.gov/historicaldocuments/frus1969-76 ve15p1/d14.

31. Presidential Directive/NSC-21, "Policy toward Eastern Europe," September 13, 1977, http://www.fas.org/irp/offdocs/pd/pd21.pdf.

32. Interview with Stuart Eizenstat, January 29–30, 1982, Jimmy Carter Presidential Oral History Project, The Miller Center, http://millercenter.org /president/carter/oralhistory/stuart-eizenstat.

33. Richard H. Cummings, *Radio Free Europe's Crusade for Freedom: Rallying Americans behind Cold War Broadcasting, 1950–1960* (Jefferson, NC: McFarland, 2010), 53–54.

34. "A Time for Choosing," October 27, 1964, http://www.reagan.utexas.edu /archives/reference/timechoosing.html.

35. "Veterans Day Address by Governor Reagan," November 10, 1967, Speeches and Articles (1967), Ronald Reagan Governor's Papers, Ronald Reagan Library.

36. Kiron K. Skinner, Annelise G. Anderson, Martin Anderson, *Reagan, in His Own Hand: The Writings of Ronald Reagan that Reveal His Revolutionary Vision for America* (New York: Free Press, 2001), 144, 152.

37. "To Restore America," March 31, 1976, http://www.ibiblio.org/sullivan/CNN /RWR/album/speechmats/restore.html.

38. Interview with Richard V. Allen, Ronald Reagan Presidential Oral History Project, May 28, 2002, The Miller Center, http://web1.millercenter.org/poh /transcripts/ohp_2002_0528_allen.pdf.

39. Howell Raines, "Carter and Reagan Open Fall Race with Praise for the Polish Workers," *New York Times,* September 2, 1980.

40. Kiron K. Skinner, Annelise G. Anderson, and Martin Anderson, *Reagan: A Life in Letters* (New York: Free Press, 2003), 375.

41. Richard Burt, "Reagan Team Says U.S. Must Deal with Any Threat," *New York Times,* November 13, 1980.

42. Peter Schweizer, *Victory: The Reagan Administration's Secret Strategy That Hastened the Collapse of the Soviet Union* (New York: Atlantic Monthly Press, 1994), 6.

43. Ronald Reagan, *The Reagan Diaries,* ed. Douglas Brinkley, pbk. ed. (New York: HarperCollins, 2009), 30.

44. "Transcript of Brezhnev's Phone Conversation with Kania," September 15, 1981, http://digitalarchive.wilsoncenter.org/document/112799; For more examples of this, see "1980–81 Polish Crisis," in the Cold War International History Project's Digital Archive, http://www.wilsoncenter.org/digital -archive.

45. National Security Council Meeting, "Further Economic Aid to Poland," September 15, 1981, http://jasonebin.com/nsc21.html.

46. Ronald Reagan, *An American Life* (New York: Simon & Schuster, 1990), 301.

47. Schweizer, *Victory,* 68.

48. National Security Council Meeting, "Poland," December 21, 1981, http:// www.thereaganfiles.com/19811221-nsc-33.pdf.

49. National Security Council Meeting, "Poland," December 22, 1981, http:// www.thereaganfiles.com/19811222-nsc-34.pdf.

50. Raymond L. Garthoff, *The Great Transition: American-Soviet Relations and the End of the Cold War* (Washington, DC: Brookings Institution Press, 1994), 548–549.

51. Jeremi Suri, "Explaining the End of the Cold War: A New Historical Consensus?," *Journal of Cold War Studies* 4, no. 4 (Fall 2002): 63.

52. NSDD-32, "U.S. National Security Strategy," May 20, 1982, http://www.fas .org/irp/offdocs/nsdd/nsdd-032.htm.

53. Schweizer, *Victory,* 76–77.

54. NSDD-75, "U.S. Relations with the USSR," January 17, 1983, http://www .fas.org/irp/offdocs/nsdd/nsdd-75.pdf.

55. National Security Council Meeting, "United States Policy toward Eastern Europe," July 21, 1982, http://www.thereaganfiles.com/19820721-nsc-56 .pdf.

56. National Security Decision Directive 54, "United States Policy toward Eastern Europe," September 2, 1982, http://www.fas.org/irp/offdocs/nsdd /nsdd-54.pdf.

57. Interview with Richard V. Allen, Reagan Oral History Project.

58. Carl Bernstein, "The Holy Alliance," *Time*, February 24, 1992.

59. Jeane Kirkpatrick, "Needed Then, Needed Now," *Washington Post*, March 8, 1993.

60. Schweizer, *Victory*, 72–74.

61. Sarah B. Snyder, *Human Rights Activism and the End of the Cold War: A Transnational History of the Helsinki Network* (Cambridge: Cambridge University Press, 2011), 12.

62. NSDD-133, "United States Policy toward Yugoslavia," March 14, 1984, http://www.fas.org/irp/offdocs/nsdd/23-2222t.gif.

63. Garthoff, *The Great Transition*, 560–561.

64. Reagan, *The Reagan Diaries*, 297.

65. Schweizer, *Victory*, 267.

66. Gregory F. Domber, "Skepticism and Stability: Reevaluating U.S. Policy during Poland's Democratic Transformation in 1989," *Journal of Cold War Studies* 13, no. 3 (Summer 2011), 58; George P. Shultz, *Turmoil and Triumph: My Years as Secretary of State* (New York: Charles Scribner's Sons, 1993), 873–875.

67. John Lewis Gaddis, *The Cold War: A New History* (New York: Penguin Press, 2005), 222.

68. Ronald Reagan, Remarks before the United Nations General Assembly Special Session Devoted to Disarmament, June 17, 1982, http://www.presidency .ucsb.edu/ws/index.php?pid=42644.

69. Garthoff, *The Great Transition*, 561–562, 577.

70. "Europe as a Common Home," Address by Mikhail Gorbachev to the Council of Europe, July 6, 1989, http://chnm.gmu.edu/1989/items/show/109.

71. Neil Reynolds, "Freed Poles Build One for the Gipper," *Globe and Mail*, July 4, 2007; Vanessa Gera, "Poland's Lech Walesa Unveils Statue of Ronald Reagan on Elegant Warsaw Street," *Associated Press*, November 21, 2011; Pablo Gorondi, "Ronald Reagan's Honored Again for Anti-Communist Efforts with a Second Statue in Budapest," Associated Press, June 28, 2011; "Prague Street on Which U.S. Ambassadors Live Renamed for Reagan," *CTK Daily News*, July 1, 2011; Florian Gathmann, "No Street, No Square, No Respect—What Does Berlin Have against Ronald Reagan?," *Spiegel Online International*, February 9, 2011.

72. "Ronald Reagan Remembered in Budapest," *MTI-EcoNews*, February 6, 2011; "Reagan Was Man of Exceptional Courage, Visions—Czech Minis-

ters," CTK National News Wire, July 1, 2011; "Guttenberg Calls on Berlin to Name a Street after Ronald Reagan," *Deutsche Welle,* December 22, 2010; "Hungarians Owe Freedom to Reagan, Says Deputy PM," *MTI-EcoNews,* June 28, 2011; M. Marini, "Fall of Berlin Wall: Great Event for Freedom of Mankind," *ATA,* November 9, 2009; Oren Dorell, "Eastern Europe Toasts Reagan's 100th Birthday, Influence," *USA Today,* June 27, 2011; "Reagan Was Speaker for Freedom Lovers from Soviet Bloc—Czech PM," *CTK Daily News,* February 9, 2011.

73. "Poles Honor Reagan, Cite His Inspiration," *Chicago Sun-Times,* November 27, 2011; Ben Birnbaum, "Reagan Feted in Hungary," *Washington Times,* June 30, 2011; "Reagan Was Man of Exceptional Courage, Visions—Czech Ministers, *CTK Daily News,* July 1, 2011; Roman Joch, "To Eastern Eyes, a Liberator," *Washington Times,* February 4, 2011.

74. Albanian Press Review, Albanian-ATA English News Service, April 9, 2009; "Czech Conservative Group against U.S. Support to Gay Parade," *CTK Daily News,* August 7, 2011; "Former Slovak PM Says U.S. Missiles Hamper Cooperation in Europe," *CTK Daily News,* June 6, 2007.

75. "Human Rights Advocates Call on Czech Rep to Back Chinese Dissident," *CTK Daily News,* June 27, 2011.

76. "Hungary to Intensify Ties, Discuss Human Rights with China, Says Deputy PM," *MTI—EcoNews,* July 1, 2011.

77. Rikard Jozwiak, "EU Foreign Ministers Divided on Wider Belarus Sanctions," *Radio Free Europe,* April 12, 2011.

78. "Reagan Was Speaker for Freedom Lovers from Soviet Bloc—Czech PM," *CTK Daily News,* February 9, 2011.

79. "Quote of the Day," *Polish News Bulletin,* January 30, 2012.

80. East Germany entered the alliance upon reunification with West Germany in October 1990. The Czech Republic, Hungary, and Poland joined in March 1999. Bulgaria, Slovakia, Slovenia, and Romania entered in March 2004. Croatia and Albania joined in April 2009.

81. "Index of Economic Freedom," Heritage Foundation and *Wall Street Journal,* http://www.heritage.org/index/about.

82. "Czechs Say Willing to Work with EU Draft Treaty," *Reuters News,* February 20, 2007; "Czech ForMin Says Iranian Threat Possible in Ten Years," *CTK Daily News,* May 8, 2007.

83. "Topolanek: Courage, Solidity and Faith," *Pravo,* January 21, 2009; Dan Bilefsky, "With Fall of the Government, a Big Moment for the Czechs Seems to Shrink," *New York Times,* April 4, 2009.

84. "Czech President Sees 'Major Mistakes in USA' behind Economic Crisis," BBC Monitoring European, from Viliam Buchert interview with Václav Klaus, in *Mlada fronta Dnes,* April 16, 2009.

85. "Germany's Bruederle: Tax Cuts 'Non-Negotiable,'" *Der Spiegel,* December 19, 2009.

86. Sali Berisha, Speech before the Israel Council on Foreign Relations, November 21, 2011, http://israelcfr.com/documents/Berisha.pdf.

5. Reagan's "March of Freedom" in a Changing World

1. Opinion polls showed initial majority support for Bush's move into Iraq, though nowhere near the level of support for the intervention in Afghanistan. That approval, however, dropped precipitously as the war wore on and, more directly, as American body bags piled up. By 2007, public approval of the war had plummeted, as did public approval of President Bush.

2. Quite unappreciated is the fact that George W. Bush had been arguing for a democratization of the Middle East long before U.S. troops failed to find expected WMD stockpiles in Iraq. In his October 2002 Cincinnati speech, a major statement on encroaching war in Iraq, Bush clearly expressed his desire to help Iraqis and "others" to "find freedom of their own," to achieve "self-government," and to "help the Iraqi people . . . create the institutions of liberty in a unified Iraq at peace with its neighbors." This would usher in an "era of new hope." To cite just one other example from even earlier, on July 12, 2001—notably, *before* September 11—Bush formally issued Proclamation 7455, marking Captive Nations Week. The first two sentences in the proclamation read: "The 21st century must become the 'Century of Democracy.' Democracy and freedom have taken root across the globe, and the United States will continue to stand for greater consolidation of pluralism and religious freedom." Among a short list of five nations, he specifically called out (for the second time since May 2001) the regimes in Iraq and Afghanistan.

3. The regime in El Salvador had been anti-communist but certainly no bastion of civil liberties. The Reagan administration's support of Salvadoran anti-communists as a bulwark against the spread of communism in Central America generated criticism that the administration was thereby also supporting Salvadoran "death squads."

4. For instance, see Václav Havel's wonderful July 4, 1994, lecture at Independence Hall in Philadelphia, or Lech Wałesa's speech at the Ronald Reagan Library on May 20, 1996.

5. Another "elsewhere" was Africa, which presented other controversial and complex challenges.

6. I wrote a book focused simply on demonstrating this Reagan intent, showing how it began long before Reagan's presidency. See Paul Kengor, *The Crusader: Ronald Reagan and the Fall of Communism* (New York: HarperPerennial, 2007).

7. NSDD-75, January 17, 1983, 1. The declassified NSDD is on file at Reagan Library. Though formally issued January 17, 1983, the document was approved by Reagan at an NSC meeting on December 17, 1982. See Norman

A. Bailey, *The Strategic Plan That Won the Cold War: National Security Decision Directive 75* (McLean, VA: Potomac Foundation, 1999), 13. Also: Interview with Norman A. Bailey, May 24, 2005. Information on the directives generally has been published in a variety of sources. The most comprehensive source is Christopher Simpson, ed., *National Security Directives of the Reagan and Bush Administrations: The Declassified History of U.S. Political and Military Policy, 1981–1991* (Boulder, CO: Westview Press, 1995). The directives are also on file at the Reagan Library.

8. See Paul Kengor, *The Judge: William P. Clark, Ronald Reagan's Top Hand* (San Francisco: Ignatius Press, 2007).

9. The Soviets learned of the directive through a leak that began with a major news article in the *Los Angeles Times*. I have written about this rather dramatic process in *The Crusader* and in subsequent articles and op-ed pieces, including Kengor, "Crucial Cold War Secret," *Washington Times*, January 13, 2008, and a Q&A that I did with Marc Zimmerman, "The Zimmerman Affair," April 18, 2008, posted at the website of the Center for Vision & Values, http://www.visionandvalues.org/2008/04/vav-qaa-on-the-zimmerman -affair/. Zimmerman was the figure at the epicenter of the drama.

10. G. Dadyants, "Pipes Threatens History," *Sotsialisticheskaya Industriya*, March 26, 1983, 3, published as "New Directive on USSR Trade 'Threatens History,'" in *FBIS*, FBIS-SOV-29-MAR-83, March 29, 1983, A5–7. "FBIS" refers to the Foreign Broadcast Information Service, a U.S. government agency that specializes in translating foreign media.

11. Vladimir Serov, "The Plans of Nuclear 'Crusaders,'" distributed by TASS, January 17, 1983. Text is printed as "Serov: Directive 'Crusade against Communism,'" in FBIS-SOV-18-JAN-83, January 18, 1983, A2.

12. See, for instance, Reagan, "Remarks at the AFL-CIO," April 5, 1982; and Reagan, "Remarks to Citizens in Hambach, Federal Republic of Germany," May 6, 1985.

13. I lay this out at length in *The Crusader*, 84–111.

14. Reagan, "Address at Commencement Exercises at Eureka College," Eureka, Illinois, May 9, 1982.

15. NSDD-32 was a summary of a report released in April 1982. The NSDD and the report are both on file at the Reagan Library. The NSDD was declassified in February 1996. Also see Simpson, *NSDDs of the Reagan and Bush Administrations*, 63–66; and Carl Bernstein, "The Holy Alliance," *Time*, February 24, 1992, 31.

16. See Keith Schneider, "Reagan-Pope Plan to Topple Warsaw Is Reported," *New York Times*, February 18, 1992; Bernstein, "The Holy Alliance," 28–35; Michael Ledeen, "This Political Pope," *The American Enterprise* 4, no. 4 (July 1993): 40–43; Peter Schweizer, *Victory: The Reagan Administration's Secret Strategy That Hastened the Collapse of the Soviet Union* (New York: Atlantic Monthly Press, 1994), xviii, 68–69; and Raymond L. Garthoff, *The Great*

Transition: American-Soviet Relations and the End of the Cold War (Washington, DC: Brookings Institution, 1994), 31–32.

17. Bernstein, "The Holy Alliance," 31.

18. See Joseph E. Persico, *Casey: From the OSS to the CIA* (New York: Viking, 1990). 236; Bernstein, "The Holy Alliance," 28–35; and Schweizer, *Victory,* xviii, 68–69.

19. Interview with Thomas C. Reed, March 14, 2005; and Thomas C. Reed, *At the Abyss* (New York: Ballantine Books, 2004), 235–237, 249.

20. Reed told me that both NSDD-32 and NSDD-75 "were the road maps."

21. Yuri Zhukov, "A Doctrine of Interference," *Pravda,* June 25, 1982, 4, published as "Reagan Policy Called 'Doctrine of Interference,'" in FBIS-6-JUL-82, July 6, 1982, A1–A3.

22. Vitaly Zhurkin speaking on Moscow's *Studio 9* television program, August 25, 1984. Transcript is published in FBIS-27-AUG-84, August 27, 1984, CC8–CC11.

23. The *Pravda* writer likely learned this from the *New York Times* article mentioned later. Y. Rusakov, "War Games and 'Peace' Games: The Path Chosen by the Reagan Administration," *Pravda,* June 1, 1984, 4, published as "Rusakov: Reagan Playing Games with War, Peace," in FBIS-5-JUN-84, June 5, 1984, A3.

24. Much more still happened in this period prior to the Westminster speech. For instance, on May 21, 1982, Bill Clark gave a crucial speech at Georgetown's Center for Strategic and International Studies. See Richard Halloran, "Reagan Aide Tells of New Strategy on Soviet Threat," *New York Times,* May 22, 1982, A1.

25. On this, see Paul Kengor, *God and Ronald Reagan* (New York: HarperCollins, 2004), 208–216.

26. Reagan expressed his shock and prayers to the pope in a May 13, 1981, cable on the assassination attempt. Cable is filed at the Reagan Library in a section on declassified NSC materials, coded as ES, NSC, HSF: Records, Vatican: Pope John Paul II, RRL, Box 41, Folder "Cables 1 of 2."

27. Interview with Bill Clark, August 24, 2001. This was the first of many such conversations I had with Clark on this subject.

28. See Kengor, *The Crusader,* 133–140; and Kengor, *God and Ronald Reagan,* 208–216.

29. Bernstein, "The Holy Alliance," 31.

30. Ibid., 28, 30.

31. See "The Pope and the President: A Key Adviser Reflects on the Reagan Administration," interview with Bill Clark, *Catholic World Reporter,* November 1999; and Bernstein, "Holy Alliance," 30.

32. Bernstein, "Holy Alliance," 30.

33. Quoted in Peter Schweizer, *Reagan's War: The Epic Story of His Forty-Year Struggle and Final Triumph over Communism* (New York: Doubleday, 2002), 213.

34. Bernstein, "The Holy Alliance," 28–35.

35. This is one of the most verifiable, indisputable elements of Reagan's Cold War strategy. For confirmation by firsthand observers, see Kengor, *The Crusader*, 84–111, 133–140; Kengor, *God and Ronald Reagan*, 208–216; and Kengor, *The Judge*, 170–174.

36. Bernstein, "The Holy Alliance," 29–31.

37. Tony Dolan has told me this numerous times. He is quick to insist upon it to anyone who asks.

38. Cannon, *Role of a Lifetime*, 272–274; Lou Cannon, *President Reagan: The Role of a Lifetime* (New York: Public Affairs, 2000).

39. See Kengor, *The Crusader*, 146–164.

40. The Crusade for Freedom was launched by Dwight Eisenhower, with Lucius Clay its first chairman. It committed the United States to a campaign to promote freedom and democracy behind the Iron Curtain. Ronald Reagan became one of its stronger spokesmen, even recording a promotion film in 1951.

41. Ibid.

42. Quoted by Steven Rottner, "Britons Reassured by Reagan's Visit," *New York Times*, June 10, 1982, A17.

43. Cannon, "Reagan Radiated Happiness and Hope," *George* 5, no. 7 (August 2000): 58.

44. V. Bolshakov, "Washington 'Crusaders' on the March," *Pravda*, January 31, 1983, 6, reprinted as "Pravda Accuses U.S. of 'Ideological Aggression,'" in FBIS-SOV-9-FEB-83, February 9, 1983, A1–A4.

45. Reagan, "Remarks at the Annual Conservative Political Action Conference," Washington, DC, February 6, 1977.

46. Probably the most authoritative statement on this figure is Stephane Courtois, ed., *The Black Book of Communism* (Cambridge, MA: Harvard University Press, 1999), 4.

47. Mikhail Gorbachev, *Memoirs* (New York: Doubleday, 1996), 457. Gorbachev has made identical or near identical remarks in "Reagan," *The American Experience*, documentary produced by PBS, WGBH-TV Boston, 1998; and Gorbachev, July 1997 statement, in *A Shining City: The Legacy of Ronald Reagan* (New York: Simon and Schuster, 1998), 222.

48. Gorbachev speaking on "Reagan," *The American Experience*.

49. Jack Matlock, who attended the dinner, relays the exchange in his *Reagan and Gorbachev* (New York: Random House, 2004), 326.

50. Gorbachev speaking on *Ronald Reagan: A Legacy Remembered*, History Channel productions, 2002.

51. Published by FBIS as "Czech President, Predecessor Express Sadness at Death of Former US President," June 5, 2004.

52. Wałesa spoke at a conference, "The Reagan Legacy," held at the Ronald Reagan Library, Simi Valley, CA, May 20, 1996. See Mack Reed, "Walesa Hails Reagan at Daylong Seminar," *Los Angeles Times*, May 21, 1996.

53. Quoted in John O'Sullivan, "Friends at Court," *National Review,* May 27, 1991, 4. For his part, Reagan called Wałesa a heroic figure. Reagan, "Remarks on Signing the Human Rights Day, Bill of Rights Day, and Human Rights Week Proclamation," December 8, 1988.

54. Interview with Lech Wałesa, April 25, 2005.

55. Wałesa, "The Reagan Legacy."

56. Speaking at the Century Plaza Hotel in Los Angeles, August 26, 1987, Reagan said: "Our goal has been to break the deadlock of the past, to seek a forward strategy for world peace, a forward strategy for world freedom."

57. I raised this possible scenario in my 2004 book, *God and George W. Bush* (New York: HarperCollins), specifically in the section "Beware Theocracy," 274–277.

58. This was a concern of Pope John Paul II, who died in April 2005, before the attacks and exodus intensified. Accounts of these attacks have been regularly carried in the *National Catholic Register,* probably the preeminent conservative Catholic publication. Also carefully chronicling the persecution is Nina Shea, first at Freedom House and currently at the Hudson Institute's Center for Religious Freedom.

59. On Buckley's (somewhat complicated) position, see Lee Edwards, *William F. Buckley Jr.: The Making of a Movement* (Wilmington, DE: ISI Books, 2010), 169–178. On Jeane Kirkpatrick, see Peter Collier, *Political Woman: The Big Little Life of Jeane Kirkpatrick* (New York: Encounter Books, 2012), 200–207. For an analysis of conservatives' antiwar positions (and liberals), see Stephen W. Knott, *Rush to Judgment: George W. Bush, the War on Terror, and His Critics* (Lawrence: University Press of Kansas, 2012).

60. On Bush and Wilson, see John Lewis Gaddis, "A Grand Strategy of Transformation," *Foreign Policy,* November–December 2002. In one of the earlier and more influential analyses, Gaddis noted that by seeking to spread democracy everywhere, Bush aimed to finish the job Woodrow Wilson started a century earlier. "The world," writes Gaddis, "quite literally, must be made safe for democracy, even those parts of it, like the Middle East, that have so far resisted that tendency."

61. This split was especially evident in the pages of the *American Conservative* versus the *Weekly Standard.*

62. In February 2007, I wrote a four-part series on this subject for the popular conservative website Townhall.com. The series was prominently displayed (and linked to by other sources) and received a huge volume of feedback, much of it very negative toward Bush. Many conservatives personally e-mailed me and expressed their outrage.

63. Charles Dunn notes that this rapid, rare use of force allowed Reagan to avoid liberal criticism of excessive force in the battle against communism. He chose prudently, selecting spots that were eminently doable. Charles W. Dunn, *The Scarlet Thread of Scandal* (Lanham, MD: Rowman & Littlefield, 2000), 150.

64. Brian Montopoli, "Three in Four Back Iraq Troop Pullout," *CBSNews.com,* November 11, 2011.

65. I know of no example of Reagan explicitly excluding Middle Easterners or Muslims from his belief that all humans are created in God's image and desirous of freedom.

6. The Beginning of a New U.S. Grand Strategy

1. See, for instance, Marc A. Celmer, *Terrorism, U.S. Strategy, and Reagan Policies* (Westport, CT: Greenwood Press, 1987); and David C. Wills, *The First War on Terrorism: Counter-Terrorism Policy during the Reagan Administration* (Lanham, MD: Rowman & Littlefield, 2003).

2. Peter Beinart, "Think Again: Ronald Reagan," *Foreign Policy,* June 7, 2010, http://www.foreignpolicy.com/articles/2010/06/07/think_again_ronald _reagan.

3. In traditional international relations theory, the systemic (international), national, and individual levels of analysis were separable entities, and most of the theorizing was done at the systemic and national levels. See J. David Singer, "International Conflicts: Three Levels of Analysis," *World Politics* 12, no. 3 (April 1960): 453–461; and Kenneth Waltz, *Man, the State, and War: A Theoretical Analysis* (New York: Columbia University Press, 1954). Along with his coauthors, Bruce Bueno de Mesquita has collapsed these distinctions and incorporated people in societies into the scientific study of international relations. This is done through an analysis of the selectorate and the winning coalition, concepts he has developed, along with his colleagues. See Bruce Bueno de Mesquita, Alastair Smith, Randolph M. Siverson, and James Morrow, *The Logic of Political Survival* (Cambridge, MA: MIT Press, 2003).

4. Jimmy Carter, "The State of the Union Address Delivered before a Joint Session of the Congress," January 23, 1980; Gerhard Peters and John T. Woolley, *The American Presidency Project,* http://www.presidency.ucsb.edu /ws/?pid=33079.

5. "Transcript of Carter Statement on Iran," *New York Times,* April 8, 1980, A6.

6. "America Remembers Desert One Heroes," Department of Defense Website: American Forces Press Service, April 25, 2005, http://www.defense.gov/news /newsarticle.aspx?id=31346.

7. Jeffrey M. Jones, "What History Foretells for Obama's First Job Approval Rating," *Gallup,* January 22, 2009, http://www.gallup.com/poll/113923/History -Foretells-Obama-First-Job-Approval-Rating.aspx; "Presidential Approval Ratings—Gallup Historical Statistics and Trends," *Gallup,* http://www.gallup .com/poll/116677/presidential-approval-ratings-gallup-historical-statistics -trends.aspx; and "Job Performance Ratings for President Carter," *Roper*

Center, http://www.ropercenter.uconn.edu/CFIDE/roper/presidential/webroot
/presidential_rating_detail.cfm?allRate=True&presidentName=Carter.

8. David Patrick Houghton, *US Foreign Policy and the Iran Hostage Crisis*
(Cambridge: Cambridge University Press, 2001), 4; and Rose McDermott,
Risk-Taking in International Politics: Prospect Theory in American Foreign Policy
(Ann Arbor: University of Michigan Press, 1998), 48–51.

9. "Kennedy Tiptoes Much Closer to a Candidacy," *New York Times,* September
16, 1979; Albert R. Hunt, "Kennedy to Start Now-Certain Campaign with a
Presidency Committee Next Week," *Wall Street Journal,* October 18, 1979;
and Albert R. Hunt, "Kennedy Opens His Bid for Presidency by Taking Aim
at Carter's Leadership," *Wall Street Journal,* November 8, 1979, 8.

10. *Guide to U.S. Elections,* 5th ed. (Washington, DC: CQ Press, 2005), 1:382.

11. Senator Edward M. Kennedy, "And the Dream Shall Never Die," August 12,
1980, http://tedkennedy.org/ownwords/event/1980_convention.

12. *Guide to U.S. Elections,* 382.

13. Ronald Reagan, "Address Accepting the Presidential Nomination at the
Republican National Convention in Detroit," *The American Presidency Project,*
July 17, 1980, http://www.presidency.ucsb.edu/ws/?pid=25970.

14. When asked about the Iranian hostage crisis during his debate with President
Carter on October 28, 1980, Governor Reagan gave his position on making
the matter a prominent issue in the campaign: "I would be fearful that I
might say something that was presently under way or in negotiations, and
thus expose it and endanger the hostages. And sometimes, I think some of
my ideas might involve quiet diplomacy, where you don't say in advance or say
to anyone what it is you're thinking of doing." See "1980 Ronald Reagan/
Jimmy Carter Presidential Debate," University of Texas, Reagan Archives,
October 28, 1980, http://www.reagan.utexas.edu/archives/reference/10.28
.80debate.html.

15. Ronald Reagan, "A Strategy for Peace in the'80s" (televised address), *The
American Presidency Project,* University of California, Santa Barbara, October
19, 1980, http://www.presidency.ucsb.edu/ws/index.php?pid=85200.

16. "1980 Ronald Reagan/Jimmy Carter Presidential Debate."

17. Ibid.

18. Ronald Reagan, "A Vision for America" (election eve address), University of
Texas, Reagan Archives, November 3, 1980, http://www.reagan.utexas.edu
/archives/reference/11.3.80.html.

19. Jimmy Carter, *White House Diary* (New York: Farrar, Straus, and Giroux,
2010), 478.

20. *The Gallup Poll: Public Opinion 1980* (Wilmington, DE: Scholarly Resources,
1981), 254. From the Associated Press, the text of the Iranian demands was
published in "Militants Accept Hostage Plan; Transfer Custody to Iranian
Government," *Boston Globe,* November 3, 1980, 1. See also "Is Hostage Crisis
Nearly Over? It Seems So, But . . . ," *New York Times,* November 2, 1980, E4.

21. Carter, *White House Diary*, 476.

22. Walter F. Mondale with David Hage, *The Good Fight: A Life in Liberal Politics* (Minneapolis: University of Minnesota Press, 2010), 259.

23. On November 7–10, 1980, a Gallup Poll question about the Iran-Iraq War was presented to the "informed public." Forty-nine percent did not have sympathies for either country. See *The Gallup Poll: Public Opinion 1980* (Wilmington, DE: Scholarly Resources, 1981), 254.

24. Kiron K. Skinner, Serhiy Kudelia, Bruce Bueno de Mesquita, and Condoleezza Rice, *The Strategy of Campaigning: Lessons from Ronald Reagan and Boris Yeltsin* (Ann Arbor: University of Michigan Press, 2007), 199–200.

25. "Case Studies in Sanctions and Terrorism: Chronology of Key Events," Peterson Institute for International Economics Website, http://www.piie .com/research/topics/sanctions/libya.cfm.

26. Margalit Fox, "David Dodge, an Early Lebanon Hostage, Dies at 86," *New York Times*, January 30, 2009, A22.

27. "Lebanon Profile: History," United States Department of State Website, January 1994, http://www.state.gov/outofdate/bgn/lebanon/7929.htm.

28. The review of Middle East terrorism against the United States in this essay draws upon numerous sources herein cited, including Michael Kirk and Peter Taylor, "Target America: Terrorist Attacks on Americans, 1979–1988," *Frontline*, program 2001, aired October 4, 2001 (Boston: WGBH Educational Foundation, 2001), http://www.pbs.org/wgbh/pages/frontline/shows /target/etc/cron.html. Hezbollah "publicly identified its ideological platforms" in 1985. Matthew Levitt, *Hezbollah: The Global Footprint of Lebanon's Party of God* (Washington, DC: Georgetown University Press, 2013), 12.

29. John Fass Morton, *Next-Generation Homeland Security: Network Federalism and the Course of National Preparedness* (Annapolis, MD: Naval Institute Press, 2012), 42.

30. "Report of the DoD Commission on Beirut International Airport Terrorist Act, October 23, 1983," Department of Defense, http://www.ibiblio.org/hyper war/AMH/XX/MidEast/Lebanon-1982-1984/DOD-Report/#page1.

31. Michael Kirk and Peter Taylor, "Target America: Terrorist Attacks on Americans, 1979–1988," *Frontline*, program 2001, aired October 4, 2001 (Boston: WGBH Educational Foundation, 2001), http://www.pbs.org/wgbh /pages/frontline/shows/target/etc/cron.html.

32. "William F. Buckley," Arlington National Cemetery Website, December 27, 1991, http://www.arlingtoncemetery.net/wbuckley.htm.

33. Kiron K. Skinner, Annelise Anderson, and Martin Anderson, eds., *Reagan: A Life in Letters* (New York: Free Press, 2003), 457. See also "A Guide to the United States' History of Recognition, Diplomatic, and Consular Relations, by Country, since 1776: Iraq," U.S. Department of State Office of the Historian, http://history.state.gov/countries/iraq.

34. Skinner, Anderson, and Anderson, *Reagan*, 457.

35. Ibid.; and "Iran-Contra Report; Arms, Hostages and Contras: How a Secret Foreign Policy Unraveled," *New York Times*, November 19, 1986, http://www .nytimes.com/1987/11/19/iran-contra-report-arms-hostages-contras-secret -foreign-policy-unraveled.html.

36. Skinner, Anderson, and Anderson, *Reagan*, 458. In this section, the analysis of the Iran-Contra scandal and the hostage crisis are based on Skinner's writing in *Reagan*, 456–459.

37. Associated Press, "Highlights of Messe's Legal Problems," Associated Press Online, July 6, 1988, http://www.apnewsarchive.com/1988/Highlights-Of -Meese-s-Legal-Problems/id-048374a638a1b801f3b7fc4902604e22.

38. Skinner, Anderson, and Anderson, *Reagan*, 459; "Final Report of the Independent Counsel for Iran/Contra Matters" (Washington, DC: U.S. Court of Appeals for the District of Columbia Circuit, August 4, 1993). http://fas.org/irp/offdocs/walsh/.

39. See the transcript of the PBS interview with Robert Oakley, http://www.pbs .org/wgbh/pages/frontline/shows/target/interviews/oakley.html; John Kifner, "23 Die, Including 2 Americans, in Terrorist Car Bomb Attack on the U.S. Embassy at Beirut; Blast Kills Driver," *New York Times*, September 21, 1984, http://www.nytimes.com/1984/09/21/world/23-die-including-2-americans -terrorist-car-bomb-attack-us-embassy-beirut-blast.html?pagewanted=all; and Wills, *The First War on Terrorism*, 84–85.

40. See Levitt, *Hezbollah*, 40–41; and "Terrorist Attacks on Americans, 1979– 1988," *Frontline*, http://www.pbs.org/wgbh/pages/frontline/shows/target/etc /cron.html.

41. William E. Smith, "Terror aboard Flight 847," *Time* Magazine Online, June 24, 2001, http://www.time.com/time/magazine/article/0,9171,142099,00.html.

42. "Bomb Kills Top Hezbollah Leader," BBC Online, February 13, 2008, http://news.bbc.co.uk/2/hi/7242383.stm; and "Terrorist Attacks on Ameri- cans, 1979–1988."

43. John W. Miller, "Five Men Convicted and Sentenced in Achille Lauro Case," Associated Press, November 18, 1985; "Terrorist Abu Abbas Dies in Iraq," Fox News, March 9, 2004, http://www.foxnews.com/story/2004/03/09/terrorist -abu-abbas-dies-in-iraq/; and David Ensor, "U.S. Captures Mastermind of Achille Lauro Hijacking," CNN, April 16, 2003, http://www.cnn.com/2003 /WORLD/meast/04/15/sprj.irq.abbas.arrested/.

44. Judy Endicott, "Raid on Libya: Operation El Dorado Canyon," Air Force Historical Studies Office, http://www.afhso.af.mil/shared/media/document /AFD-120823-032.pdf.

45. For a detailed review of the Reagan administration's deliberations on Libya and terrorism related to these activities, see George P. Shultz, *Turmoil and Triumph: My Years as Secretary of State* (New York: Charles Scribner's Sons, 1993), 669–688.

46. Anne Swardson, "Lockerbie Suspects Delivered for Trial," *Washington Post* Online, April 6, 1999, http://pqasb.pqarchiver.com/washingtonpost/doc /408476294.html?FMT=ABS&FMTS=ABS:FT&date=Apr+6%2C+1999 &author=Swardson%2C+Anne&pub=The+Washington+Post&edition=&st artpage=&desc=Lockerbie+Suspects+Delivered+For+Trial%3B+Sanctions +on+Libya+Suspended+by+U.N.

47. See Office of the Secretary of State, "The Year in Review," April 1991, *Patterns of Global Terrorism*, http://fas.org/irp/threat/terror_91/review.html.

48. "Abdelbaset Al-Megrahi Dead: Lockerbie Bomber Dies of Cancer in Libya," The Huffington Post Online, May 20, 2012, http://www.huffingtonpost.co .uk/2012/05/20/lockerbie-bomber-abdelbaset-al-megrahi-dead_n_1530759 .html.

49. Felicity Barringer, "Libya Admits Culpability in Crash of Pan Am Plane," *New York Times,* August 16, 2003, http://www.nytimes.com/2003/08/16 /international/middleeast/16NATI.html; and "Libya Compensates Terror Victims," BBC News, October 31, 2008, http://news.bbc.co.uk/2/hi/americas /7703110.stm.

50. Ronald Reagan, *The Reagan Diaries,* ed. Douglas Brinkley (New York: HarperCollins, 2007), 688, 690.

51. Ronald Reagan, *An American Life* (New York: Simon and Schuster, 1990), 491–492.

52. Ibid., 492.

53. Ibid.

54. Rachel Bronson, *Thicker Than Oil: America's Uneasy Partnership with Saudi Arabia* (Oxford: Oxford University Press, 2006), 161.

55. Mattia Toaldo, "The Reagan Administration and the Origins of the War on Terror: Lebanon and Libya as Case Studies," *New Middle Eastern Studies* (April 4, 2012): 13.

56. SNIE 11/2-81, "Soviet Support for International Terrorism and Revolutionary Violence," May 27, 1981, 1–2, http://www.foia.cia.gov/sites/default /files/document_conversions/89801/DOC_0000272980.pdf.

57. George P. Shultz, "Power and Diplomacy in the 1980s," *Current Policy* 561 (April 3, 1984).

58. George P. Shultz, "Terrorism and the Modern World," *Current Policy* 629 (October 25, 1984).

59. Ibid.

60. "Low-Intensity Warfare: The Challenge of Ambiguity," *Current Policy* 783 (January 15, 1986).

61. Ibid.

62. "The Uses of Military Power," *The Uses of Military Power: Secretary Weinberger on the Uses of Military Power (excerpts)* 27, no. 1 (November 28, 1984): 32–35, http://dx.doi.org/10.1080/00396338508442218.

63. For a recent analysis of the Weinberger Doctrine, see Gail E. S. Yoshitani, *Reagan on War: A Reappraisal of the Weinberger Doctrine, 1980–1984* (College Station, TX: Texas A&M University Press, 2012).

64. Caspar Weinberger, *In the Arena: A Memoir of the 20th Century* (Washington, DC: Regnery, 2001), 309.

65. Caspar Weinberger, *Fighting for Peace: Seven Critical Years in the Pentagon* (New York: Warner Books, 1990), 154.

66. For NSDD 138, see "National Security Decision Directive 138: Combating Terrorism," The White House, April 3, 1984, http://www.thereaganfiles.com /nsdd-138.pdf. For NSDD 179, see "National Security Decision Directive 179: Task Force on Combating Terrorism," The White House, July 20, 1985, http://www.fas.org/irp/offdocs/nsdd/nsdd-179.htm. This July 20, 1985, directive created the Vice President's Task Force on Combating Terrorism, which is discussed later in this chapter.

67. White House Fact Sheet, April 26, 1984; Ronald Reagan, "Message to the Congress Transmitting Proposed Legislation to Combat International Terrorism," April 26, 1984, http://www.reagan.utexas.edu/archives/speeches /1984/42684a.htm.

68. Ronald Reagan, "National Security Decision Directive 138: Combating Terrorism," The White House, April 3, 1984, http://www.thereaganfiles.com /nsdd-138.pdf.

69. Quoted in Robert C. Toth, "Preemptive Anti-Terrorist Raids Allowed," *Washington Post,* April 16, 1984, A19.

70. George P. Shultz, "Power and Diplomacy in the 1980s," *Current Policy,* 561, U.S. Department of State, April 3, 1984; James P. Terry, "'Operationalizing' Legal Requirements for Unconventional Warfare," *JFQ* 52 (First quarter, 2009): 136–137.

71. Robert C. McFarlane, "Terrorism and the Future of Free Society," speech, National Strategic Information Center, Defense Strategy Forum, Washington, DC, March 25, 1985, reprinted in *Terrorism* 8, no. 4 (1986): 315–326.

72. Office of the Press Secretary, "To the Congress of the United States," The White House, April 26, 1984, http://www2.gwu.edu/~nsarchiv/NSAEBB /NSAEBB55/nsdd138congress.pdf.

73. "Bill Summary & Status, 98th Congress (1983–1984), H.R.5689," Library of Congress Online, http://thomas.loc.gov/cgi-bin/bdquery/z?d098:HR05689:; "Bill Summary & Status, 98th Congress (1983–1984), H.R.5690," Library of Congress Online, http://thomas.loc.gov/cgi-bin/bdquery/z?d098:HR05690: @@@D; and "Bill Summary & Status 98th Congress (1983–1984) H.J.RES.648," Library of Congress Online, http://thomas.loc.gov/cgi-bin /bdquery/z?d098:HJ00648:@@@L&summ2=m&.

74. It should be noted that in November 1972 the U.S. Senate ratified the Montreal Convention. See "President's Anti-Terrorism Legislation Fact

Sheet," The White House, April 26, 1984, http://www2.gwu.edu/~nsarchiv/NSAEBB/NSAEBB55/nsdd138legislation.pdf; and "Convention for the Suppression of Unlawful Acts against the Safety of Civil Aviation, Signed at Montreal, on 23 September 1971 (Montreal Convention 1971)," September 23, 1971, http://www.mcgill.ca/files/iasl/montreal1971.pdf.

75. See "Statement on Signing the 1984 Act to Combat International Terrorism," University of Texas, Reagan Archives, October 19, 1984, http://www.reagan.utexas.edu/archives/speeches/1984/101984a.htm; and "Bill Summary & Status, 98th Congress (1983–1984) H.R.6311," Library of Congress Online, http://thomas.loc.gov/cgi-bin/bdquery/z?d098:HR06311:@@@L&summ2=m&.

76. See "Message to the Congress Transmitting Proposed Legislation to Combat International Terrorism," April 26, 1984, http://www.reagan.utexas.edu/archives/speeches/1984/42684a.htm; "Bill Summary & Status, 98th Congress (1983–1984) S.2626," Library of Congress Online, http://thomas.loc.gov/cgi-bin/bdquery/z?d098:SN02626:@@@L&summ2=m&; and "Bill Summary & Status, 98th Congress (1983–1984) H.R.5613," Library of Congress Online, http://thomas.loc.gov/cgi-bin/bdquery/z?d098:HR05613:@@@L&summ2=m&.

77. William H. Schaap, *Covert Action* (New York: Ocean Press, 2003), 80.

78. "National Security Decision Directive 179: Task Force on Combating Terrorism," Homeland Security Digital Library, https://www.hsdl.org/?abstract&did=443007; and https://www.hsdl.org/?view&did=443007.

79. Ibid.

80. For a complete outline of the vice president's task force on terrorism, see "National Security Decision Directive 207," Homeland Security Digital Library, January 20, 1986, https://www.hsdl.org/?abstract&did=463170.

81. "Study on Terrorist Groups," *Congressional Record*, February 8, 1989, http://thomas.loc.gov/cgi-bin/query/z?r101:S08FE9-135:.

82. Andrew Feickert, "U.S. Special Operations Forces (SOF): Background and Issues for Congress," *Congressional Research Service*, June 22, 2009, https://www.fas.org/sgp/crs/natsec/RS21048.pdf.

83. Lee Allen Zatarain, *Tanker War: America's First Conflict with Iran, 1987–1988* (Philadelphia: CASEMATE, 2008).

84. Shultz, *Turmoil and Triumph*, 925–935.

85. James P. Terry, "'Operationalizing' Legal Requirements for Unconventional Warfare," *JFQ* (October 2009): 137.

86. "The President," 60, no. 16, *Presidential Documents*, January 23, 1995, http://www.treasury.gov/resource-center/sanctions/Documents/12947.pdf.

87. Ronald Reagan, "National Security Decision Directive 138: Combating Terrorism," The White House, April 3, 1984, http://www.thereaganfiles.com/nsdd-138.pdf.

88. "Prohibiting Transactions with Terrorists Who Threaten to Disrupt the Middle East Peace Process," 63, no. 164, Presidential Documents, August 20, 1998, http://www.gpo.gov/fdsys/pkg/FR-1998-08-25/pdf/98-22940.pdf.

89. Richard J. Newman et al., "America Fights Back." *U.S. News & World Report* 125, no. 8 (August 31, 1998): 38.

90. George W. Bush, "Commencement Address at the United States Military Academy in West Point, New York," *The American Presidency Project,* June 1, 2002, http://www.presidency.ucsb.edu/ws/?pid=62730; and "The National Security Strategy of the United States of America," September 2002, http://www.state.gov/documents/organization/63562.pdf. For other statements in defense of preemption as a means of combating terrorism, see the president's speeches at West Point on May 27, 2006, and December 10, 2008.

91. John Lewis Gaddis, *Surprise, Security, and the American Experience* (Cambridge, MA: Harvard University Press, 2005).

92. George W. Bush, "Commencement Address at the United States Military Academy in West Point, New York," The American Presidency Project, June 1, 2002, http://www.presidency.ucsb.edu/ws/?pid=62730; and Arnel B. Enriquez, "The US National Security Strategy of 2002: A Use-of-Force Doctrine?," *Air and Space Power Journal* (Fall 2004): 8, http://www.airpower.maxwell.af.mil/airchronicles/apj/apj04/fal04/enriquez.html.

93. "Creation of the Department of Homeland Security," Department of Homeland Security, http://www.dhs.gov/creation-department-homeland-security; and Alberto Gonzales, "Transcript: AG Alberto Gonzales on 'FOX News Sunday,'" July 24, 2005, http://www.foxnews.com/story/2005/07/24/transcript-ag-alberto-gonzales-on-fox-news-sunday/.

94. Andrew Glass, "Bush Signs the Patriot Act Oct. 26, 2001," *Politico,* April 9, 2013, http://www.politico.com/news/stories/1007/6564.html.

95. "History—U.S. Strategic Command," U.S. Strategic Command, http://www.stratcom.mil/history/; and "U.S. Northern Command," About US-NORTHCOM, http://www.northcom.mil/AboutUSNORTHCOM.aspx.

96. For similar analysis, see Richard Jackson, "Culture, Identity and Hegemony: Continuity and (the Lack of) Change in U.S. Counterterrorism Policy from Bush to Obama," *International Politics* (March–May 2011): 390–408. See also Joe Scarborough, "President Obama Embraces George W. Bush's Anti-Terror Tactics," Politico, January 17, 2014, http://www.politico.com/story/2014/01/president-obama-national-security-102334.html.

7. Ronald Reagan and American Defense

1. Lou Cannon, *President Reagan: The Role of a Lifetime* (New York: Public Affairs, 2000), 404.

2. "A Strategy for Peace in the '80s," October 19, 1980, http://www.reagan.utexas.edu/archives/Reference/10.19.80.html.

3. Ronald Reagan to Kenneth J. Hoover, December 27, 1982, in Kiron K. Skinner, Annelise Anderson, and Martin Anderson, eds., *Reagan: A Life in Letters* (New York: Free Press, 2003), 391.

4. "Address to the Nation on Defense and National Security," March 23, 1983, http://www.reagan.utexas.edu/archives/speeches/1983/32383d.htm. This is the speech announcing the Strategic Defense Initiative.

5. "Remarks at a Cemetery Commemorating the 40th Anniversary of the Normandy Invasion, D-day," June 6, 1984, http://www.reagan.utexas.edu /archives/speeches/1984/60684a.htm.

6. Quoted in Skinner, Anderson, and Anderson, *Reagan,* 534.

7. Ronald Reagan to Mark L. Smith, November 8, 1982, in ibid., 265.

8. See Caspar Weinberger, *Fighting for Peace* (New York: Warner Books, 1990), 52–56.

9. See Daniel Wirls, *Buildup: The Politics of Defense in the Reagan Era* (Ithaca, NY: Cornell University Press, 1992), 36; also Lawrence J. Korb, "The Reagan Defense Budget and Program: The Buildup That Collapsed," in David Boaz, ed., *Assessing the Reagan Years* (Washington, DC: Cato Institute, 1988), 83–94, for a good short summary of the numbers.

10. Korb, "The Reagan Defense Budget," 84.

11. "Address to Members of the British Parliament," June 8, 1982, http://www .reagan.utexas.edu/archives/speeches/1982/60882a.htm.

12. On Reagan's long-standing anxieties about thermonuclear war, see Cannon, *President Reagan,* 248–250 and passim.

13. See Donald R. Baucom, *The Origins of SDI, 1944–1983* (Lawrence: University Press of Kansas, 1992).

14. "Republican National Convention," August 19, 1976, http://www.reagan .utexas.edu/archives/reference/8.19.76.html.

15. Ronald Reagan to VADM (ret.) Marmaduke Bayne, September 12, 1983, in Skinner, Anderson, and Anderson, *Reagan,* 410.

16. George P. Shultz, *Turmoil and Triumph: My Years as Secretary of State* (New York: Charles Scribner's Sons, 1993), 646ff.

17. Ibid., 648.

18. Caspar W. Weinberger, *Fighting for Peace: Seven Critical Years in the Pentagon* (New York: Warner Books, 1990), 397–402.

19. Colin Powell with Joseph E. Persico, *My American Journey* (New York: Random House, 1995), 302–303.

20. One text of this widely reprinted speech is in Weinberger, *Fighting for Peace,* 433–445.

21. Powell, *My American Journey,* 303.

22. George P. Shultz, "The Ethics of Power," in Ernest W. Lefever, ed., *Ethics and American Power: Speeches by Caspar W. Weinberger and George P. Shultz* (Washington, DC: Ethics and Public Policy Center, 1985), 13.

23. Carl von Clausewitz, *On War,* trans. and ed. Michael Howard and Peter Paret, (Princeton, NJ: Princeton University Press, 1976), 86–88, book I, chapter 1, on war as an act of policy and the importance of understanding the nature of any individual conflict.

24. Ibid., book III, chapter 7, 193. "In war more than anywhere else things do not turn out as we expect."

8. A World of Fewer Nuclear Weapons

1. See "Ronald Reagan: Pre-Presidential Papers: Selected Radio Broadcasts, 1975–1979," April 1977 to September 1977, Box 2, Ronald Reagan Library, Simi Valley, CA; and Kiron K. Skinner, Annelise Anderson, and Martin Anderson, eds., *Reagan, in His Own Hand* (New York: Free Press, 2001), 10–12.

2. For Fischer and Lettow, this is a primary focus of their work. See Beth A. Fischer, *The Reagan Reversal* (Columbia: University of Missouri Press, 2000); and Paul Lettow, *Ronald Reagan and His Quest to Abolish Nuclear Weapons* (New York: Random House, 2005). Important secondary works include Melvyn Leffler, *For the Soul of Mankind* (New York: Macmillan, 2007); and David E. Hoffman, *The Dead Hand: The Untold Story of the Cold War Arms Race and Its Dangerous Legacy* (New York: Random House, 2010).

3. Reagan, "Acceptance Speech at Republican National Convention," July 17, 1980.

4. Among international sources, the literature from the Soviet side is very revealing and very rich. The Reagan-Gorbachev relationship and their dealings and negotiations are illuminated by the many Soviet memoirs relating to the period. Among others, see A. Adamishin, *Human Rights, Perestroika, and the End of the Cold War* (Washington, DC: United States Institute of Peace Press, 2009); G. Arbatov, *The System: An Insider's Life in Soviet Politics* (New York: Three Rivers Press, 1993); N. Baibakov, *The Cause of My Life* (Moscow: Progress, 1987); V. Bakatin, *Izbaveleine ot KGB* (Moscow: Novosti, 1992); A. Bovin, *Notes from a Non-Professional Ambassador* (Moscow: Zacharov, 2001); A. Chernyaev, *My Six Years with Gorbachev* (State College: Pennsylvania State University Press, 2000); A. Dobrynin, *In Confidence* (New York: Random House, 1995); Y. Dubinin, *Time of Change: The Notes of the Ambassador to the United States* (Moscow: Aviarus-XXI, 2003); V. Falin, *Politische Errinerungen,* translated from Russian to German by Heddy Press-Veerth (Munich: Dreemer Knaur, 1993); M. Gorbachev, *Memoirs* (New York: Doubleday, 1996); R. Gorbachev, *I Hope: Reminiscences and Reflections* (New York: HarperCollins, 1992); A. Grachev, *Final Days: The Inside Story of the Collapse of the Soviet Union* (Boulder, CO: Westview Press, 1995); A. Grachev, *Gorbachev's Gamble: Soviet Foreign Policy and the End of the Cold War* (Cambridge: Polity, 2008); S. Grigoriev, *The International*

Department of the CPSU Central Committee: The Central Party Apparatus under Gorbachev (Cambridge, MA: Harvard University Press, 1995); A. Gromyko, *Memoirs* (New York: Doubleday, 1990); R. Khasbulatov, *The Struggle for Russia: Power and Change in the Democratic Revolution* (New York: Routledge, 1993); V. Kryuchkov, *Lichnoye Delo: A Personal File* (Moscow: Olimp, 1996); A. Lebed, *General Alexander Lebed: My Life and Country* (Washington, DC: Regnery, 1997); Y. Ligachev, *Inside Gorbachev's Kremlin: The Memoirs of Yegor Ligachev* (Boulder, CO: Westview Press, 1996); E. Mawdsley and S. White, *The Soviet Elite from Lenin to Gorbachev: The Central Committee and Its Members* (Oxford: Oxford University Press, 2000); D. Mikheev, *The Rise and Fall of Gorbachev* (Washington, DC: Hudson Institute, 1992); P. Palazchenko, *My Years with Gorbachev and Shevardnadze: The Memoir of a Soviet Interpreter* (State College: Pennsylvania State University Press, 1997); B. Pankin, *The Last Hundred Days of the Soviet Union* (New York: I. B. Taurus, 1996); B. Ponomarev, *Winning for Peace: The Great Victory* (Moscow: Progress, 1986); Y. Primakov, *Russian Crossroads: Towards the New Millennium* (New Haven, CT: Yale University Press, 2004); E. Shevardnadze, *The Future Belongs to Freedom* (London: Sinclair-Stevenson, 1991); S. Stankevich, *Perestroika: Through the Eyes of a People's Deputy* (Moscow: Novosti Press, 1990); A. Yakovlev, *Striving for Law in a Lawless Land: Memoirs of a Russian Reformer* (Armonk, NY: M. E. Sharpe, 1996); B. Yeltsin, *Against the Grain* (New York: Simon and Schuster, 1990); B. Yeltsin, *The Struggle for Russia* (New York: Crown, 1995); and I. Zemcov, *Chernenko: The Last Bolshevik* (Piscataway, NJ: Transaction, 1989).

5. Mikhail Gorbachev, July 1997 statement, in Ronald Reagan, *A Shining City: The Legacy of Ronald Reagan* (New York: Simon and Schuster, 1998), 222.

6. John Lewis Gaddis, *The United States and the End of the Cold War* (New York: Oxford University Press, 1994), 62, 130.

7. Cannon in Kenneth W. Thompson, ed., *Leadership in the Reagan Presidency: Seven Intimate Perspectives* (Lanham, MD: Madison Books, 1992), 125.

8. Cannon interviewed on C-SPAN's *American Presidents* series, December 6, 1999.

9. Don Oberdorfer speaking at a 1993 Hofstra University conference on the Reagan presidency, published in Eric J. Schmertz et al., eds., *President Reagan and the World* (Westport, CT: Greenwood Press, 1997), 130. Hereafter referred to as "Hofstra collection."

10. Fred I. Greenstein, *The Presidential Difference: Leadership Style from FDR to Clinton* (New York: Free Press, 2000), 150; and Greenstein in Hofstra collection, 473.

11. Jack F. Matlock, *Autopsy of an Empire* (New York: Random House, 1995), 77.

12. Interview with Ed Meese, March 23, 1998. Also see Edwin Meese, *With Reagan: The Inside Story* (Washington, DC: Regnery Gateway, 1992), 21.

13. Martin Anderson, *Revolution* (New York: Harcourt, 1988), 284–285.

14. Reagan diary entry, April 6, 1982. First published in Ronald Reagan, *An American Life* (New York: Simon and Schuster, 1990), 572.

15. Don Oberdorfer, *The Turn* (New York: Poseidon Press, 1991), 17–19, 22, 37, 141, 188–189, 438.

16. Reagan weekly radio address, September 29, 1984, published in Fred L. Israel, ed., *Ronald Reagan's Weekly Radio Addresses,* vol. 1 (Wilmington, DE: Scholarly Resources, 1987), 248.

17. A favorite anecdote of Reagan's son Michael is when his father lost his 1976 bid for the Republican presidential nomination and told Michael that his greatest regret was that he would not get a chance to sit down with Brezhnev and let Brezhnev finally hear the word "Nyet" from a U.S. president. Yes, Reagan wanted to sit down with Brezhnev, but he did not want to give the Soviet leader everything Moscow wanted.

18. A book that influenced Reagan's thinking was *The Treaty Trap,* a 1969 work by Laurence W. Beilenson. He cited the book often. See Skinner, Anderson, and Anderson, *Reagan, in His Own Hand,* 8, 48–54; and Paul Kengor, *God and Ronald Reagan* (New York: HarperCollins, 2004), 76.

19. See Edmund Morris, *Dutch: A Memoir of Ronald Reagan* (New York: Random House, 1999), 598–599; Reagan, *An American Life,* 676–677; and "Memcons from Reykjavik Summit," Ronald Reagan Library, Box 92140, Folders 2 and 3.

20. Quoted in Oberdorfer, *The Turn,* 285.

21. See my extended analysis in Kengor, *God and Ronald Reagan,* 264–269.

22. Reagan, *An American Life,* 569–570.

23. Gaddis, *The United States and the End of the Cold War,* 62, 125.

24. Reagan, "Interview with Ann Devroy and Johanna Neuman of USA Today," January 17, 1985.

25. Donald Regan, *For the Record* (San Diego, CA: Harcourt Brace Jovanovich, 1988), 294.

26. Source: Multiple interviews and conversations with Dolan. Also see Kengor, *God and Ronald Reagan,* 244–249, and Paul Kengor, *The Crusader: Ronald Reagan and the Fall of Communism* (New York: HarperPerennial), 140–144.

27. Anthony R. Dolan, "Premeditated Prose: Reagan's Evil Empire," *The American Enterprise* (March–April 1993): 24–26.

28. I have talked to Dolan about this on many occasions.

29. Dolan did not specify which passage was "too searing."

30. Ibid.

31. Reagan, *An American Life,* 628.

32. Gromyko, *Memoirs,* 279–280.

33. Ibid.

34. Here are three examples from just one week in May 1968: Reagan, "Speech to Republican State Central Committee Luncheon," Hilton Plaza, Miami, May 21, 1968; "Speech to Republican State Central Committee Finance

Dinner," Sheraton-Cleveland Hotel, Cleveland, May 22, 1968; and "Speech to the U.S. Chamber of Commerce for Businessmen," Fairmont Hotel, San Francisco, May 27, 1968. Later in 1968, see Reagan, "Speech at Price for Congress Rally," Amarillo, Texas, July 19, 1968. Speeches filed at Ronald Reagan Library, "RWR—Speeches and Articles (1968)," vertical files.

35. Reagan, "Speech to Members of Platform Committee," Republican National Convention, July 31, 1968. Speeches filed at Reagan Library, "RWR—Speeches and Articles (1968)," vertical files.

36. See Skinner, Anderson, and Anderson, *Reagan, in His Own Hand*, 99–102.

37. For the 1970s, see (among others) James S. Brady, ed., *Ronald Reagan: A Man True to His Word* (Washington, DC: National Federation of Republican Women, 1984), 32–33.

38. "Where Reagan Stands, Interview on the Issues," *U.S. News & World Report*, May 31, 1976, 20.

39. Professor Phil Williams, my adviser in my doctoral program at the University of Pittsburgh, frequently used the phrase, "Reagan built up in order to build down."

40. Quote is published in Brady, *Ronald Reagan*, 38.

41. Reagan said this in Anaheim, California. See "Reagan Proposes Arms Approach," United Press International, published in the *Washington Post*, April 17, 1977, A5.

42. Quoted in Ronnie Dugger, *On Reagan: The Man & His Presidency* (New York: McGraw Hill, 1983), 395. Reagan said the same in a May 1979 radio broadcast. See Skinner, Anderson, and Anderson, *Reagan, in His Own Hand*, 104–105.

43. From the 1980 campaign, also see "Reagan: 'It Isn't Only Washington . . . ,'" *National Journal*, March 8, 1980, 392.

44. Lou Cannon, "Arms Boost Seen as Strain on Soviets," *Washington Post*, June 19, 1980, A3.

45. Ibid.

46. Published in Kenneth W. Thompson, ed., *Leadership in the Reagan Presidency, Pt II: Eleven Intimate Perspectives* (Lanham, MD: United Press of America, 1993), 59, 65.

47. Cannon, "Arms Boost Seen as Strain on Soviets," A3.

48. See Skinner, Anderson, and Anderson, *Reagan, in His Own Hand*, 470–479. Text also available at the Reagan Library: "Reagan-Bush 1980 Campaign Papers, 1979–80," Box 949.

49. Ibid.

50. Reagan, "First Inaugural Address," January 20, 1981.

51. Reagan, "The President's News Conference," January 29, 1981.

52. "More Signals to the World," *Time*, February 16, 1981, 18.

53. Reagan, "Excerpts from an Interview with Walter Cronkite of CBS News," March 3, 1981.

54. Letter is located in Executive Secretariat (ES), National Security Council (NSC), Head of State Files (HSF): Records, USSR, Box 37, Folder 8100630, Ronald Reagan Library.

55. Reagan, *An American Life*, 269.

56. These drafts and memoranda are ES, NSC, HSF: Records, USSR, Box 37, Folders 8190199–8190201, 8190202–8190203, 8190204–8190205, and 8100630, Ronald Reagan Library.

57. Reagan, *An American Life*, 273.

58. Letter is located in ES, NSC, HSF: Records, USSR, Box 37, Folder 8190204–8190205, Ronald Reagan Library.

59. Reagan, *An American Life*, 302.

60. Letter is located in ES, NSC, HSF: Records, USSR, Box 37, Folder 8106115, Ronald Reagan Library.

61. The September letter is located in ES, NSC, HSF: Records, USSR, Box 37, Folders 8103556–8105534 and 8105567–8105658, Ronald Reagan Library.

62. There were November 16 and 17 drafts of the November 18 letter. The near-final draft version on November 17 also includes many Reagan edits. See drafts located in ES, NSC, HSF: Records, USSR, Box 37, Folder 8106607, Ronald Reagan Library.

63. Reagan, "The President's News Conference," June 16, 1981.

64. Reagan, "Remarks at the Bicentennial Observance of the Battle of Yorktown in Virginia," October 19, 1981.

65. The initial draft was written by speechwriter Aram Bakshian. Reagan completely overhauled it via multiple drafts. The final version is almost unrecognizable from the first. The initial introduction by Bakshian invoked the "moving words from the Book of Common Prayer: 'Give to all nations unity, peace and concord.'" Reagan slashed that entire first paragraph, all of the second, and half of the third, composing his own intro, which he excerpted from his April letter to Brezhnev. Drafts are located in Presidential Handwriting File (PHF), Presidential Speeches (PS), Box 2, Folders 35–36, Ronald Reagan Library.

66. Reagan, *An American Life*, 273.

67. Ibid., 293.

68. PHF, Presidential Records (PR), Box 2, Folder 35, Ronald Reagan Library.

69. See Laurence I. Barrett, *Gambling with History: Ronald Reagan in the White House* (New York: Doubleday, 1983), 313–315.

70. Morris, *Dutch*, 454.

71. Barrett, *Gambling with History*, 314.

72. For an excellent treatment of negotiations during this period, see ibid., 315–325.

73. Not all of the letters dealt with negotiations. Letters located in ES, NSC, HSF: Records, USSR, RRL, Box 37, Folders 8200225–8204854, 8190038–

8190057, 8190210, and 8190211–8290212. On Reagan being enraged over Soviet actions regarding martial law in Poland, see Kengor, *The Crusader.*

74. Peter Schweizer, *Victory: The Reagan Administration's Secret Strategy That Hastened the Collapse of the Soviet Union* (New York: Atlantic Monthly Press, 1994), 29, 31; Richard Pipes, *Vixi: Memoirs of a Non-Belonger* (New Haven, CT: Yale University Press, 2006), 170–172.

75. Throughout the 1980s, Reagan's concern about Soviet treaty obligations was a constant theme, reinforced in reports by the Defense Department and State Department contending that Moscow was violating various treaties, particularly the ABM Treaty but also the ban on chemical weapons and portions of the (unsigned) SALT II Treaty.

76. Reagan, "Address at Commencement Exercises at Eureka College in Illinois," May 9, 1982.

77. Ibid.

78. Ibid.

79. Reagan made the annotation on page 10 of a May 5 draft. The draft is located in PHF, PS, Box 4, Folder 79, Ronald Reagan Library.

80. Reagan, "Remarks from the Reagan Ranch, Near Santa Barbara, CA," May 29, 1982.

81. Reagan, *An American Life,* 552.

82. Letter located in ES, NSC, HSF: Records, USSR, Box 37, Folder 8290289–8290342, Ronald Reagan Library.

83. Letter is located in PHF, PR, Box 3, Folder 40, Ronald Reagan Library. It was declassified June 28, 2000.

84. See, for instance, Reagan, "Remarks to the People of Berlin," June 11, 1982.

85. There was also, of course, a mixed reception to the "walk-in-the-woods" by the media.

86. Eugene Rostow, *A Breakfast for Bonaparte* (Washington, DC: National Defense University Press, 1993), 422–426.

87. Ibid.

88. George Shultz, *Turmoil and Triumph* (New York: Scribner, 1993), 164–165.

89. Dobrynin, *In Confidence,* 521.

90. Ibid., 517–520.

91. Ibid.

92. Shultz speaking on "Reagan," *The American Experience,* PBS-WGBH, 1998.

93. Ibid.

94. Dobrynin acknowledges this as well. See Dobrynin, *In Confidence,* 520.

95. Shultz speaking on "Reagan," *The American Experience.*

96. Reagan, "Question-and-Answer Session with Members of the Sperling Breakfast Group," February 23, 1983. Also see Reagan, "Remarks at the Annual Washington Conference of the American Legion," February 22, 1983.

97. Given space limitations, I cannot quote from those letters here. The letters are located at the Reagan Library in ES, NSC, HSF: Records, USSR, RRL, Boxes 37 and 38, Folders 8304209–8308981 and 8290913–8391032.

98. I intend to elaborate on these details in a future book on this subject.

99. All of these were major actions by Reagan, especially the January 16, 1984 speech. Among others, see Fischer, *The Reagan Reversal.*

100. Reagan, *An American Life,* 589.

101. Letters located in ES, NSC, HSF: Records, USSR, Box 39, Folders 8401238 and 8490236–8490546, Ronald Reagan Library.

102. These documents are located in ES, NSC, HSF: Records, USSR, Box 39, Folders 8401238 and 8490236–8490546, Ronald Reagan Library.

103. Document located in ES, NSC, HSF: Records, USSR, Box 39, Folder 8490236–8490546, Ronald Reagan Library.

104. These documents were declassified in 1999 and 2000. Here are the letters: Chernenko to Reagan, June 6; Reagan to Chernenko, July 2; Chernenko to Reagan, July 7; Reagan to Chernenko, July 18; Chernenko to Reagan, July 26; Reagan to Chernenko, late July (exact date unclear); and Chernenko to Reagan, July 31. Letters are located in ES, NSC, HSF: Records, USSR, Box 39, Folders 8470695, 8490757, 8490829, 8490847–8491054, Ronald Reagan Library.

105. See Reagan, *An American Life,* 603–605; Shultz, *Turmoil and Triumph,* 482; Gromyko, *Memoirs,* 309; and Skinner, Anderson, and Anderson, *Reagan, in His Own Hand,* 496–498.

106. Reagan received a November 7 letter from Chernenko, which is located in ES, NSC, HSF: Records, USSR, Box 39, Folder 8401238, Ronald Reagan Library. Chernenko wrote a November 17 letter to Reagan limited to Nicaragua, with the president responding on December 20. Reagan sent a letter pushing dialogue and negotiations on December 7. The general secretary responded to Reagan's December 7 letter on December 20. These four letters are located in ES, NSC, HSF: Records, USSR, Box 39, Folders 8491175–8491234 and 8491237–8491334, Ronald Reagan Library.

107. Reagan, "Question-and-Answer Session."

108. Again, because of space limitations, I cannot chronicle every Reagan move in this period. Two other critical meetings in the immediate days before Gorbachev's arrival was a March 4 NSC meeting and a March 7 meeting of Reagan, a few staffers, Dobrynin, and other Soviet officials. See Reagan, *An American Life,* 610–611.

109. Lou Cannon and David Hoffman, "Gorbachev Endorses Idea of a Summit Meeting," *Washington Post,* April 2, 1985.

110. I detail this at length in Kengor, *The Crusader,* 228–262.

111. Reagan, "The President's News Conference," January 9, 1985.

9. Building Up and Seeking Peace

1. For example, see National Security Decision Directive (NSDD)-12, "Strategic Forces Modernization Program," October 1, 1981, and NSDD-32, "US National Security Strategy," May 20, 1982, http://www.fas.org/irp /offdocs/nsdd. See also Ronald Reagan, "Address to the Nation: Arms Reduction and Deterrence," November 22, 1982, *Weekly Compilation of Presidential Documents (WCPD)* 18, *1982,* 1517–1521.

2. Richard Halloran, "Weinberger Begins Drive for Big Rise in Military Budget," *New York Times,* March 5, 1981; Richard Halloran, "Reagan to Request $38B Increase in Military Outlays," *New York Times,* March 5, 1981; and Hedrick Smith, "US Priorities: Basic Reversal," *New York Times,* March 5, 1981.

3. Reagan, Address, November 22, 1982, *WCPD* 18, 1516–1521; Ronald Reagan, Address to the United Nations General Assembly, September 24, 1984, *American Foreign Policy: Current Documents (AFP:CD), 1984,* 220–227; Halloran, "Weinberger Begins Drive."

4. Reagan, Address, November 22, 1982, *WCPD* 18, 1519.

5. Secretary of State George P. Shultz, "US-Soviet Relations in the Context of US Foreign Policy," Remarks before the Senate Foreign Relations Committee, June 15, 1983, *AFP:CD, 1983,* 508.

6. Ronald Reagan, "The US-Soviet Relationship," January 16, 1984, *Department of State Bulletin* 84: 2083, 1–4.

7. Ronald Reagan, Address before the Japanese Diet in Tokyo, November 11, 1983, *The Public Papers of President Ronald Reagan,* http://www.reagan.utexas .edu/archives/speeches/1983/111183a.htm.

8. Martin Anderson and Annelise Anderson, *Reagan's Secret War: The Untold Story of His Fight to Save the World from Nuclear Disaster* (New York: Crown, 2009), 93–94.

9. Reagan, *An American Life* (New York: Pocket Books, 1990), 13, 547, 550.

10. Martin Anderson, *Revolution* (New York: Harcourt Brace Jovanovich, 1987), 72.

11. Reagan, Address, March 23, 1983, *WCPD* 19, 447.

12. For example, see the February 10, 1987, NSC meeting in Jason Saltoun-Ebin, ed., *The Reagan Files* (CreateSpace Independent Publishing Platform, 2010), 365–373.

13. Ronald Reagan, Address, March 23, 1983, *Public Papers of the Presidents of the United States, Ronald Reagan, 1983* (Washington, DC: Government Printing Office, 1984), 442–443.

14. Reagan, *An American Life,* 550.

15. Shultz, *Turmoil and Triumph: My Years as Secretary of State* (New York: Charles Scribner's Sons, 1993), 466.

16. Ibid., 509.

17. McFarlane, "Consider What Star Wars Accomplished," *New York Times*, August 24, 1993.

18. For example, see the February 10, 1987, NSC meeting in Saltoun-Ebin, *The Reagan Files*, 365–373.

19. Matlock remarks, Princeton Oral History Conference on the Ending of the Cold War (February 26–27, 1993), Session II, 81–82.

20. Carlucci remarks, Princeton Conference, Session II, 54.

21. The Politburo was unable to undertake reform until 1985, however, owing to a rapid turnover in leadership.

22. Mikhail Gorbachev, as cited in Vladislav M. Zubok, "Soviet Foreign Policy from Détente to Gorbachev," in Melvyn P. Leffler and Odd Arned Westad, eds., *The Cambridge History of the Cold War*, vol. 3 (Cambridge: Cambridge University Press, 2010), 110; Nina Tannenwald, ed., *Understanding the End of the Cold War, 1980–1987*, Oral History Conference, Brown University, May 7–10, 1998, 81.

23. Makhmut Gareyev, "The Revised Soviet Military Doctrine," *Bulletin of the Atomic Scientists* (December 1988): 33.

24. Jonathan Schell, *The Gift of Time: The Case for Abolishing Nuclear Weapons* (New York: Metropolitan Books, 1998).

25. Mikhail S. Gorbachev and Zdenek Mlynar, *Conversations with Gorbachev on Perestroika, the Prague Spring, and the Crossroads of Socialism* (New York: Columbia University Press, 2002), 139.

26. Mikhail S. Gorbachev, *Mandate for Peace* (Toronto: PaperJacks, 1987), 330.

27. Andrei Grachev, *Gorbachev's Gamble: Soviet Foreign Policy and the End of the Cold War* (Cambridge: Polity Press, 2008), 81.

28. Velikhov, as quoted in Robert D. English, *Russia and the Idea of the West* (New York: Columbia University Press, 2000), 217.

29. Grachev, *Gorbachev's Gamble*, 81.

30. See Roald Z. Sagdeev, *The Making of a Soviet Scientist* (New York: John Wiley and Sons, 1994), 123–124, 209–211; Nikolai Detinov, in Tannenwald, Brown Conference, 37–39; Yevgeny Velikhov, Roald Sagdeev, and Andrei Kokoshin, eds., *Weaponry in Space: The Dilemma of Security* (Moscow: Mir, 1986); Matthew Evangelista, *Unarmed Forces: The Transnational Movement to End the Cold War* (Ithaca, NY: Cornell University Press, 1999), 234–236; and David E. Hoffman, *The Dead Hand: The Untold Story of the Cold War Arms Race and Its Dangerous Legacy* (New York: Anchor Books, 2009), 215–218.

31. Vladimir Slipchenko, in Tannenwald, Brown Conference, 51.

32. Hoffman, *The Dead Hand*, 214–215.

33. Grachev, *Gorbachev's Gamble*, 94.

34. Nikolai Detinov, in Tannenwald, Brown Conference, 37–39.

35. Velikhov, as quoted in Hoffman, *Dead Hand*, 217–218.

36. Slipchenko in Tannenwald, Brown Conference, 51–52.

37. Ibid.

38. Skeptics might argue that SDI drove Gorbachev to seek a cost-effective response to Reagan's initiatives. But this causal logic is faulty. It is akin to arguing, "I wanted it to rain. It rained. Ergo, I caused the rain." Soviet documents, memoirs, and oral testimony from Soviet officials demonstrate that there were many internal factors that prompted Moscow to seek an end to the arms race. For more details see Beth A. Fischer, *Triumph: Ronald Reagan's Legacy and American Politics Today* (forthcoming).

39. Jack F. Matlock, *Autopsy on an Empire: The American Ambassador's Account of the Collapse of the Soviet Union* (New York: Random House, 1995), 148–149 (advance copy).

40. John Mueller, "When Did the Cold War End?," paper presented to the annual meeting of the Society for the Historians of American Foreign Relations (SHAFR), Princeton University, June 24–26, 1999, 7 and figure 2, 18.

41. Ronald Reagan, handwritten letter to Mikhail Gorbachev, November 28, 1985, in Saltoun-Ebin, *The Reagan Files,* 286–290.

42. Aleksandr Bessmertnykh, Princeton Conference, 125–127, 160.

10. Ronald Reagan, Liberalism, and the Politics of Nuclear War and National Security, 1981–1985

1. For examples of this work, see Paul Lettow, *Ronald Reagan and His Quest to Abolish Nuclear Weapons* (New York: Random House, 2005); Martin Anderson and Annelise Anderson, *Reagan's Secret War: The Untold Story of His Fight to Save the World from Nuclear Disaster* (New York: Crown, 2009); Jay Winik, *On the Brink: The Dramatic behind the Scenes Saga of the Reagan Era and the Men and Women Who Won the Cold War* (New York: Simon & Schuster, 1996). For a trenchant critique of the literature about Reagan and his quest for nuclear abolition, see Doug Rossinow, "The Legend of Reagan the Peacemaker," *Raritan* (Winter 2003): 56–76.

2. Beth Fisher, *The Reagan Reversal: Foreign Policy and the End of the Cold War* (Columbia: University of Missouri Press, 1997).

3. Sean Wilentz, *The Age of Reagan: A History 1974–2008* (New York: Harper, 2008).

4. Frances Fitzgerald, *Way Out There in the Blue: Reagan, Star Wars, and the End of the Cold War* (New York: Touchstone, 2000); Steve Kotkin, *Armageddon Averted: The Soviet Collapse, 1970–2000* (New York: Oxford University Press, 2008).

5. This chapter draws on material that appeared in Julian E. Zelizer, *Arsenal of Democracy: The Politics of National Security—From World War II to the War on Terrorism* (New York: Basic Books, 2010), 300–332.

6. I examine the historiography of conservatism in Julian E. Zelizer, "Rethinking the History of American Conservatism," *Reviews in American History* 38 (2010): 367–392.

7. Martin Schram, "Schizophrenia Politica," *Washington Post,* June 29, 1981.

8. Deborah Hart Strober and Gerald S. Strober, *Reagan: The Man and His Presidency* (Boston: Houghton Mifflin, 1998).

9. Transcript, *Face the Nation,* March 8, 1981, Ronald Reagan Library, Simi Valley, CA, Elizabeth Dole Files, Box 18, File: Defense.

10. Richard Halloran, "Plan for Military Spending Is Major Shift for Peacetime," *New York Times,* February 19, 1981.

11. Daniel Wirls, *Buildup: The Politics of Defense in the Reagan Era* (Ithaca, NY: Cornell University Press, 1992), 54; Michael Schaller, *Reckoning with Reagan: America and Its President in the 1980s* (New York: Oxford University Press, 1992), 127.

12. Robert M. Collins, *Transforming America: Politics and Culture during the Reagan Years* (New York: Columbia University Press, 2007), 198. For the best work on the freeze movement, see Larry Wittner, *Toward Nuclear Abolition: A History of the World Nuclear Disarmament Movement, 1971 to the Present* (Stanford, CA: Stanford University Press, 2003).

13. David Treadwell and Doyle McManus, "More in U.S. Warming to Arms Freeze," *Los Angeles Times,* March 3, 1982.

14. Richard Sobel, *The Impact of Public Opinion on U.S. Foreign Policy since Vietnam* (New York: Oxford University Press, 2001), 40–41, 101–142; Robert D. Schulzinger, *A Time for Peace: The Legacy of the Vietnam War* (New York: Oxford University Press, 2006).

15. Richard Wirthlin to James Baker, March 29, 1982, James Baker Papers, Chief of Staff Series, Box 65, Folder 7.

16. "O'Neill Sees Close Vote on Nicaragua," *Los Angeles Times,* July 26, 1983.

17. "A Public Affairs Program to Support the Administration's Nuclear Policy," May 5, 1982, RRL, Sven Kraemer Files, Box 90100, file: Nuclear Freeze, April 28, 1982.

18. Richard Wirthlin to James Baker, March 29, 1982, James Baker Papers, Chief of Staff Series, Box 65, Folder 7.

19. Hedrick Smith, "New House Seems Less in Tune with Reagan," *New York Times,* November 4, 1982.

20. Bernard Weinraub, "Congress Renews Curbs on Actions against Nicaragua," *New York Times,* December 23, 1982.

21. Rushworth Kidder, "Poll Shows Public's Still Warm about Nuclear Freeze," *Christian Science Monitor,* January 17, 1983.

22. Jay Keyworth to Ronald Reagan, July 29, 1982, RRL, George Keyworth Files, Box 5-7, Folder: Edward Teller 1/1981–1982 (1 of 3).

23. Edward Teller to President Reagan, July 23, 1982, RRL, George Keyworth Files, Box 5-7, Folder: Edward Teller 1/1981–1982 (1 of 3).

24. Edward Teller, with Judith Shoolery, *Memoirs* (Cambridge, MA: Perseus, 2001), 508–509.

25. William Safire, "Farewell to Dempsey," *New York Times,* March 31, 1983.

26. Arthur Finkelstein and Associates to the High Frontier, February 1984, RRL, Star Wars Open Collection, Box 1, File: SDI 1984 (1).

27. George Keyworth to Caspar Weinberger, December 9, 1983, RRL, George Keyworth File, Box 3-5, File: Presidents SDI.

28. Ronald Reagan to Lt. General Victor H. Krulak, September 5, 1985, in Kiron K. Skinner, Annelise Anderson, and Martin Anderson, eds., *Reagan: A Life in Letters* (New York: Free Press, 2003), 427.

29. Edward Kennedy and Mark Hatfield to Colleague, March 2, 1982, RRL, Richard Darman Files, Box 1, File: Nuclear Freeze.

30. These events and their impact on Reagan are covered by Fischer in *The Reagan Reversal*.

31. Newt Gingrich to Ronald Reagan, September 1, 1983, in RRL, Kenneth Duberstein Files, Box 9, File: Memos: September 1983 (3).

32. Martin Tolchin, "In Congress, Bitter Words and Demand for Sanctions," *New York Times*, September 13, 1983.

33. Dale R. Herpsring, *The Pentagon and the Presidency: Civil-Military Relations from FDR to George W. Bush* (Lawrence: University Press of Kansas, 2005), 279–280.

34. George P. Shultz, *Turmoil and Triumph: My Years as Secretary of State* (New York: Scribner's 1993), 311.

35. "Draft Reagan Campaign Action Plan," October 27, 1983, JBF, Chief of Staff Series, Box 136, File: 43.

36. Peter Perl, "'The Day After': Nation Girds for Firestorm," *Washington Post*, November 20, 1983.

37. Diary Entry, November 18, 1983, in Ronald Reagan, *The Reagan Diaries*, ed. Douglas Brinkley (New York: HarperCollins, 2007), 199.

38. Philip Taubman, "White House Quits Rebel Aid Battle," *New York Times*, July 25, 1984.

39. Diary Entry, July 24, 1983, in Reagan, *The Reagan Diaries*.

40. Minutes, National Security Planning Group Meeting, June 25, 1984, National Security Online Archive.

41. Ibid.

42. Julian E. Zelizer, "How Conservatives Learned to Stop Worrying and Love Presidential Power," in Julian E. Zelizer, ed., *The Presidency of George W. Bush: A First Historical Assessment* (Princeton, NJ: Princeton University Press, 2010), 25–30.

43. Herbert Meyer to the Director of Central Intelligence, June 28, 1984, RRI, William Clark Files, Box 9, File: U.S. Soviets Relations Papers (16).

44. Bernard Weinraub, "Mondale Pledges Immediate Effort for Arms Freeze," *New York Times*, September 6, 1984.

45. David S. Foglesong, *The American Mission and the "Evil Empire"* (New York: Cambridge University Press, 2007), 188.

46. Rudy Abramson, "Democrats Fail to Seize Edge on Arms Issue," *Los Angeles Times*, September 30, 1984.

47. The American Political Report, "Grenada and the New 1984 Politics of Foreign Policy," November 4, 1983, RRL, Michael Baroody File, Box 4, File: Lebanon/Grenada (3 of 5).

48. Richard Wirthlin to Michael Deaver, JBP, Presidential Campaigns, Box 137, File: 4.

49. Julian E. Zelizer, *On Capitol Hill: The Struggle to Reform Congress and Its Consequences, 1948–2000* (New York: Cambridge University Press, 2004), 214–215.

50. The INF Treaty closely resembled the zero-zero option that Reagan had proposed in 1981, when there was little possibility that it would become the basis of agreement with the Soviets and the president offered little evidence of anything but a proposal that he knew would be rejected, offering him a pretext to then expand the number of missiles in Europe.

11. Ronald Reagan's Approach to the United Nations

Special thanks to Janice A. Smith, Special Assistant to the Distinguished Fellow and Policy Coordinator for the Vice President of Foreign and Defense Policy Studies at The Heritage Foundation, for research and editing support.

1. Robert C. Johansen, "The Reagan Administration and the U.N.: The Costs of Unilateralism," *World Policy Journal* 3, no. 4 (Fall 1986): 601–641, http://www.jstor.org/stable/40209032.

2. Nick Madigan, "Reagan: U.S. Troops Complete Mission in Grenada," United Press International, November 3, 1983.

3. Personal interview with former Attorney General Ed Meese, February 4, 2011. See also Tim Weiner, "Jeane Kirkpatrick, Reagan's Forceful Envoy, Dies," *New York Times*, December 9, 2006, http://www.nytimes.com/2006/12/09/washington/09kirkpatrick.html?ex=1323320400&en=721b7bd24a2c694d&ei=5090; and Peter Collier, *Political Woman: The Big Little Life of Jeane Kirkpatrick* (New York: Encounter Books, 2012), 168.

4. Ronald Reagan, The Reagan Diaries, ed. Douglas Brinkley (New York: HarperCollins, 2007), 33.

5. David Bosco, *Five to Rule Them All: The UN Security Council and the Making of the Modern World* (New York: Oxford University Press, 2009), 143–144.

6. Ibid.

7. Ibid.

8. Address before United Nations General Assembly Special Session Devoted to Disarmament, June 17, 1982, http://www.reagan.utexas.edu/archives/speeches/1982/61782a.htm.

9. Ibid.

10. "Reagan Tells ILO Workers and Employers Both Need Freedom," United Press International, June 8, 1981. See also Kimberly Ann Elliott and Richard

B. Freeman, *Can Labor Standards Improve under Globalization?* (Washington, DC: Institute for International Economics, 2003), 108: "Ronald Reagan turned to the ILO as a tool for helping workers in communist countries form free unions thereby undermining state control. In 1982, with strong backing from the United States, ILO conference delegates voted to initiate an Article 26 complaint against Poland for its treatment of the Solidarity trade union."

11. Elaine Sciolino, "President Orders Moscow's Missions to U.N. Reduced," *New York Times,* March 8, 1986, 1.

12. Bosco, *Five to Rule Them All,* 142. See also Jeane J. Kirkpatrick, "UN Mugging Fails," *New York Times,* March 31, 1983, reprinted in *Legitimacy and Force,* vol. 1 (New Brunswick, NJ: Transaction Books, 1988), 229.

13. Nicholas Laham, *Crossing the Rubicon: Ronald Reagan and U.S. Policy in the Middle East* (Aldershot, UK: Ashgate, 2004), 61.

14. U.S. Ambassador to the United Nations Vernon A. Walters, "Introduction," *Report to Congress on Voting Practices in the United Nations* (1988), http://www .princeton.edu/~sbwhite/un/1988-I.pdf.

15. United Nations Peacekeeping, "History of Peacekeeping," http://www.un .org/en/peacekeeping/operations/history.shtml.

16. Calculations from "Report of the Open-Ended Working Group on the Question of Equitable Representation on and Increase in the Membership of the Security Council and Other Matters Related to the Security Council," GAOR 58th Session, Suppl. 48 (A/58/47).

17. Ronald Reagan, "Excerpts from an Interview with Walter Cronkite of CBS News," The American Presidency Project (University of California, Santa Barbara), March 3, 1981, http://www.presidency.ucsb.edu/ws/?pid=43497.

18. Address before the 38th Session of the United Nations General Assembly.

19. Roger Pilon, a Reagan administration official in the State Department's Bureau of Human Rights and Humanitarian Affairs, who currently is the Cato Institute's vice president for legal affairs, writes: "President Ronald Reagan went on the offensive, using the U.N. Commission on Human Rights as a forum for public diplomacy against some of the worst regimes of the Cold War, including the Soviet Union." See Roger Pilon, "Wrong about Human Rights," philly.com, September 1, 2010.

20. "Introduction," U.S. Department of State, *State Department Country Reports on Human Rights Practices for 1981* (1982).

21. Jeane J. Kirkpatrick, *The Reagan Phenomenon* (Washington, DC: American Enterprise Institute, 1983), 49.

22. "Introduction," *State Department Country Reports on Human Rights Practices for 1981.*

23. Ibid.

24. New Zealand Ministry of Foreign Affairs and Trade, *United Nations Handbook 1996,* 34th ed. (Wellington, NZ: G P Print, 1996), 89–93.

25. As explained by Ambassador James Malone, Reagan's chief negotiator, in James Malone, "Who Needs the Sea Treaty?," *Foreign Policy* 54 (Spring 1984): 44–45.

26. "Statement on United States Participation in the Third United Nations Conference on the Law of the Sea," January 29, 1982, www.reagan.utexas.edu /archives/speeches/1982/12982b.htm.

27. Ibid.

28. Ibid. A subsequent statement issued by Reagan on March 10, 1983, did not alter or amend his stated objections here in any manner. See "Statement on United States Oceans Policy," March 10, 1983.

29. Reagan, *The Reagan Diaries,* 91.

30. Personal interview with former attorney general and Reagan adviser Ed Meese, February 4, 2011.

31. "Statement on United States Oceans Policy, March 10, 1983," *The Public Papers of President Ronald W. Reagan,* Ronald Reagan Presidential Library.

32. E.g., former Secretary of State George Shultz, in a letter to Senator Dick Lugar on June 28, 2007, said: "It surprises me to learn that opponents of the treaty are invoking President Reagan's name, arguing that he would have opposed ratification despite having succeeded on the deep sea-bed issue. During his administration, with full clearance and support from President Reagan, we made it very clear that we would support ratification if our position on the sea-bed issue were accepted." See http://www.virginia.edu /colp/pdf/ShultzLetter.pdf. Former legal adviser John Bellinger testified on June 14, 2012, before the Senate Foreign Relations Committee that the Bush administration had reviewed the specific concerns Reagan had raised and that all "of these concerns had been satisfactorily addressed by the amendments made to the Convention in 1994." Moreover, he said, "Reagan had said that if U.S. concerns were addressed, 'my Administration will support ratification.'" See http://www.foreign.senate.gov/imo/media/doc/John_Bellinger _Testimony.pdf.

33. For further explanation, see William P. Clark and Edwin Meese," Reagan and the Law of the Sea," *Wall Street Journal,* October 8, 2007, http://online .wsj.com/article/SB119179903218351465.html. Judge Clark served in the Reagan administration in several capacities, including as national security adviser. See Paul Kengor and Patricia Clark Doerner, *The Judge: William P. Clark, Ronald Reagan's Top Hand* (San Francisco: Ignatius Press, 2007).

34. The White House, "Letter of Transmittal to the Senate Regarding Protocol II Additional to the Geneva Conventions of 12 August 1949," dated January 29, 1987.

35. Ibid.

36. Ibid.

37. Ibid. Theodor Meron, in *War Crimes Law Comes of Age: Essays* (New York: Oxford University Press, 1998), 176n5, lists the concerns of the Department

of Defense: "In addition to provisions of Protocol 1 on liberation movements, privileges of irregular combatants and reprisals, other issues involved in the military review include: (1) which provisions codify existing customary law and which are new law, and whether the latter are militarily acceptable; (2) the problems posed by the codification of the rules on the conduct of hostilities, such as those limiting permissible collateral damage, and whether these problems can be effectively addressed through military manuals, statements of understanding or reservations; (3) whether the ambiguity regarding the application of the Protocol to nuclear warfare (most of the participants in the diplomatic conference had intended to limit it to conventional warfare but did not spell it out in the Protocol's text) might weaken nuclear deterrence, since military experts believe that it would not be possible to conform the use of nuclear weapons to the provisions on proportionality and collateral damage to civilians; and whether this problem can be remedied by an understanding or a reservation (to be sure, the question of the legality of the use of nuclear weapons arises also under the customary law of war, apart from Protocol 1); (4) what in practical terms is involved by the apparently increased obligation for armed forces to care for all sick and wounded regardless of the availability of civilian medical facilities; (5) the practical effect of the new regime on the operation of medical aircraft and the implementation problems in light of modern technology; (6) the practicality and military acceptability of the newly revised annex on identification of medical and religious personnel, involving the use of distinctive protective emblems and signals to facilitate identification of medical aircraft, vessels and facilities; and (7) the seriousness of the ambiguity built into several provisions of the Protocol and the possibility of its leading to contradictory, and sometimes extreme, interpretations."

38. Personal interview, February 4, 2011.

39. Ed Pilkington, "Bradley Manning's Treatment Was Cruel and Inhuman, UN Torture Chief rules," *Guardian,* March 12, 2012, http://www.guardian.co .uk/world/2012/mar/12/bradley-manning-cruel-inhuman-treatment-un.

40. Paul Lewis, "Disarmament Parley Ends in Discord," *New York Times,* June 27, 1988.

41. See George Shultz, "Letter from U.S. Secretary of State George Shultz to UNESCO Director-General Amadou-Mahtar M'Bow, announcing the decision of the U.S. government to withdraw its membership from UNESCO," dated December 28, 1983, *Journal of Communication* 34, no. 4 (1984): 82, 84. See also Thomas McPhail, *Global Communication: Theories, Stakeholders, and Trends,* 3rd ed. (Oxford: John Wiley and Sons, 2010), 73.

42. Francis X. Clines, "State Department Bids Reagan Act to Leave UNESCO," *New York Times,* December 24, 1983, 1. See also Paul Lewis, "Jean Gerard, 58, Reagan Envoy Who Led U.S. to Leave Unesco," *New York Times,* August 6, 1996: "Mrs. Gerard was appointed representative to the United Nations

Educational, Scientific and Cultural Organization in 1981 with a mandate from the Reagan Administration to clean up an agency that in its view was badly managed and had become increasingly politicized and anti-Western under its director general, Amadou Mahtar M'Bow of Senegal."

43. See Table 2, "Sample Countries' Actual Peacekeeping Payments to the United Nations, 1976–1996: Selected Years (current U.S. dollars)," in Jyoti Khanna, Todd Sandler, and Hirofumi Shimizu, "Sharing the Financial Burden for U.N. and NATO Peacekeeping, 1976–1996," *Journal of Conflict Resolution* 42, no. 2 (April 1998): 176–195.

44. This occurred from fiscal year 1981 to 1983 and realized a one-time U.S. budget reduction of over $400 million. See U.S. General Accounting Office, "Delaying U.S. Payments to International Organizations May Not Be the Best Means to Promote Budget Restraint," *Report to the Chairman, Committee on Foreign Relations, United States Senate,* No. GAO/ID-83–26, February 15, 1983.

45. Public Law 99-93.

46. Ronald Reagan, "Statement on Signing the Foreign Relations Authorization Act, Fiscal Years 1986 and 1987," August 17, 1985, posted on Gerhard Peters and John T. Woolley, *The American Presidency Project,* http://www.presidency.ucsb.edu/ws/?pid=39005.

47. Walters, "Introduction," *Report to Congress on Voting Practices in the United Nations.*

48. "Last month President Reagan ordered the immediate payment of $44 million in outstanding United States dues owed for fiscal 1988, which ended Sept. 30, saying he was satisfied that the United Nations was making good progress toward carrying out an agreed program of administrative changes. Congress had made the release of this money conditional on such a Presidential finding." Paul Lewis, "U.S. Holding Back Part of U.N. Dues over Budget Issue," *New York Times,* October 15, 1988, http://www.nytimes.com/1988/10/15/world/us-holding-back-part-of-un-dues-over-budget-issue.html.

49. Marjorie Ann Browne and Kennon H. Nakamura, "United Nations System Funding: Congressional Issues," *CRS Report for Congress* RL33611, updated November 13, 2008, 18.

50. The most recent *Annual Report on United States Contributions to the United Nations System* was for fiscal year 2010. It reported total contributions that year of $7,691,822,000 to the UN system from 17 U.S. departments and agencies. See Jacob Lew, "FY 2010 U.S. Contributions to the United Nations System," Executive Office of the President, Office of Management and Budget, June 6, 2011, 2, http://www.whitehouse.gov/sites/default/files/omb/assets/legislative_reports/us_contributions_to_the_un_06062011.pdf.

51. Statement delivered by Ambassador Terry Kramer during the World Conference on International Telecommunications in Dubai, UAE, December 13, 2012, http://www.state.gov/r/pa/prs/ps/2012/12/202037.htm.

52. For a fuller discussion of this approach, see Kim R. Holmes, "Smart Multilateralism: When and When Not to Rely on the United Nations," in Brett D. Schaefer, ed., *ConUNdrum: The Limits of the United Nations and the Search for Alternatives* (Lanham, MD: Rowman & Littlefield, 2009), 9–30.

12. Ronald Reagan, the Pragmatic Internationalist

1. Although my memory is still vivid about Mondale calling for the lower dollar to expand exports and increase jobs and the gist of the Reagan campaign's quick response, I am unable to date or provide the exact wording of the Mondale speech and the text of the Reagan campaign reply. The statements of a sitting president are carefully recorded, though campaign statements are more difficult to locate. Nonetheless, any such statement was consistent with Reagan's remarkably consistent statements about the value of the dollar in 1984. Some examples follow:

> The sharp rise in the value of the dollar since 1980 has made it cheaper for Americans to purchase products from overseas, thereby helping us fight inflation. But the dollar's sharp rise has made it difficult for American businesses and farmers to compete in world markets.
>
> I am also firmly opposed to any attempt to depress the dollar's exchange value by intervention in international currency markets. Pure exchange market intervention cannot offset the fundamental factors that determine the dollar's value. Intervention in the foreign exchange market would be an exercise in futility that would probably enrich currency speculators at the expense of American taxpayers. . . . The dollar must therefore be allowed to seek its natural value without exchange market intervention. ("Message to Congress Transmitting the Annual Economic Report of the President," *Public Papers of the Presidents of the United States: Ronald Reagan,* February 2, 1984, 146, 148 [1984, Book 1] [Washington, DC: U.S. Government Printing Office, 1987].)
>
> Now, lately, the pessimists have been sounding a new alarm: The dollar is so strong, they say, that exporters can't export, and we'll have no chance for lasting growth. Well, the facts are—as Secretary Don Regan has pointed out—the dollar is strong because of people's confidence in our currency, our low rate of inflation, and the incentives to invest in the United States. No American should undermine confidence in this nation's currency. A strong dollar is one of our greatest weapons against inflation. Anyone who doubts the value of a strong currency should look at the postwar performances of Japan, Switzerland, and West Germany. ("Remarks at the Annual Conservative Political Action Conference Dinner," *Public Papers of the Presidents of the United States: Ronald Reagan,* March 2, 1984, 288, 290.)

Fundamentally, the dollar is strong because the U.S. economy is strong. ("Written Responses to Questions Submitted by *France Soir* Magazine," *Public Papers of the Presidents of the United States: Ronald Reagan,* November 3, 1984, 1740, 1743.)

2. See the quotation from the President's Message to Congress Transmitting the Annual Economic Report of the President in note 1.

3. Yoichi Funabashi, *Managing the Dollar: From the Plaza to the Louvre* (Washington, DC: Institute for International Economics, 1988), 10. This section's discussion about the G-5 process and results draws heavily upon this excellent book.

4. Ibid., 23.

5. George P. Shultz, *Turmoil and Triumph: My Years as Secretary of State* (New York: Charles Scribner's Sons, 1993), 751.

6. Lou Cannon, *President Reagan: The Role of a Lifetime* (New York: Simon & Schuster, 1991), 687.

7. Ibid., 689; Schultz, *Turmoil and Triumph,* 772.

8. Shultz, *Turmoil and Triumph,* 780.

9. See George P. Shultz, William J. Perry, Henry A. Kissinger, and Sam Nunn, "A World Free of Nuclear Weapons," *Wall Street Journal,* January 4, 2007; "Toward a Nuclear Free World," *Wall Street Journal,* January 15, 2008; President Barack Obama, "Remarks by President Barack Obama," Prague, Czech Republic, April 5, 2009.

10. Arms Control Association, "The Intermediate-Range Nuclear Forces (INF) Treaty at a Glance," http://www.armscontrol.org. This and other ACA publications provide helpful analysis and detail.

11. The eventual agreement, which started as the Law of the Sea Negotiations, was called a "convention," which is another name for a treaty. Conventions are usually treaties with several parties.

12. The history in this section draws considerably on the discussion in Barry E. Carter and Allen S. Weiner, *International Law,* 6th ed. (New York: Aspen-Kluwer, 2011), 813–875.

13. One nautical mile is equal to 1.151 miles or 1.852 kilometers. Unless indicated otherwise, references here to a "mile" or "miles" are to nautical miles.

14. According to the American Law Institute, customary international law "results from a general and consistent practice of states followed by them from a sense of legal obligation." See American Law Institute, *Restatement of the Foreign Relations Law of the United States,* 3rd ed. (Philadelphia: American Law Institute, 1987). There is some debate over how long and consistent the practice need be.

15. Commission's final report: http://govinfo.library.unt.edu/oceancommission /documents/full_color_rpt/000_ocean_full_report.pdf.

16. For example, see Doug Bandow, "Don't Resurrect the Law of the Sea Treaty," CATO Institute Policy Analysis No. 552 (2005). One of the other speakers who joined me at the Reagan Centennial Conference in February 2011, hosted in Washington by the University of Virginia's Miller Center, also expressed his opposition.

17. A thorough comparison can be found in Bernard H. Oxman, "The 1994 Agreement and the Convention," *The American Journal of International Law* 88 (1994): 687. Oxman concludes, "The 1984 Agreement substantially accommodates the objections of the United States and other industrial states to the deep seabed mining provision of the . . . Convention" (695).

Acknowledgments

The editors would like to thank the University of Virginia's Miller Center for its support of this volume, which emanated from the Miller Center's 2011 Ronald Reagan Centennial Conference. We extend special thanks to Rosemary P. Galbraith and John W. Galbraith for their generous support of the conference and their steadfast commitment to preserving our nation's history. We also thank the Ronald Reagan Presidential Library and Foundation and the Ronald Reagan Centennial Commission for initiating the Reagan Centennial conference series.

We wish to thank the following individuals for their continuous encouragement, adroit insights, and candid reviews throughout the course of this volume's production: Governor Gerald L. Baliles, W. Taylor Reveley IV, Andrew Chancey, Arthur Milnes, Duke Blackwood, and Stewart McLaurin. We are grateful to Kathleen McDermott and the staff at Harvard University Press as well as the reviewers who devoted their time and talents to improving the manuscript. This volume underwent a rigorous review process that required time and patience.

As always, we wish to thank our families for providing the kind of love and encouragement that we do not deserve, but which we have come to rely on as we continue our scholarly pursuits.

And finally, we thank the authors included in this volume, not only for their outstanding contributions to understanding the enduring legacy of Ronald Reagan, but for their persistence in improving the manuscript and their commitments to public service and the advancement of knowledge.

Contributors

THE RIGHT HONOURABLE BRIAN MULRONEY served as Canada's eighteenth prime minister from 1984 to 1993.

BARRY E. CARTER was professor of law at Georgetown University Law Center and director of the Center on Transnational Business and the Law.

JEFFREY L. CHIDESTER is director of policy programs and corporate secretary to the Governing Council and Foundation Board at the Miller Center, University of Virginia.

ELIOT A. COHEN is Robert E. Osgood Professor of Strategic Studies at Johns Hopkins University's School of Advanced International Studies.

ALFRED E. ECKES JR. is eminent research professor emeritus, Ohio University.

BETH A. FISCHER is on the faculty at the Munk School of Global Affairs at the University of Toronto.

KIM R. HOLMES is a distinguished fellow at the Heritage Foundation, where he served as vice president for Foreign and Defense Policy.

PAUL KENGOR is professor of political science at Grove City College, a private liberal arts college in Grove City, Pennsylvania, and executive director of the college's Center for Vision & Values.

HENRY R. NAU is professor of political science and international affairs at the Elliott School of International Affairs, The George Washington University.

KIRON K. SKINNER is a research fellow at the Hoover Institution and associate professor of political science at Carnegie Mellon University.

PETER TRUBOWITZ is professor of international relations at the London School of Economics and Political Science and co-head of the United States International Affairs Programme at LSE IDEAS.

JULIAN E. ZELIZER is Malcolm Stevenson Forbes, Class of 1941 Professor of History and Public Affairs, Princeton University.

Index